FUTURA

Edited by Petra Eisele,
Annette Ludwig, Isabel Naegele

FUTURA

THE TYPEFACE.

LAURENCE KING PUBLISHING

BAUERSCHE GIESSEREI

FUTURA

BLACK

FUTURA

FUTURA
NEGRA

FUNDICIÓN TIPOGRÁFICA
BAUER
FRANKFURT·M (ALEMANIA)

SERRA HERMANOS
Representantes Exclusivos
para los Estados del Plata
BUENOS AIRES · MONTEVIDEO

FÜR

FUTURA
FUTURA
FUTURA
FUTURA
FUTURA
FUTURA
FUTURA
FUTURA
FUTURA
FUTURA
FUTURA
FUTURA
FUTURA
FUTURA
FUTURA
FUTURA

TO
GE

BAUER TYPE
FOUNDRY · INC

235 EAST 45TH STREET · NEW YORK
Frankfurt am Main, Germany · Madrid and Barcelona, Spain

FUTURA
FUTURA
FUTURA
FUTURA
FUTURA
FUTURA
FUTURA
FUTURA
FUTURA
FUTURA
FUTURA
FUTURA
FUTURA

A

ABGRŒars KLMNO
vwxchck!?

I. Korr.

KYZÆŒ

ÇØ$ÄÖÜ

aabcdefgghijklmmnno

pqrsʃtuvwxyzchckʄffifl

Aʃʃliʃß&æœøçr

1234567890

1234567890

.,-:;!?'«»(*§†

^ ^ ^ ..

II Korr. Bschckx

60

Gutenberg-Museum
Richard Wagner
Hotel Schweizerhof
Winterfahrplan
abcdefghijklmnop
qrsſtuvwxyzæœç
chckﬀﬁﬂﬀﬁﬁﬆﬁßß

äüöáàâéèêëìíîï
òóôùúûãõñå

Corps 60 Magere Futura / 18. Juni 1928

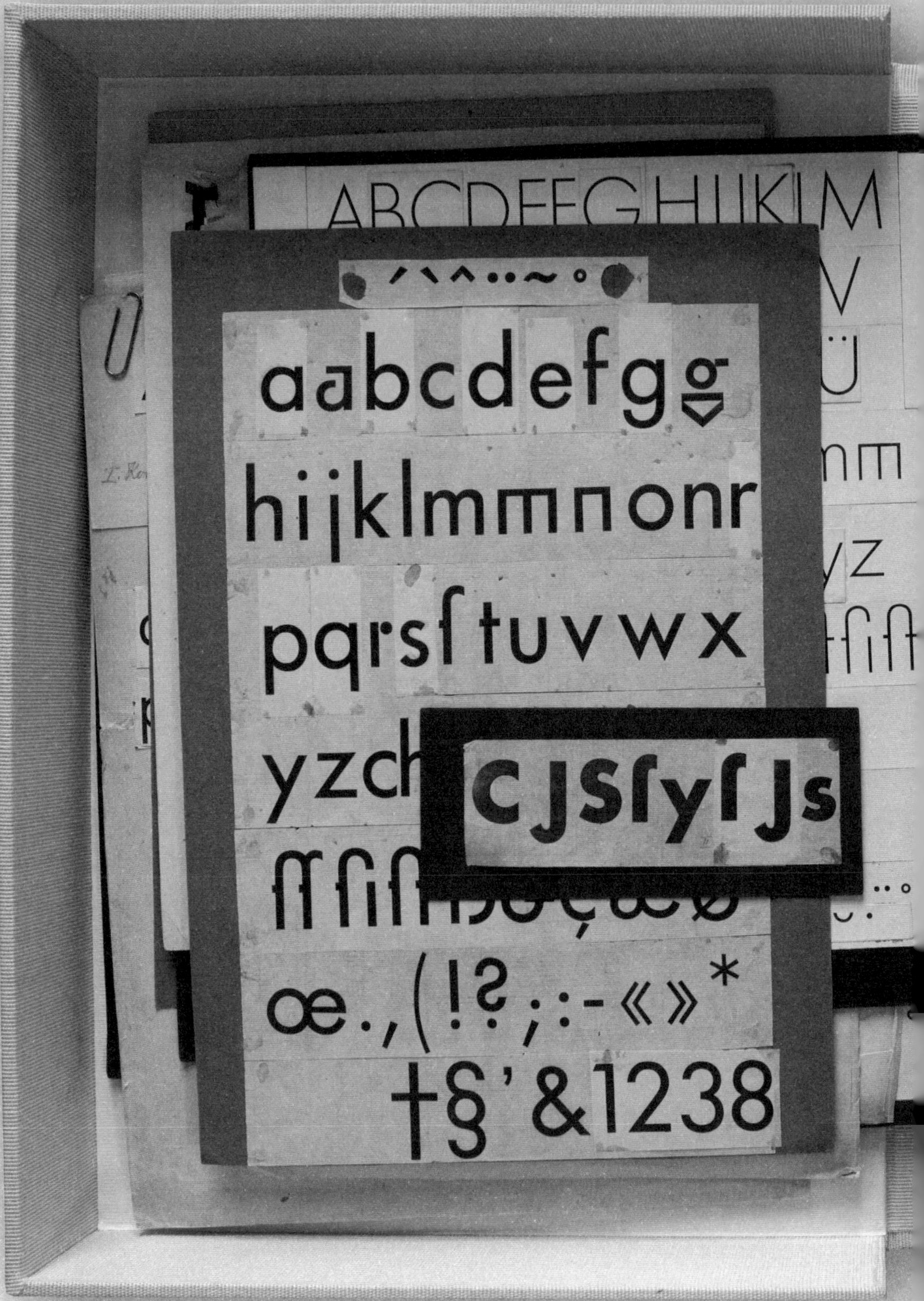

ABCDEFGHIJKLM

^^^ .. ~ ∘

aabcdefg

hijklmmnonr

pqrsʃtuvwx

yzch

cJsʃyʃjs

œ.,(!?;:-«»*

†§'&1238

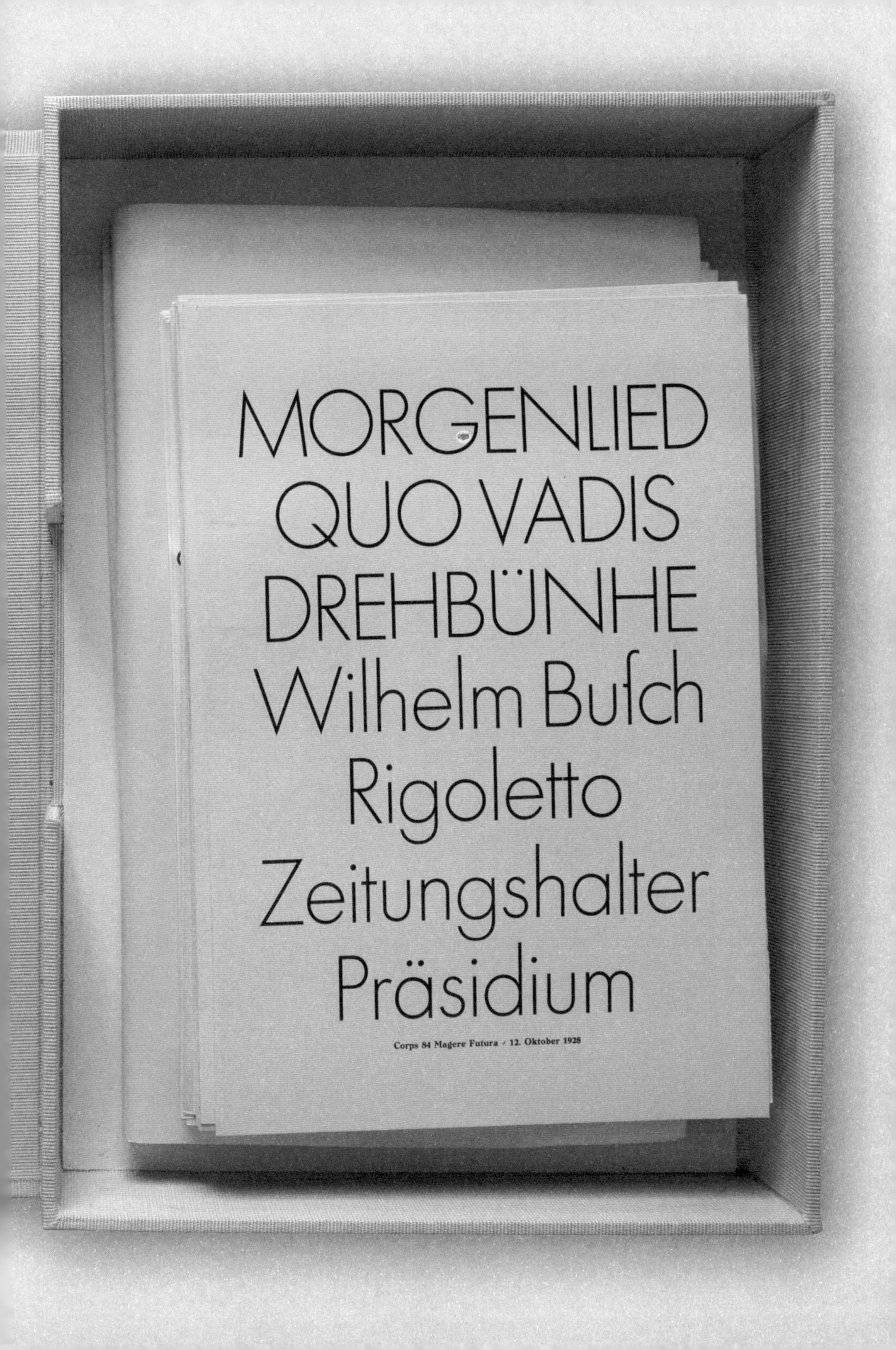

MORGENLIED
QUO VADIS
DREHBÜNHE
Wilhelm Buſch
Rigoletto
Zeitungshalter
Präsidium

Corps 84 Magere Futura / 12. Oktober 1928

P. 4 et seq. Specimens and revisions of Futura.

FOREWORD

The present volume is intended as a homage to the typeface Futura and to all the people who have contributed to its international success. The Futura owes its existence to an artist and a businessman. The book was originally developed as a catalogue, a reference source to accompany an exhibition of the same name at the Gutenberg Museum in Mainz, and both catalogue and exhibition were structured identically – as a journey around the world, with stopovers in various capital cities, from Frankfurt to Hanover, Berlin and Munich, followed by Vienna, Prague, Paris, New York and even as far as the moon, with the typeface's travels functioning as an introduction to its biographical details. The concept of travel, in fact, sums up the decentralized nature of the avant-garde in the 1920s and 1930s, with design innovations being developed in Germany, beyond the metropolis of Berlin, in other key cities throughout the country. Futura itself was synonymous with breakthrough, timelessness and the future, its most appropriate colour being a shiny metallic silver. This, along with the iconic look of 'futuristic' interior design and the pastel shades of some of its contemporary applications, therefore also determined the design of the accompanying catalogue.

The exhibition and catalogue were made possible by the loan of valuable items and the extensive collections of the Gutenberg Museum, which acquired about 2,000 typeface specimens from the estate of the book designer Philipp Bertheau (1927–2009) in 2010. At the same time, the 'Weltmuseum der Druckkunst' (World Museum of Printing) established its new emphasis on typography by holding special exhibitions and symposiums.

In 1928 Jan Tschichold postulated that a group of people would be required to develop the typeface of the future successfully. The exhibition and the book dedicated to this group also constitute a truly collective work. I would like to give my deepest thanks to Prof. Dr Petra Eisele and Prof. Dr Isabel Naegele from the University of Applied Sciences Mainz for their dedicated work as co-editor and co-curator. I would also like to thank wholeheartedly all the public organizations and private individuals who loaned materials to us for their generosity and trust; the authors for their knowledgeable contributions; and the sponsors and patrons for their financial support. Warm thanks go to the museum's team for its committed involvement. Special thanks go to Senator Wolfgang Hartmann. His grandfather Georg Hartmann was one of the patrons of the Gutenberg commemorative publication of 1925 published by the museum's director, Aloys Ruppel. This book, whose contributors included László Moholy-Nagy and El Lissitzky, as well as Paul Renner and other typographers, outlines the mission of the Gutenberg Museum, which is once again exhibiting the Futura catalogue and presentation materials. The museum, founded in 1900, 'collects ... not only objects from the incunabulum period, but also objects related to the development of the black art right up to the present day', which it 'wishes to demonstrate through specimens and tools'. We hope that FUTURA. THE TYPEFACE will be enjoyed by many readers, and that the institution will 'win many friends, colleagues and supporters' as it grows to become – as it was described in the foreword of the 1925 publication – 'the museum of the future'.

Dr Annette Ludwig, Director of the Gutenberg Museum

INTRODUCTION

With his typeface Futura, Paul Renner's (1878–1956) reputation began to grow at the end of the 1920s; he went on to become one of the best-known type designers of his time. As a leading member of Deutscher-Werkbund (a German association of architects, artists, designers and industrialists) and head of Meisterschule für Deutschlands Buchdrucker (Trade School for Book Printers of Germany) in Munich, he was at the centre of a new media and advertising industry — a position that he also used to criticize the propagandist strategies of the National Socialists.

'FUTURA – the typeface of our time.' FIG.26 P.48

However, Renner's work cannot be unreservedly grouped together with the radical design trends of the Bauhaus or the New Typography, even though he was sympathetic to the typographic avant-garde. Renner was too rooted in the design traditions of the liberal humanist bourgeoisie, and it was from this position that the conception of Futura arose. Renner did not base the development of his typeface on the well-known sans-serif types that had hitherto been used for simple printed material and were therefore considered to be inferior; his approach was determined much more by antique inscriptions, and particularly by the Roman Capitalis Monumentalis.

'FUTURA – an international success.' <u>FIG.48</u> <u>P.126</u>

Unlike many avant-garde designers, who saw their experiments with type as manifestations of a new way of thinking, and either drew typefaces manually or used existing text in a playful way, Renner operated as a typographic specialist. His extensive experience with typefaces made it clear to him that a typeface could be successful only if the upper- and lower-case letters gave rise to a formal aesthetic whole. On the basis of this observation, he systematically derived the structures of his lower-case letters from the geometrical principles of Roman upper-case Antiqua. With this reference to antiquity, Renner managed to design a truly 'modern' geometrical typeface, which both met the requirements of the New Typography and suited the tastes of more conservative designers. From a historical point of view, therefore, Futura was a true typographic design innovation that anticipated the future while being rooted in its own time.

'FUTURA – a typeface conquers the world.' <u>FIG.12</u> <u>P.184</u>

The enormous success of Futura was owed to the risks taken by Georg Hartmann, the professional care given to the typeface by Heinrich Jost, and the marketing of the typeface through the marketing strategies of the Bauer Type Foundry in Frankfurt. Fritz Wichert's idea to name the new typeface Futura – the future – was certainly also ingenious. It is no coincidence that this name was devised in the context of the New Frankfurt project, since, at this time, the city was turning into a hotspot of innovative design.

Another contributor to the typeface's rapid success in Germany was the economic prosperity being experienced in that country, which led to a booming advertising scene that quickly became professional. With its elegant, modern and classic appearance, Futura seemed destined to become the typeface of the 'modern' look. With the internationalization of this new way of experiencing life, the typeface, which was quickly expanded by the Bauer Type Foundry into a varied typeface family, became a successful export product.

FUTURA – a typeface travels the world.

This book invites you to go on a visual journey through a handful of international metropolises that will illuminate typographic ideas and discourses from the 1920s to the 1960s, from different perspectives, yet through the example of a single typeface.

The journey will allow you to view designs, drawings, documents and letters from important private collections, state archives, libraries, museums and institutions, some of which have never before been documented, or placed in their historical design context. These originals are supplemented by Renner's own texts, which provide insight into his theoretical explorations during the development of his typeface. Most of all, we are delighted to present numerous impressive applications of Futura, which not only testify to the outstanding typographic quality of this typeface, but also demonstrate – even 90 years later – the enormous innovative power that the 'modernist' design movement has to this day, and to which this typeface gave its valuable support.

Petra Eisele, Annette Ludwig, Isabel Naegele

FUTURA. A JOURNEY AROUND THE WORLD

'The most supreme of the European types are the Roman capitals, consisting of circles, triangles and squares, which are the simplest and most antithetical forms imaginable. Rarely does the light of this type's elegant simplicity shine as far as our times, like the last shimmer of the bright intellectuality of ancient Rome. There is nothing more simple than what gives the Roman script its unparalleled élan.'

PAUL RENNER
Typografie als Kunst (Typography as Art), 1922.

ABCD
EFGHI
LMNO
PQRST
VXYZ

PETRA EISELE

THE WORKSHOP AND THE COMMISSION 1920–1924

Like many typographers of his time, Renner initially worked as a painter after completing his studies, producing illustrations for – among other customers – the Munich satirical magazine *Simplicissimus*, which began to publish in 1896. The magazine criticized bourgeois values and Wilhelmine politics.

Inspired by the contemporary demand for the applied use of art, the young artist also became involved in book design. Between 1907 and 1917 he was artistic director of the publisher Georg Müller Verlag in Munich, which had close connections with the so-called book art movement and worked as a producer and supplier of books.[1]

During this time, Renner also founded the Münchner Schule für Illustration und Buchgewerbe (Munich School of Illustration and Publishing) with Emil Preetorius, in 1911. This was a private school that later merged with the Debschitz School of Fine and Applied Arts. One of Renner's pupils at this school was Heinrich Jost, who was later to take on an important role at the Bauer Type Foundry.

Renner had examined typography in detail prior to his conception of Futura in *Typografie als Kunst* (Typography as Art), published in 1922.[2] He not only described the historical development of type in this work, but also presented the rules of typography, although he did not address the topic of sans serif types.

Renner had therefore already made a name for himself as a type designer when Siegfried Buchenau[3] and Jakob Hegner[4] paid him a visit in the summer of 1924 at his workshop in Pasinger.[5] After they examined some samples of Renner's work, Hegner announced spontaneously that Renner should now tackle the task that he himself had already engaged two other painters to complete.[6] Renner should design a typeface that could be considered the 'typeface of our time'.[7]

With this brief, Hegner clearly chose the right words. Over the next few days, Renner drew the sentence 'The typeface of our time' in five different versions, from which Buchenau selected one design; this would be used to develop what would become Futura.[8] Renner sent the drawings to Hegner, who was particularly impressed by the ﬀ ligature, which reminded him of a horseshoe magnet. Renner subsequently drew the remaining letters on blue graph paper and promised Hegner that he would deliver them to the type foundry immediately.[9]

Thus, the first drawings of the typeface that would become Futura were completed in the summer of 1924.[FIG.3 P.30] However, when Renner received no news for several months, he requested that his drawings be returned. He then sent them to his former pupil Heinrich Jost,[10] who, since 1922, had been the artistic director of the Bauer Type Foundry in Frankfurt. In late autumn, Renner showed his drawings for the 'typeface of our time' to Georg Hartmann, the then owner of the Bauer Type Foundry, who accepted it.

In the winter of 1924/25, the first experimental designs, containing unusual – and sometimes highly eccentric – characters, were submitted. The typeface was subsequently revised and individual alternate letters were developed.

1

P.27 – portrait of Paul Renner, c. 1930.

2

Roman Capitalis Monumentalis type, a classic form from the Trajan period.

3

Denis Megaw published this image in 1938 in his article '20th Century Sans Serif Types', in the British periodical *Typography*, as Paul Renner's 'first designs for Futura'. According to Christopher Burke, Megaw was a typographer from Belfast with good connections with German type foundries. Burke therefore does not find it entirely unlikely that Megaw might have received the originals, or a reproduction of Futura, from the Bauer Type Foundry for his article. The

original drawings from 1924 have been lost. This illustration is the earliest evidence of the so-called Ur-Futura. The original drawings were probably destroyed by the bombing of Frankfurt-Bockenheim on 11 February 1944, as a result of which – according to Heinrich Jost, in a letter to Paul Renner – the Bauer Type Foundry suffered great losses.

bottom right:
Futura in a version after 1930.

ABCDEFG
HIJKLMN
OPQRST
UVWXYZ
1234567890
&-»!?*§(,,

3

ABCDEFGHIJKLMNO
PQRSTUVWXYZabcd
efghijklmnopqrſstuvwxyz
1234567890ffckß£«»*§!()

BETWEEN ANTIQUITY AND THE AVANT-GARDE

Paul Renner was a recognized expert in the history of typography and held a committed and historically grounded position in many publications on the Fraktur–Antiqua dispute and the question of German type. As early as 1922, two years before the commission to create the 'typeface of our time', he had published his thoughts on the art of writing and printing in *Typografie als Kunst* (Typography as Art), describing how he saw in Roman inscriptions an example of perfection that could never grow old.[11] Renner described Roman Capitalis as the prime inspiration and basis for determining the forms of Futura:

'Unlike the Constructivists, who had become fashionable at that time, I did not want ... to extol the virtues of the pair of compasses as a tool, but rather to rescue form from its vulgarization and bring it back to its original roots. In classical Roman capitals I saw the most intellectually inspired combination of the basic geometric shapes, with all the finer requirements that a typeface should fulfil.'[12]

This specific comparison with the Capitalis Monumentalis of Trajan's Column proves Renner's intention to devise a conceptual solution using these basic geometric shapes as his foundation. However, it should be noted that the Capitalis consists of only upper-case letters. Thus, in an article from 1925, 'Neue Ziele des Schriftschaffens' (The New Objectives of Type Design), when comparing the upper-case and lower-case letters of Romans, Renner sees 'two fundamentally different sets of formal laws as well as two fundamentally different viewpoints held by men regarding their relationship with their fellow human beings and with the world as a whole'.[13]

Although our Latin lower-case letters come from Roman capitals, they came about only after a thousand years of development. They are a type of their own and follow their own rules of form. From **H**, **M** and **N**, came **h**, **m** and **n**; although the opposition to the basic shapes is mitigated, the formation of ascenders and descenders aids legibility and gives the words easily recognizable contours. The perpendicular and the horizontal are predominant and remain assertive, even in the arcs; the diagonal strokes are limited to the letters **k**, **v**, **w**, **x**, **y**, **z**, where the correspondences with Futura are already present in a more reduced form.[14]

4

Georg Hartmann later paid tribute to Capitalis Monumentalis with an inscription of the lettering on Trajan's Column (AD 113) at the entrance of the Bauer Type Foundry on Hamburger Allee in Frankfurt.

The reason for this is: 'So long as we use upper-case and lower-case letters next to each other, the artist has the task of executing the same formal motifs in both of these very different alphabets. Since almost nothing can be done to alter the form of the Roman capitals, the motif of their contrasting forms must be transferred to the lower-case letters as well.'[15]

The transfer of the formal motif, as Renner referred to it, from the Roman capitals to the lower-case letters must surely be the most original and revolutionary aspect of the design of Renner's typeface. Accordingly, he tried to bring not only the capitals but also the lower-case letters back to the 'simplest, most elementary, geometric, basic shapes'.[16]

The first draft FIG.3 P.30 contains many interesting and innovative lower-case letters. These include four variations of lower-case **a** (three versions as a two-storey **a**, and a version that already bears close resemblance to the later single-eyed **a**).

Two versions of lower-case **g** even comprise three storeys and are very striking in their construction. Lower-case **e** does not have a closed eye and is reminiscent of the lower-case **e** of the Stefan-George-Schrift.[17] Different versions of lower-case **o**, **b**, **d**, **p** and **q** are offered with varying proportions. The **m** and **n** are constructed using right angles with no arcs, and the two variants of the lower-case **r** consist of a stem and a ball in two different sizes. The **f** is generally very wide, with a wide hook and crossbar. The **v**, **w** and **z** already have tapered peaks and apexes, but capital **A**, **M** and **N** of Futura Light and Medium acquired this elegant attribute only in a revision of around 1925. FIG.19 P.43

In 1940 Renner described his design approach in a letter to the Bauer Type Foundry, at a time when there were copyright disputes with Berthold, as follows: 'I simply do not subscribe to the idea of differentiating between basic weights and hairlines and the integration of feet, which led me to pursue the most extreme simplicity. While this of course bears some similarities to the grotesque, I did not take the grotesque as my starting point, but rather, clear, logical principles derived from Roman capitals.'

THE TYPEFACE OF OUR TIME IS EXACT, PRECISE AND IMPERSONAL

Paul Renner's second inspiration was the forms popular at that time, and he explained that the 'typeface of our time cannot be derived from handwriting. ... A typeface that corresponds to the contemporary mood should thus be exact, precise and impersonal. It should be functional and simply be what it is without any fuss. If it is a printed type, it should not mimic any kind of handwriting. Our printed script in machine printing consists of machine-manufactured metal letters, which are symbols rather than a script as such. Our printed script is not an expressive gesture in the way handwriting is; every movement that exerts pressure from left to right, every expansion and contraction of the stroke, which can only be incorporated into a script using a cut reed or quill pen, has no place in printed script. We must at last accept the consequence imposed by the invention of the letterpress.'[18] In accordance with this idea, the design of Ur-Futura avoids any upstrokes and downstrokes and is notable for its reduction of the stroke to a minimum. The lower-case letters consist primarily of circles, strokes, right angles, diagonals and a small number of arcs. Renner justified this with his very own theory as regards the reading process:

'We must become accustomed to the idea that printed script has nothing to do with writing, that it is the pressing of metal blocks [of letters] and symbols which give rise to the formation of words. The eye, when it reads, does not follow the line of the individual characters. It cannot be guided by the characteristics of the individual forms. Rather, it captures the dormant word pictures on the paper as it flies above them. ... Futura has attempted to meet this requirement for the first time. It has taken away from the lower-case letters the impulse that drives them from left to right, thereby giving them stillness, which previously had been the exclusive attribute of the upper-case letters.'[19]

The upper- and lower-case **O/o** consist of geometric circles, as do the lower-case **a**, **b**, **d**, **p** and **q** – each of which is supplemented with a straight stroke (stem). The lower-case **t**

5

The special characters/alternates of
Ur-Futura (1924) and the final versions
of the lower-case letters used to develop
Neufville Digital (Futura ND), 2015.

consists of two crossed straight strokes. One characteristic of Futura – the long, straight i – is already present, but with a square dot.

According to Renner, it is not the small hooks (starting and ending strokes) but a 'spiritual bond' that holds the many individual forms of the letters together and connects them in one overall form.[20] Accordingly, all the starting and ending strokes, hooks and ears that could possibly be reminiscent of handwriting were reduced to a minimum in the first design.FIG.6 P.36

TYPE REFORM AND THE SPECIAL CHARACTERISTICS OF GERMAN SPELLING

The third idea that was to be decisive for Futura arose from Renner's intense engagement with German orthography. From 1920 he had grappled fiercely with the idea of spelling reform, and particularly with the topic of the 'two alphabets' – upper-case and lower-case letters. In the *Gutenberg-Jahrbuch* (Almanac) of 1925, he writes: 'We Germans have unfortunately insisted on gracing every noun with a capital letter since the end of the 17th century. We must urgently do away with this obsequious habit and instil a true democracy.'[21] Accordingly, he advocated: 'We should therefore limit the use of capitals to the beginning of sentences and proper nouns, as we used to do in the past and as is the custom everywhere else in the world. After a brief period of adjustment, the legibility of the script will only improve, because the beginning of sentences will be emphasized and names will be distinctly indicated.'[22] However, despite many prominent supporters and advocates for spelling reform, German orthography remained largely unchanged. Proposals to shorten the spelling of phonemes such as **sh** instead of **sch**, **f** instead of **ph**, **v** instead of **w**, and the abolition of long vowels, were generally not implemented.[23] Renner honoured the frequent use of **Ch**, **ch** and **ck** combinations in the German language with vertical terminals in capital **C** and lower-case **c**, which enabled the two letter pairs **c-h** and **c-k** to be closely connected.FIG.14 P.39

Renner attempted to harmonize the two alphabets in the design of his typeface in such a way that they could stand directly next to each other, both expressing the same origins and speaking the same language of form. In his text 'Drei Jahre Futura' (Three Years of Futura, 1930), he justified the prominent ascenders of some lower-case letters, such as **b**, **d**, **f**, **h**, **k**, **l** and **ß**, and of the ligatures, which overshoot even the capitals, as a reaction to the particularities of German orthography, with its frequent use of capital letters. He based this argument on the historical precursor of humanist Antiqua: 'how powerfully the lower-case letters assert themselves against the capitals.'[24]

One special exception is the relatively 'short' **t**. Yet this very discreet speciality was the subject of much feedback – and not all positive – received by the Bauer Type Foundry: 'How many letters I received following the release of the typeface, complaining that I should improve this single error. Georg Hartmann did not let these letters lead him astray; he thought, as I did, that this difference in length was good, and had no intention of sacrificing this good to his enemies for the sake of a supposed improvement.'[25] FIG.7 P.36

All in all, three fundamental ideas can be observed in the 1924 design of Futura. The first is the reference to 'the oldest alphabet of the scripts still in use today': Roman capitals; the second is the rejection of any suggestion of handwriting in the lower-case letters; and lastly, there is the concern for the particular characteristics of German orthography. What resulted was a type that combined the timeless elegance of the Roman canon of forms with a formal reduction of both alphabets.

FUTURA – DEVELOPMENT OF THE TYPEFACE OF OUR TIME

In the winter of 1924/25 a collaboration that would last many years began between Renner and the Bauer Type Foundry. With Heinrich Jost, the design was revised and rebalanced according to optical considerations over a period of almost three years. In the spring of 1925, Renner was engaged by the Kunstschule (School of Art) in Frankfurt, and so found himself regularly in that

aa gg uu ll tt

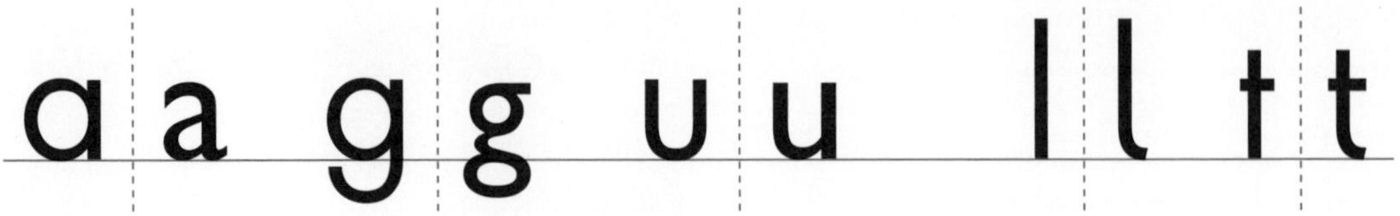

Bb Dd Ff Hh Kk Ll Tt

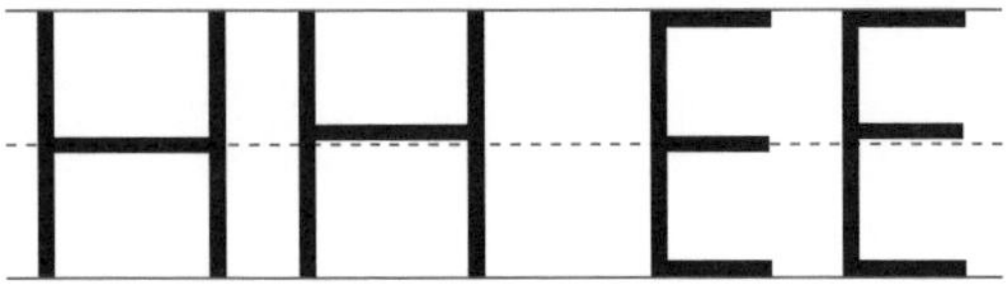

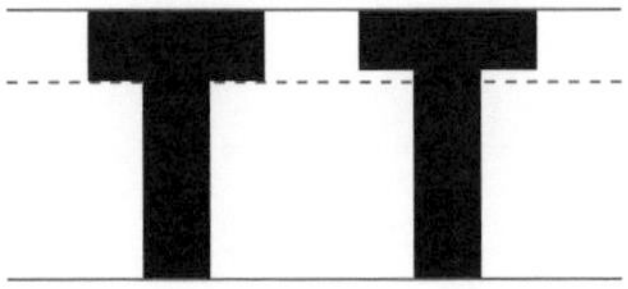

HH EE   TT

HAOT

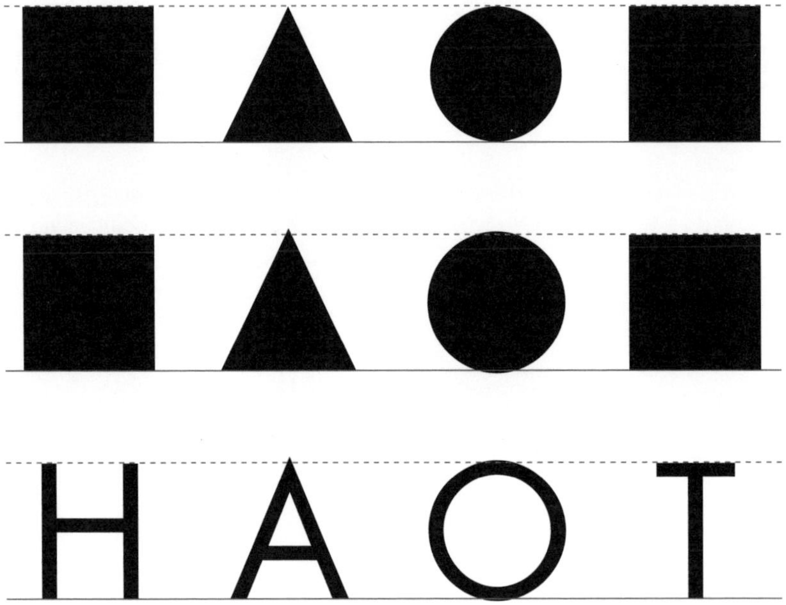

6

Paul Renner frees the lower-case letters from any reminders of handwriting, such as starting and ending strokes, and adjusts the dynamic of the type's direction by reducing the stroke to a minimum. This is a comparison of Futura/Gill Sans and Futura/Futura ND Alternate.

7

A special characteristic of Futura is the long ascenders of the lower-case **b**, **d**, **f**, **h**, **k** and **l**, which overshoot the cap height, and which initially drew much criticism. An exception is the lower-case **t**, with its asymmetrical crossbar and much lower ascender.

8

The crossbars on the left in each case are positioned in the mathematical centre, while the crossbars to their right are in the visual centre. The crossbars appear somewhat raised when visually centred.

9

Monoline on the left, and visually corrected on the right. With the same stroke weight, the horizontal appears wider than the vertical. The horizontal bar has been narrowed accordingly in the visually corrected version.

10

With the same height, the triangle and circle appear smaller than the square. To balance this effect visually, the apex of the **A** and the round of the **O** on the second line are raised slightly above the cap height, with the **O** also undershooting the baseline.

11

To prevent so-called spots, or 'irradiation', care should be taken when curves and stems meet by narrowing the arches and/or the width of the stroke at the point where it joins the stem. The stroke weight then changes accordingly in mathematical terms, but appears monolinear from a visual point of view.

12

The lower-case **ö** has been optically balanced. The outer line is circular, but the inner circle is more oval than round. Since the horizontal appears wider than the perpendicular, this has been optically corrected accordingly.

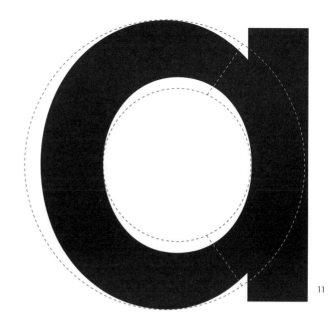

11

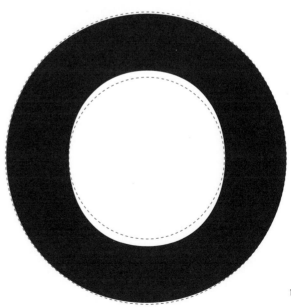

12

ABCDEFGHIJKLM
NOPQRSTUVW
XYZÆŒÇÄÖÜ
aabcdefgghijklmm
nnopqrsſtuvwxyz
æœçchck ff fi fl ffi ffl fi ffl

1234567890

1234567890

.,;:;-!?')†§&G*»«& ˆˊˇˉ˜ ̈ ˙

13

Futura Light, proof, c. 1926. Type specimen sheets with glued-on letters, with later versions pasted over some earlier designs. Featuring numerous alternate characters, ligatures and oldstyle figures.

14

Futura Medium, proof, c. 1926/27, first revision, with pencil markings indicating the changes to the lower-case **s**, **x** and **c**.

15

Futura Medium, proof, c. 1926/27, second revision. The revised versions of **B**, **s**, **ch**, **ck** and **x** are presented separately.

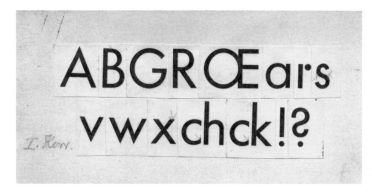

14

15

16

17

16

Proofs of Futura Bold, c. 1926/27, first and second revisions pasted on, with pencil markings in some places and corrections made in white ink, such as for the **s**. The provisional designs of the long **s** and long **ss** are of particular interest, as is the **s-t** ligature. The **J** has a long descender.

17

Proofs of Futura Medium, c. 1927/28, presenting some early alternate forms. Corrected versions of the lower-case **a**, **b**, **d**, **e**, **g**, **p**, **q** and **s** have been pasted over their previous versions, giving them a lighter background. A more conventional version of the **r** has also been pasted at the edge of the page.

18

Proofs of Futura Medium, c. 1927/28, presenting some early alternate forms. Revised versions of characters such as **E**, **F**, **Q**, **S** and lower-case **a**, **b**, **d**, **g**, **k**, **p** and **q** have been pasted over their previous versions, giving them a lighter background. They are all somewhat less round when compared with their first publication in 1927. The more conventional version of the **r** has been added to the sixth row. The numbers **1**, **2**, **3** and **8** are already significantly different from the first publication in 1927. The original longer horizontal arm of the figure **1** can still be seen through the paper.

ABCDEFGHIJK
LMNOPQRSTUV
WXYZÇŒ Æ ÄÖÜØ$
aabcdefgghijklm
mnnopqrsſtuvwx
yzæœçøchckfffiflr
ftſſſiſtß&&
1234567890
1234567890
§†?!(*«»’-:;,.
72

18

city. But soon after, in May 1926, he accepted the position of head of the Berufsschule für das Graphische Gewerbe (Technical College of Graphic Trades) in Munich. The corrections to Futura were sent by post no later than this period, and there is evidence of the interim stages in the form of numerous proofs. [CF. P.369 ET SEQ.]

Renner's concept corresponded to a mono-line sans serif, free of any reminders of handwriting, such as starting and ending strokes, including in the lower-case letters, as well as a 'subjugation and obliteration' of any dynamic movement, and a reduction of the stroke to a minimum. [26] Futura underwent optical corrections and many tests prior to its first publication – particularly the original alternate lower-case letters.

IRRADIATION

Renner wrote: 'While the strokes of FUTURA are never perfectly equal (when measured with the aid of a magnifying glass), this variation is not based on the technical requirements of writing and is not outside the particular realm of printed type. The various weights of the stroke are selected so carefully that all the strokes appear to be of the same weight.' [27] And 'we also require a printed type of an even, pearly grey; no letters should be of a darker black than the others, and there should be no spots anywhere within the body of a letter.' [28]

Renner had already addressed the problem of irradiation in *Typografie als Kunst* in 1922. 'Wherever two strong bars cross at right angles or form an angle at an apex, a zone forms which is not, or minimally, brightened by the irradiation. This results in dark spots; they can be observed in almost all printed types.' [29]

When a curve meets a straight or diagonal stroke, so-called knots or spots occur for the viewer, and these can be optically corrected by balancing the stroke weight at the point where the lines join together. [30] As a result, the weight of the line, including in Futura, after its revision, is strictly speaking no longer monolinear, and thereby appears more unified. [FIG.11 P.37]

THE HORIZONTAL AND THE PERPENDICULAR

According to optical rules, equal weights of stroke appear wider on the horizontal than they do on the perpendicular. To balance this effect optically and achieve stroke weights that appear to be the same, the horizontal must be made somewhat lighter. This applies not only to straight strokes but also to round forms and diagonals. While the right diagonal must be somewhat wider than the vertical when making optical corrections, the left diagonal must be relatively narrower than the vertical. [31] [FIG.9 P.36]

THE VISUAL CENTRE

When a plane is divided into mathematically exact halves, the upper half will appear to be larger than the lower half. In typographical design this means that, for example, in the capital **H**, the crossbar must be technically positioned somewhat higher so that optically it appears to sit in the middle. This also applies to the crossing of the **X** and the horizontal middle bar of the **E**. [32] [FIG.8 P.36]

CIRCLE, TRIANGLE, SQUARE

When the round and triangular capitals are the same mathematical height, they appear smaller when compared to a right-angled character. The **G** and **A**, for example, were therefore made somewhat taller so that they extend over the cap line and baseline and appear optically to be the same height as the right-angled letters (e.g. **H**, **T**, **U**). This applies particularly to the sharp apex of the **A**, **N** and **M** (of Futura Light, Medium and Book), which can be observed from 1925 on in the specimen sizes and first printed materials, such as an invitation to a lecture in Frankfurt on 3 July 1925. [FIG.4 P.67]

The detailed work of optical correction can be observed in the proofs from 1926 and 1927.

19

Type specimen of Renner Futura Medium, c.1925/26. The apex of the **A** is already sharp, and the upper arc of the lower-case **f** is still very wide. The alternates for **a**, **g**, **r**, **m** and **n** are tested against one another, including the 'stroke-and-ball' **r**.

RENNER-FUTURA

An der Spitze aller euro-
paischen Schriften stehen
die romischen Versalien,
aufgebaut aus Kreis und

An der Spitze aller euro-
paischen Schriften stehen
die romischen Versalien,
aufgebaut aus Kreis und

20

21

20

Futura type specimen, 1927, in light and medium weights. Futura Bold is said to be 'in development'.

21

Supplement for a 'more conventional' **r** in addition to the 'stroke-and-ball' **r**.

22

Futura type specimen, 16 point, Futura Medium, 11 February 1927. The alternates are tested in running text. The two versions of the **s** in particular are juxtaposed. The long **s** with many ligatures changes the appearance of the script significantly, with the emphasized upper lengths. The alternates for **a**, **g**, **m**, **n** and **&** were still in the test phase. The stroke-and-ball **r** and long **s** were also included in the regular character set in the first publication in November 1927. The other alternates were provided only upon request. The curve of the **f** is very wide, and the **2** forms an almost closed circle.

23

Futura type specimen with word combinations using the existing types. Futura Light 60 point, 18 June 1928. After the second publication of type specimens at the beginning of 1928, which no longer offered any alternates apart from the long **s**, additional tests of the innovative lowercase letters were carried out.

22

23

ABCDEFGHIJKLMNO
PQRSTUVWXYZÄÖÜ
abcdefghijklmnopqrſst
uvwxyzäöüchckﬀﬁﬂﬀﬅﬆﬆß

mager 1234567890 &.,-:;·!?'(*†«»§

Auf Wunsch liefern wir Mediäval-Ziffern 1234567890

ABCDEFGHIJKLMNO
PQRSTUVWXYZÄÖÜ
abcdefghijklmnopqrſst
uvwxyzäöüchckﬀﬁﬂﬀﬅﬆﬆß

halbfett 1234567890 &.,-:;·!?'(*†«»§

Auf Wunsch liefern wir Mediäval-Ziffern 1234567890

ABCDEFGHIJKLMNO
PQRSTUVWXYZÄÖÜ
abcdefghijklmnopq
rſstuvwxyzäöüchck
ﬀﬁﬂﬀﬅﬆﬆß
1234567890
fett &.,-:;·!?'(*†«»§

46

Futura mager

A B C D E F G H I J K L M N O P
Q R S T U V W X Y Z Ä Ö Ü Æ Œ Ç
a b c d e f g h i j k l m n o p q r ſ s t u v w
x y z ä ö ü ch ck ff fi fl ffl ſi ß æ œ ç
1 2 3 4 5 6 7 8 9 0 & . , - : ; · ! ? (' « » § † *

Auf besonderen Wunsch liefern wir auch nachstehende Figuren

a g m n ä & 1 2 3 4 5 6 7 8 9 0

Sie sind im Gradverzeichnis jeweils in der letzten Zeile verwendet

Futura halbfett

A B C D E F G H I J K L M N O P
Q R S T U V W X Y Z Ä Ö Ü Æ Œ Ç
a b c d e f g h i j k l m n o p q r ſ s t u v w
x y z ä ö ü ch ck ff fi fl ffl ſi ß æ œ ç
1 2 3 4 5 6 7 8 9 0 & . , - : ; · ! ? (' « » § † *

Auf besonderen Wunsch liefern wir auch nachstehende Figuren

a g m n ä & 1 2 3 4 5 6 7 8 9 0

Sie sind im Gradverzeichnis jeweils in der letzten Zeile verwendet

spätere Form

25

26

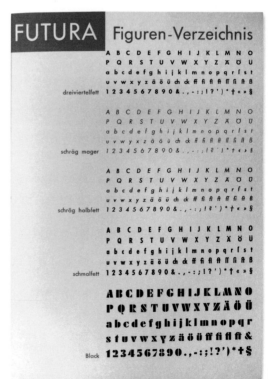

27

24

P.46 – Futura type specimen, 1930.
Overview of the index of characters
for Futura Light, Medium and Bold. In
this publication, the stroke-and-ball **r** is
replaced by the conventional **r**, and the innovative alternates are no longer offered.
Oldstyle figures could be ordered specially. Some letters have been discreetly
revised. For example, the lower-case **b**,
d, **p** and **q** are less round than in the first
edition. The figures **2** and **8** have also
been revised.

25

P.47 – Futura type specimen, 1927.
Overview of the character sets for the light
and medium faces. The accompanying
right-hand page states that Futura Bold
is still undergoing development. The two
special characters, the stroke-and-ball **r**
and the long **s**, are integral parts of the
character set, while the innovative alternates and oldstyle figures are available
upon request.

26

'Futura: Die Schrift unserer Zeit'
(Typeface of our Time), type
specimen, 1930.

27

The additional weights, type
specimen, 1930.

28

'Futura: Die grossen Grade'
(The Large Sizes), c. 1930.

28

SPECIAL CHARACTERS/ALTERNATES

While the capitals of the first design were revised to only a minor extent, many changes and revisions were made to the lower-case letters. The most bizarre characters of Ur-Futura, such as the **g**, **a**, **ɛ** and the various versions of **b**, had already been singled out and were removed early on in the production process. The **a**, **g**, **m**, **n**, **ä**, **&** and the long **s** were tested at the same time as the more conventional characters, until their publication in November 1927.

The relevant literature contains numerous references indicating that the light, medium and bold faces were released simultaneously. However, the Bauer Type Foundry had in fact already registered Renner-Futura Light and Medium on 26 February 1926 with the Verein Deutscher Schriftgiessereien (Association of German Type Foundries) in Leipzig and Offenbach/Main, but not at the same time as the bold face. Publication followed on 14 November 1927, at the same time as the typeface's release for sale through sales representatives.[33]

The overview of the characters indicates that **a**, **g**, **m**, **n**, **ä**, **&** and the oldstyle figures were available only upon special request. The bold face had already been announced in the advertising brochures of November 1927. The single-eyed **a** and two-storey **g** were already established. The unconventional lower-case **r**, consisting of a stroke and a ball, had been prepared in time for the first release.

Futura Light, Medium and Bold were first advertised in February 1928, in relevant magazines such as *Gebrauchsgraphik*. The type-specimen brochure entitled *Futura – The Typeface of our Time* included an exclusive offering of Futura Bold as well. The **r** and the long **s** were added as standard to the index of characters for Futura Bold. The oldstyle figures were made available upon request in the light and medium weights. The first portfolio offered many sample commercial applications of Futura Light and Medium for viewing.

Some letters and figures were revised in 1930 in the programmatic, silver second portfolio, *Futura – die sich die Welt erobert* (Futura – how it conquered the world). The capital **J** had been

shortened, the lower-case 'stroke-and-ball' **r** had been replaced by the more conventional form with ears, and the figures **2**, **3** and **8** were less striking. The proportions of the lower-case **a**, **b**, **d**, **g**, **q** and **p** were further revised and their basic geometric shape altered, with the circle eventually becoming an oval. The oldstyle figures were included in the standard set, and the special characters/alternates were no longer listed.

Renner seems to have adhered for a while longer to the alternate characters **m**, **n** and, in particular, the idiosyncratic "stroke-and-ball" **r**, which is used in proofs of the type and in his book *Mechanisierte Grafik* (1931). [34]

29

29
Verein Deutscher Schriftgiessereien (Association of German Type Foundries): index cards with the registration dates of new types and submissions of type specimens. Renner-Futura Light and Medium were registered on 26 February 1926. The print was submitted on 4 November. The main tasks of the association included the settlement of disputes between type foundries. Georg Hartmann was vice-chairman of the association from 1926 to 1934.

30
'Futura Oblique Points in New Directions', type specimen, 1930.

DIE SCHRÄGE FUTURA WEIST NEUE WEGE

Die Ergänzung unserer Futura-Schriften durch einen schrägen Schnitt wurde von den Notwendigkeiten typographischer Technik gefordert. Der Buchdrucker braucht als Auszeichnungsschrift eine der Futura ebenbürtige Type, eine Schrift von gleicher Prägnanz und Schönheit. Aus der folgerichtigen Gestaltung klar erkannter Gesetzmäßigkeiten entstand eine Schrift von ausgezeichneter Wirkung, die dem Druckwerk Kraft und Leben verleiht. Jene kristallklare Reinheit der Form, die das typische Kennzeichen der Futura-Schriften ist, offenbart in diesem schrägen Schnitt neue Schönheiten. Der modernen Satzgestaltung sind durch die schräge Futura neue Wege eröffnet worden.

BAUERSCHE GIESSEREI · FRANKFURT A·M

30

'Nothing could be further from my intention than the design of a sans serif typeface.'

PAUL RENNER
'From Georg-Müller-Buch to Futura and the Master School. Memories of Paul – Renner from 1918 to 1927', 1940.

PETRA EISELE

THE FADING STAR OF THE CLASSIC TYPES

FROM THE CLASSICAL ANTIQUA TO THE MODERN SANS SERIF

Although sans serif typefaces had been developed in German in the nineteenth century, their proportions were generally reminiscent of bold Antiqua types and were not highly regarded, primarily because they were clearly subject to the industrialized aesthetic of that century. Looking back, Renner wrote:

'When I designed this typeface [i.e. Futura] the term "sans serif type" was not part of my vocabulary; ... The sans serifs were for people who were familiar with printed types because of their work on the Good Book. It was a proletarian typeface family that had no renowned predecessors, good for newspaper headlines; but which book artists at that time saw any indication of an artistic endeavour in the typographic design of an advertisement? Nothing could be further from my intention than the design of a sans serif typeface. No, I took the Roman capitals as my starting point.'[35]

How did sans serif types, which had previously been regarded as inferior, come to be assessed in a new and positive light, and eventually advocated by avant-garde designers? What caused Renner to take greater account of them? In Renner's opinion – and in the opinion of many progressive contemporaries – a letter could be designed with the utmost objectivity by focusing on the use of the basic shapes (circle, square, triangle).

This return to the basic shapes and colours demonstrates an attempt to go back to the origins of design. The aim was to discard the weight of history by concentrating on abstract forms and rethinking design from the ground up.

Thus, the engagement with basic geometric shapes at the beginning of the twentieth century was an essential principle in progressive artistic and design training.[36] The Viennese teacher of type Rudolf von Larisch had, for example, reduced the form of letters to the circle, stroke, triangle and square,[37] while Adolf Hölzel had devised elementary design rules in art, and his research included the circle, square and triangle – a tradition that was continued by his pupil Johannes Itten at the Bauhaus.[38]

In his book *Über das Geistige in der Kunst* (On the Spiritual in Art; 1912), Wassily Kandinsky had described geometric shapes such as the square, circle, triangle, rhombus or trapezium as purely abstract entities and 'equal citizens of the abstract realm'.[39] In his teaching at the Bauhaus, he systematized these theories on art in concrete form and ascribed a specific primary colour to the triangle, square and circle: yellow for the dynamic triangle, red for the static square, and blue for the calm circle.[40] These three basic color-and-shape associations subsequently developed into a leitmotif that typified the Bauhaus approach.

From a historical perspective, Walter Porstmann's book *Sprache und Schrift* (1920) is also informative. In it, he called for an even greater 'simplification of the character': 'Any attempts to create new types and shorthand types are based on stroke combinations. The ultimate unit of the letter, as well as of all geometric shapes and all artistic forms, is the simple stroke, the line, whether straight or curved.'[41]

The topic of sans serif types did not play any role in Renner's textbook published in 1922 and set in Ungar-Fraktur, *Typografie als Kunst* (Typography as Art). Instead, he concentrated on basic, elementary geometric shapes, in accordance with contemporary concerns in art and design pedagogy: 'If we were to see which shapes are most securely present in our minds, the shapes that come to our minds most quickly and clearly at any time, we would all come to the same conclusion. They are the simplest bodies: the sphere, cylinder, cone, cube, spindle and the like.'[42] In terms of type design, Renner understandably preferred the Roman capitals.

The Bauhaus exhibition for which Walter Gropius devised the motto 'Kunst und Technik – eine neue Einheit' (Art and Technology – a New Unity) marked a turning point. The school's new approach to typography followed hitherto unknown design motifs that focused on the organization of elementary design methods and was approved by typography professionals such as Jan Tschichold: sans serifs; capitals constructed with a ruler; grotesque types that had not been widely used in book design, particularly Venus[43] and Akzidenz-Grotesk; justified text; and the use of type elements as vertical or horizontal structural bars. The rhythm achieved on flat surfaces is also the result of large geometric symbols such as the circle, square and triangle, often in combination with the three primary colours. Although varied and modified for individual use, these elementary design methods, combined with the new 'typesetting style',[44] led to recurring motifs in the work of the Bauhaus, which in turn meant that the general public perceived a coherence or unity in the school's output.

For Renner, the motivation behind the creation of a new type of script was clearly to reproduce the 'machine-like smoothness made easily possible by modern technology' in a new 'Antiqua' type.[45] He declared as much in 1925, despite some uncertainty, when he embarked

32

upon his search: 'it may be possible one day to reduce the upper-case and lower-case letters to a single formal principle. I hope to be able to speak about this possibility in a few months, when my own first typeface will be ready.'[46]

The actual problem that Renner had challenged himself to solve in the design of Futura was how to determine the forms of the lower-case letters based on formal rules derived from Roman capital script. What makes Futura truly innovative, therefore, is the way that the upper- and lower-case letters follow a consistently unified, elementary language of form. In this way, Futura fulfilled the requirements of its time, both as a type design and in terms of a radical reduction of form.

31

STAATLICHES BAUHAUS IN WEIMAR 1919-1923

33

31

László Moholy-Nagy: prospectus, 1925 (invitation to subscribe to the catalogue *Staatliches* [State] *Bauhaus in Weimar 1919–1923.*)

32

Oskar Schlemmer: first page of a four-page prospectus, *Das staatliche Bauhaus*, 1922.

33

Herbert Bayer: cover design for *Staatliches Bauhaus in Weimar 1919–1923*, catalogue for the Bauhaus exhibition, 1923.

bbb

Alternate designs for lower-case **b**
Ur-Futura, 1924.

1

One clear example of the broad scope of his work, and the responsibility it bore, is the enormous number of titles (287) published in 1913 alone.

2

Renner had previously published typographic rules in his industry's press, and they were the subject of much discussion among his peers. His *Typografie als Kunst* (Typography as Art) provided further explanations and opinions regarding these rules. Cf. [Paul Renner]: 'Vom Georg-Müller-Buch bis zur Futura und Meisterschule. Erinnerungen Paul Renners aus dem Jahrzehnt 1918 bis 1927'. In: *Imprimatur* (Munich), vol.IX, 1940, pp.2–3 [supplement].

3

Buchenau was a publisher, book designer and editor of the almanac *Imprimatur*, the mouthpiece of the bibliophiles; cf. note 2.

4

Hegner was a publisher from Gartenstadt Hellerau, near Dresden, where he founded his own publishing house in 1913. Cf. Georg Kurt Schauer: 'Das Bauhaus und Paul Renner'. In: *Deutsche Buchkunst 1890 bis 1960*, vol.1, Hamburg 1963, p.236 et seq.

5

Cf. Günter Gerhard Lange: 'Weg, Werk und Zeitgenossen Paul Renners'. In: Philipp Luidl and Günter Gerhard Lange (eds): *Paul Renner. A special publication of the Munich Typography Society*, Munich 1978, p.48.

6

The two painters are purported to be Lyonel Feininger and Karl Schmidt-Rottluff.

7

Paul Renner: 'Vom Georg-Müller-Buch bis zur Futura und Meisterschule'. In: *Gebrauchsgraphik* (Berlin), vol.20, May 1943/44, no.5, page not specified, and [Renner]: 'Vom Georg-Müller-Buch bis zur Futura und Meisterschule. (Imprimatur)', p.5. Hegner was convinced that only one painter could create the 'typeface of our time'; cf. Christopher Burke: *Paul Renner: The Art of Typography*, London 1998, p.87; Andreas Hansert: *Georg Hartmann (1870-1954). Biografie eines Frankfurter Schriftgiessers, Bibliophilen und Kunstmäzens*, Vienna/Cologne/Weimar 2009, pp.84–85.

8

[Renner]: 'Vom Georg-Müller-Buch bis zur Futura und Meisterschule. (Imprimatur)', p.5; Günter Gerhard Lange: 'Weg, Werk und Zeitgenossen Paul Renners'. In: Luidl and Lange (eds): *Paul Renner*, p.48; also cf. Burke: *Paul Renner*, p.87, and Hansert: *Georg Hartmann*, p.85.

9

[Renner]: 'Vom Georg-Müller-Buch bis zur Futura und Meisterschule. (Imprimatur)', p.5, and Renner: 'Vom Georg-Müller-Buch bis zur Futura und Meisterschule' (Gebrauchsgraphik).

10

Heinrich Jost visited the Schule für Illustration und Buchgewerbe (Munich School of Illustration and Publishing) and the Debschitzschule (Debschitz School), directed by Paul Renner and Emil Preetorius, both in Munich. Cf. Robert Diehl: *Heinrich Jost (Deutsche Buchkünstler und Gebrauchsgraphiker der Gegenwart)*, Leipzig 1926, p.xvii.

11

In 1940, in retrospect, Renner described his encounter with inscriptions engraved in stone during a stay in Rome in the first year of his marriage as having had the strongest artistic impression ever made on him. In almost all typesetting guidelines since Edward Johnston's manual *Writing & Illuminating & Lettering*, the inscription on Trajan's Column has been referred to as the finest example of Roman monumental script. Renner certainly knew the work. He later described how his pupils would always set Roman capitals using 'a tool that could produce the same stroke weight in any direction'.

12

Letter from Paul Renner to the Bauer Type Foundry on 14 March 1940. Archive of Andrea Haushofer, Munich.

13

Paul Renner: 'Neue Ziele des Schriftschaffens'. In: *Die Bücherstube* (Munich), vol.4, 1925, no.1, pp.18–28.

14

Paul Renner: *Die Kunst der Typografie*, Berlin 1939.

15

Paul Renner: 'Das Formproblem der Druckschrift'. In: *Imprimatur* (Munich), vol.I, January 1930, pp.27–33.

16

Letter from Renner to the Bauer Type Foundry on 14 March 1940.

17

The so-called Stefan-George-Schrift was based on George's handwriting. It was developed in 1903 and used for the first time in 1904. There has been a digital version of the George typeface since 2003. Samples were used from a collection of type models from 1907 published by the Berlin publishing house Otto von Holten. The book of type models has fortunately been preserved, and is held in the Berlin State Library. The publishing house and printing press were destroyed at the end of World War II. Cf. Roland Reuss/Institut für Textkritik Heidelberg 2003: www.textkritik.de.

18

Paul Renner: 'Die Schrift unserer Zeit'. In: *Die Form* (Berlin), vol.2, 1927, no.4, pp.109–10.

19

[Paul Renner]: 'Paul Renner on his typeface "Futura"'. In: *Börsenblatt für den deutschen Buchhandel* (Leipzig), vol.94, 20 September 1927, no.220, pp.1134–35.

20

Paul Renner, 'Über die Schrift der Zukunft'. In: *Typographische Mitteilungen* (Berlin), vol.25, August 1928, no.8., pp.189–192.

21

Paul Renner: 'Revolution der Buchschrift'. In: Gutenberg commemorative publication, *Gutenberg-Jahrbuch* (Almanac), to celebrate the 25th anniversary of the Gutenberg Museum in Mainz 1925, ed. by A[loys] Ruppel, Mainz 1925, pp.279–82.

22

Paul Renner: 'Schrift und Rechtschreibung'. In: *Pandora* (Ulm), 1946, pp.31–37.

23

Ibid.

24

Paul Renner: 'Drei Jahre Futura'. In: *Type specimen Futura: die Ergänzungsgarnituren*. Frankfurt am Main: 1930/31.

25

Paul Renner: 'Aus der Geschichte der neuen deutschen Typografie'. Lecture at the annual assembly of Grafisches Gewerbe (graphic industry) in Freiburg im Breisgau, 1947. Copy of a typewritten manuscript, 13 p. Gutenberg Museum, Mainz.

26

Letter from Paul Renner to the Bauer Type Foundry on 14 March 1940.

27

Renner: 'Über die Schrift der Zukunft', pp. 189–192.

28

Renner: 'Schrift und Rechtschreibung', pp. 31–37.

29

Renner: 'Das Formproblem der Druckschrift', pp. 27–33.

30

Jost Hochuli: *Das Detail in der Typografie. Buchstabe, Buchstabenabstand, Wort, Wortabstand, Zeile, Zeilenabstand, Kolumne*, Munich 1990, pp. 20–23.

31

Ibid.

32

Ibid.

33

On 25 November 1927 the general representative of the Bauer Type Foundry wrote to the Kreysing company in Leipzig, informing it that the type foundry could now offer specimens of the light and medium weights of Futura, and that Futura Bold was also in development.

34

Paul Renner: *Mechanisierte Grafik. Schrift, Typo, Foto, Film, Farbe*, Berlin 1931.

35

[Renner]: 'Vom Georg-Müller-Buch bis zur Futura und Meisterschule.(*Imprimatur*), p. 5, and Renner: 'Vom Georg-Müller-Buch bis zur Futura und Meisterschule' (*Gebrauchsgraphik*), page not specified.

36

These are based in turn on the teaching reforms of the nineteenth century, under which leading figures of the later design and/or artistic avant-garde – including Wassily Kandinsky – were educated. Cf. J. Abbott Miller: 'Elementar-Schule'. In: Ellen Lupton and J. Abbott Miller (eds): *The ABCs of the Bauhaus. The Bauhaus and Design Theory*, London 1993, p. 6 et seq.

37

Albert Kapr: *Schriftkunst. Geschichte, Anatomie und Schönheit der lateinischen Buchstaben*, Dresden 1996, p. 209.

38

Itten's research resulted in the book *Geist der Primäruntersuchung* (The Spirit of Primary Investigation) and is strongly concerned with the attempt, akin to the spirit of expressionism, to return to the original experiences of childhood; cf. Miller: 'Elementar-Schule', p. 20; Rainer Wick emphasized that Itten was also obsessed by Kandinsky's *On the Spiritual in Art*, and so taught the same colour classification as Kandinsky. Cf. Rainer Wick: *Bauhaus – Kunstschule der Moderne*, Ostfildern-Ruit 2000, p. 214.

39

Wassily Kandinsky: *Über das Geistige in der Kunst*. With an introduction by Max Bill. 10th ed., Bern 1980, p. 70. The book was published at the end of 1911 but was dated 1912; the manuscript had been completed in 1910.

40

To address any doubts, Kandinsky conducted surveys among the students as well as the general population. He summarized the essence of his teachings on the Bauhaus in 1926 in *Point and Line to Plane*. Cf. Wassily Kandinsky: *Punkt und Linie zu Fläche. Contribution to an analysis of painting-related aspects* (Bauhaus-Buch no. 9). Munich 1926.

41

Walter Porstmann: *Sprache und Schrift*, Berlin 1920, pp. 82–83.

42

Paul Renner: *Typografie als Kunst*, Munich 1922, p. 33.

43

Venus plays an important role in the New Typography; see fig. 50, p. 478, Venus in the Futura Schmuck specimen, with a quotation from Moholy-Nagy about Venus.

44

Heinrich Jost: 'Zweifel'. In: *Klimschs Jahrbuch* (Frankfurt am Main), 1933, p. 6.

45

Paul Renner: 'Das Ende des Historismus'. In: *Gebrauchsgraphik* (Berlin), vol. 1, September 1925, no. 9, p. 47.

46

Renner: 'Neue Ziele des Schriftschaffens', p. 23.

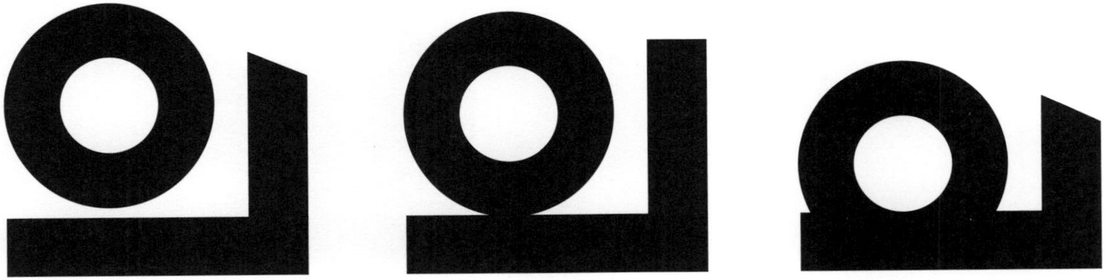

Alternate designs for lower-case **a**
Ur-Futura, 1924.

KAMA
DER
ELEGANTE
SCHUH

KARL MATTHIAE

KAMA
SCHUHHAUS

KAMA
SCHUHHAUS

KARL MATTHIAE

KARL MATTHIAE

FRANK FURT

From the mid-1920s, a new kind of architecture began to appear. In Dessau, the new Bauhaus building, with its spectacular 'curtain wall', and the Meisterhäuser (Masters' Houses) were opened. In Stuttgart, intense preparations were under way for the Werkbund exhibition at the Weissenhof housing estate, which demonstrated 'the application of new production techniques for the construction of residential housing' under the direction of Ludwig Mies van der Rohe.[1]

From 1925 to 1930 Ernst May was head of urban planning and building in Frankfurt am Main. Under his leadership, the largest experiment of the 'New Architecture' was carried out, involving the construction of several independent satellite towns on the outskirts of the city, with approximately 12,000 modern apartments, for which the Viennese architect Margarete Schütte-Lihotzky developed a rationally planned built-in kitchen – the so-called Frankfurt kitchen.[2]

The 'May Brigade' attracted renowned architects of the time, among them Martin Elsässer, Max Bromme, Ferdinand Kramer, Herbert Boehm and Adolf Meyer; in addition, internationally renowned architects such as Walter Gropius, Max Taut and Mart Stam worked on individual projects. Both the urban-planning concept of housing estates themselves and, more importantly, the aesthetic and functional attributes of the homes and utilities, including the interior fittings, were designed to be standardized and to serve as a model suitable for mass production. Major special exhibitions, such as 'Die neue Wohnung und ihr Innenausbau' (The New Apartment and its Interior Design), which was held in 1927 on the occasion of the Frankfurt Spring Fair, demonstrated the advantages of the New Living convincingly.[3]

Renner was very impressed by these efforts to devise a socially orientated concept of design based on rationalization and standardization, as a statement made during his time in Frankfurt clearly shows: 'we need many new and cheap apartments. The things we need to be comfortable are not all that different. It must therefore be possible to improve the construction of residential buildings and make them cheaper by means of the mass production of carefully tested models, such as is already the case for bicycles and cars. This will lead to the standardization of building components.'[4]

Renner's discussions with the May 'brigade' of architects, and his observations of their design projects, inspired him and influenced his attitude towards Futura, which became even more rooted in a technical and functional rationale, with a thoroughly revolutionary verve. He wanted to create something new; a clear break had to be made with the old. To achieve this break, he wanted to reduce the form of every letter to its function. In addition, technical parameters, such as the raw material of the type, the printing technique and the purpose of the type's use, should inform the 'objective' design: 'A typeface that corresponds to the contemporary mood should thus be exact, precise and impersonal. It should be functional and simply be what it is without any fuss. If it is a printed type, it should not mimic any kind of handwriting.'[5]

PE

1
Margarete Schütte-Lihotzky: the Frankfurt kitchen.

2
Partial view of the Höhenblick housing estate, Frankfurt am Main, 1927. Architect: Ernst May, with Carl-Hermann Rudloff.

3
Part of the Bruchfeldstrasse housing estate, seen from the courtyard. Architect: Ernst May, with Carl-Hermann Rudloff.

PETRA EISELE
ISABEL NAEGELE

NEW FRANKFURT – NEW ARCHITECTURE

Renner recalled that directly after the Bauer Type Foundry granted its approval in winter 1924/25, the first sample of Futura was developed and his type became 'visible in every street and discussed enthusiastically within the book-making industry', even before his appointment to the Frankfurter Kunstschule (Frankfurt School of Art).[6] Since he had taught courses in February at two major printing houses in Cologne, as well as in Mönchen-Gladbach, and had also been invited to give lectures in various towns in the Rhine region, he brought with him 'slides of the first preliminary designs of the type', ready to tell the whole world what had led him to this new form of type.[7] Renner's sample of Futura had also already been used in the setting of the invitations.[8]

In fact, applications of the first samples of Futura appeared in the summer of 1925. One example is an invitation card, which still survives, for a lecture to be given by Renner on 3 July at the Frankfurt group of the Bildungsverbandes der Deutschen Buchdrucker (Educational Association of German Letterpress Printers) on the topic of 'Tote oder lebende Schrift?' (Dead or Living Type?). The card was set using the samples of Futura, probably by Philipp Albinus at the Frankfurter Kunstschule.[9] Another example appeared in July 1925: 'Vorprobe der noch unfertigen Renner-Futura' (Samples of the still unfinished Renner-Futura), in Fritz Helmuth Ehmcke's book *Schrift* (Type).[10]

THE FRANKFURTER KUNSTSCHULE

After the art historian Fritz Wichert became head of the Frankfurter Kunstschule in 1923, he reformed the school according to the model of the Weimar Bauhaus. He merged the Kunstschule and the Kunstgewerbeschule (Arts and Crafts School) with the aim of combining them under the name 'Hochschule für freie und angewandte Kunst' (University of Fine and Applied Arts), although in the end the institution became known as the 'Frankfurter Kunstschule'.[11] Even though Wichert had failed to move the Bauhaus to Frankfurt in 1924, he was able, because of the Bauhaus's move to Dessau, to attract important Bauhaus teachers, such as Josef Hartwig, Christian Dell and Karl Peter Röhl, as well as Adolf Meyer, an employee close to Walter Gropius at his private construction firm. Meyer was head not only of the school's construction course but also of the construction advisory department of the city's construction authority, until his early death in 1929.

The Frankfurter Kunstschule had no need to be concerned about being compared unfavourably to the Bauhaus. The Kunstschule strove to collaborate with industry, as the Bauhaus did, and its fine and applied arts were considered to be of equal importance. And, as at the Bauhaus, students were required to take

EINLADUNG zum Vortrag
des Herrn Paul Renner aus München:
TOTE ODER LEBENDE SCHRIFT?
am Freitag, den 3. Juli abends 8 Uhr
im großen Saale des Löwenbräu
Große Gallusstraße 17
Bildungsverband der deutschen
Buchdrucker Ortsgruppe Frankfurt

4

VON SCHREIBKUNST UND DRUCKSCHRIFT
An der Spitze der europäischen Schriften stehen
die römischen Versalien, aufgebaut aus Dreieck,
Kreis und Geviert, den denkbar einfachsten und
denkbar gegensätzlichsten Formen.

PAUL RENNER: VORPROBE DER NOCH UNFERTIGEN RENNER-FUTURA
BAUERSCHE GIESSEREI, FRANKFURT A. M. 1925

5

Ausstellung
Aseun stugel snuste Agenstues
nustesg eu Ageln sugeste leun
gleu stengel une Astung stulleg
Ausstellung stulle neu eugenus

Aeglnsust

Corps 20 Renner-Futura / 5. Februar 1926

6

4
Use of the Futura type specimen on an invitation card for a lecture given by Renner on the topic 'Tote oder lebende Schrift?' (Dead or Living Type?), 24 point, original size, July 1925. In both samples the pointed apex and vertex of the A, N and M are crisp, and the top of the R's leg is diagonal and near the stem. Early versions of the innovative alternates, such as the lower-case a, e, g, n, r and s, are used.

5
'Sample of the still-unfinished Renner-Futura', in: Fritz Helmuth Ehmcke, *Schrift. Ihre Gestaltung und Entwicklung in neuerer Zeit*. Munich 1925, p.66.

6
Futura type specimen with word combinations using the existing types, 20 point, 5 February 1926. The letters of the word 'Ausstellung' (exhibition) are recombined as an anagram, using the innovative n and g alternates and the s-t ligature. The typeface is still very unbalanced and blotchy.

7

The New Frankfurt. Monthly magazine
for urban design: covers no. 1 (1926/27)
to 7 (October/December 1927); double
spread 'Neue Reklame [advertisements] in
Frankfurt am Main', no. 3, pp. 60–61; and
'Eine Bauausstellung auf der Frankfurter
Frühjahrsmesse' (A Building Exhibition
at the Frankfurt Spring Fair), no. 3,
pp. 90–91.

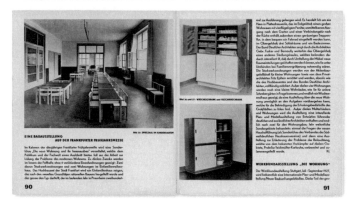

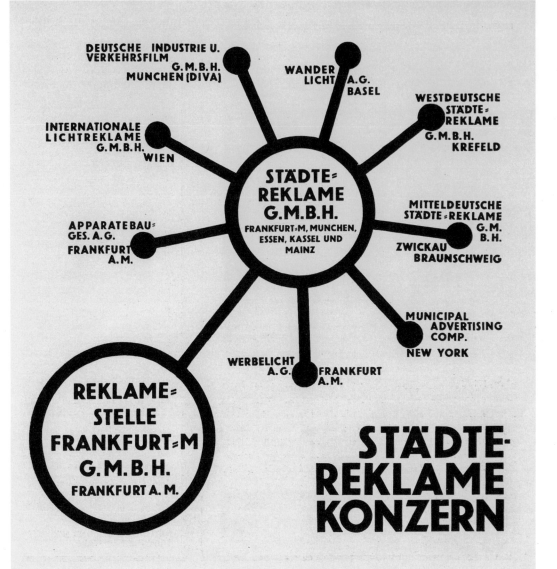

8

8

The Städte-Reklame-Konzern in Frankfurt
am Main, *DNF*, no. 3, 1926/27.

9

Walter Dexel: telephone box and clock
column at day and night, Frankfurt am
Main, 1928.

an initial foundation course for two terms before continuing most of the rest of their education in the workshops.

Although architecture became a teaching subject at Dessau only in 1927, in Frankfurt an architecture course directed by Meyer was offered as early as 1926.[12] Ernst May directed the master studio personally.[13] The Housing and Interior Design course, directed by Franz Schuster from 1928, was particularly important. Students on this course were required to develop commercially viable furniture suited to industrial production, which would therefore be affordable for much of the population. A comparison with the Bauhaus is also worth making in this regard because its second director, Hannes Meyer, merged the metal, carpentry and mural studios into a development studio only in 1929, in faithful accordance with his motto 'Volksbedarf statt Luxusbedarf' (Real-life needs, not luxury needs). Important employees of the city building authority, such as Martin Elsässer and Ferdinand Kramer, also took on teaching responsibilities in Frankfurt and executed projects together with the students.[14]

The Frankfurter Kunstschule was also a good place to study typography and advertising. While the Bauhaus was able to set up a studio for printing and advertising only after its move to Dessau, typography and graphic design for advertising was already on offer in Frankfurt in 1924.[15] Paul Renner was made director of this course at the Kunstschule in May 1925, together with Max Beckmann and Adolf Meyer. And it was at the school that Renner publicly presented his Futura samples.[16]

The content of this course for typography and graphic design for advertising, which was 'always one of the school's strongest departments in terms of numbers',[17] was geared towards a 'general education in the artistic treatment of flat planes: elementary compositions with black and white, colour, line, lettering, images, photographs, figure drawings. Designs for the entire advertising industry with consideration towards reproduction methods. Technical training in typesetting, printing, wood and linoleum blocks.'[18]

Interaction was encouraged not only between the building authority and the architects, as well as the school's interior designers, but also between the building authority and the typography and graphic design course. Hans Leistikow, head of the city's graphic design office, taught at the Kunstschule, and Renner also reported that he gave a sample of his Futura to the urban planning authority.[19]

TYPOTECHTURE:[20] WALTER DEXEL

Advertisements played an increasingly important role in urban planning in the second half of the 1920s. Accordingly, a 'City Advisory Office' was created, led

9

by Adolf Meyer. Its task was to unify the city's advertisements according to current design principles into an 'organized advertising design'.[21]

In 1926 the art historian, graphic artist, painter and former head of the Jena Art Association, Walter Dexel, was appointed by the urban planning authority as an 'advisor for advertising design in the city'. He developed a consistent style of advertising for Frankfurt's public spaces, and also devised basic guidelines for the regulation of advertising in the city.[22]

An enthusiastic proponent of the 'New Typography',[23] Dexel battled in particular against 'calligraphy, scripts that imitate handwriting and ornate scripts', because they 'draw the eye of passers-by but focus their attention on the typeface itself rather than on the content of the text. This kind of type demands too much attention for itself, the form dominates the content, the means dominates the purpose, the "art" asserts itself but its purpose remains unachieved.'[24] Dexel fought with dedication against pictorial components and advocated for a purely typographic design.[25] His advertising rules, developed from 1927 and implemented in a milder

form in 1928, recommended few sans serif types for use in outdoor spaces. He considered Café de Unie, by Jacobus Johannes Pieter Oud, and Wachthof, by Arthur Korn for the Berliner Wach- und Schliessgesellschaft (Berlin Security Company), to be exemplary models.[26] Dexel designed illuminated street signs, advertising clocks,[27] illuminated advertisements, telephone boxes and tram stops for the city of Frankfurt – all in simple sans serif types constructed using a ruler.

When Renner accepted his position in Frankfurt, he relates that he 'redesigned the alphabets of Futura for the municipal building authority', and 'duplicated them for distribution to all type painters as a model for the city's lettering'.[28]

In fact, 'modern' sans serif types dating from the second half of the 1920s – unusual at that time – can be found in public spaces in varying degrees of quality and execution. All are set in capitals and are very similar in terms of form.

10

left: Jacobus Johannes Pieter Oud: Café de Unie, Rotterdam, 1925/26
right: declarative facade of the Wach- und Schliessgesellschaft, Berlin. Architect: Arthur Korn.

11

Walter Dexel: advertising lamp in Jena, produced by the Mechanische Werkstätten (Mechanical Workshops) of the city gasworks.

12

Walter Dexel: illuminated advertising column, produced by the Mechanische Werkstätten of the city gasworks.

13

Walter Dexel: public kiosk, Frankfurt am Main, 1927.

10

11

12

13

54

14
Double spread from *DNF*, no. 3, 1927, with
advertising specimens by Werner Epstein; architecture by Karl Wiehl and Hans Leistikow.

Bild 19: Hans Leiftikow, **WERBEDRUCKSACHEN** für die Lotterie „Haus der Jugend", Frankfurt a·M.

55

Bild 15 und 16: Walter Dexel,
REKLAMEUHREN
der Sternwartezeit G. m. b. H.

53

15

Double spread from *DNF*, no. 3, 1927,
with advertising clocks by Walter Dexel.

Bild 20 und 21: Walter Dexel,
REKLAMEUHREN
der Sternwartezeit G. m. b. H.

56

16

17

All in all, it should be noted that, owing to their simple construction, sans serif types set in capitals had been in use since the nineteenth century by sign painters, who painted them by hand or produced them according to templates in various materials to be used on facades and in displays. This tendency became more widespread in the 1920s as a result of the demands of the New Typography.

FERDINAND KRAMER

In this context, Ferdinand Kramer's sign for the hat shop Hutlager G. Kramer, which the shop commissioned in connection with its renovation, should also be considered. It used a capital alphabet similar to the capitals of Futura.[29] A 98 per cent reduced copy of a blueprint and a design drawing on graph paper have survived. The latter was made before the reconstruction and shows capitals with corrections made to some letters. This sheet has given rise to speculation over whether Kramer himself designed these capitals for the sign, to what extent their form may have influenced Futura, or vice versa,[30] and whether the design drawing is one of the samples that Renner gave the municipal building authority.[31]

The fact that the only known image of Kramer's hat-shop sign is ascribed to Renner in the magazine *Das Neue Frankfurt* (The New Frankfurt)[32] suggests that Kramer himself considered Renner to be the author.[33] The fact that another sign in capitals on the facade of a pastry shop is shown on the same page, 'containing the same typographic characteristics' and also ascribed to Renner, supports the

theory that both signs were made according to Renner's templates. [34]

In any case, it is clear that Renner had become acquainted with Ferdinand Kramer as early as the spring of 1925, through Ernst May. During this time, the first samples of Futura were developed and preparations made for the first prints. FIG.4 P.67 In 1925 Kramer was made head of the newly founded

18

16
Design drawing of an upper-case alphabet on graph paper.

17
Paul Renner: exterior adverts for Kramer's hat shop. The capital **R**, **K** and **A** in the uppermost row differ from Futura and from the design drawing in Fig. 16.

18
Outdoor sign in Futura-Grotesk by Paul Renner.

standardization department, where one of his tasks was to design inexpensive objects, such as standardized freestanding, modular furniture for Städtische Hausrat GmbH that would fit the measurements of the houses being built for the New Frankfurt.

As lectures he gave towards the end of 1925 clearly indicate, Renner was impressed by the new ideas and uncompromisingly modern aesthetic of the New Architecture, and by the way that Kramer and his New Frankfurt colleagues applied them in their constructions and installations. Renner was also greatly influenced and inspired by them over the two-year period of the development of his typeface. A few sentences from a report on these lectures have been preserved: 'as a direct result of machine engineering, far from the path of the artist, technical possibilities have been invented that are heralding the start of a new stylistic period. A new kind of form has been produced by the machines, the cars and aeroplanes, the glass buildings, the concrete slabs, the radio towers, etc. ... And in type design, too, there is a return to the beginning, to the elements, to the circle, the square and the triangle.'[35]

It is certain that Renner and Kramer maintained an open and friendly relationship, and that Renner admired the work and design approach of the Frankfurt architect. This is evidenced in an article entitled 'On the Works of Ferdinand Kramer',[36] in which Renner refers to him as 'a model to follow' of the new style, which had been freed entirely from historical shackles as well as from a 'dogmatic formalism'[37] for the purpose of creating functional furniture: 'He reflects passionately on the practical usability, the new possibilities offered by materials and techniques. And so his furniture achieves the most modern standards of comfort.'[38] Renner continues: 'Kramer's furniture constitutes possibly the best household objects for the simple, cubic, plain spaces of the new architecture, with the smooth plywood panels of its doors; they are inspired by the modern style in which the inhabitants of these buildings dress their fit bodies.'[39]

Renner praised Kramer as a visionary product and furniture designer, but did not see him as a typographer or a type designer. Indeed, Kramer was not particularly known as a typographer. Like many of his architect colleagues, he designed lettering for facades to suit the character of his reconstruction and interior design projects, so although his involvement with type was important, it played a relatively marginal role in his architectural work. Since Kramer clearly did not favour any one particular type during this time, it can be assumed that he used various capital types in the reconstruction of the stamp and signage plant Mosthaf, as well as for the fur company Rosenblum & Co. on Biebergasse and for Bender Cigarettes in the Hauptwache plaza in Frankfurt.[40]

The use of typography for signage contrasts with the labour-intensive development of a typeface in lead through innumerable design procedures and reiterations, with all the different sizes and faces being drawn and cut so that they could be cast and sold. The harmonious play of upper-case and lower-case letters within a self-contained face must be achieved, and the legibility of the type remained the prime concern.

Renner recognized, in the adjustment of the lower-case letters to be formally consistent with the upper-case letters, the actual type-design challenge that he had to meet: 'It [i.e. Futura] has subjected the lower-case letters to the formal principle of the simplest elementary planes, which take inspiration from Roman capitals for their easy legibility. The capitals now no longer disrupt the picture of the lower-case letters because of their own rhythm and foreign shapes; that is an advantage that will be of great benefit to German texts, with their frequent use of capitals.'[41]

In fact, Renner's innovation was the way in which he derived formal principles from the capitals of Roman Antiqua and transferred them to the lower-case letters. Thus, he did not – as type-design innovators like Herbert Bayer demanded – construct a type out of purely geometric shapes with the same stroke weight. Rather, he optically adjusted the entire alphabet. As Renner wrote in a letter some years later, 'unlike the Constructivists, who had become fashionable at that time', he had not wanted 'to extol the virtues of the pair of compasses as a tool, but rather to rescue form from its vulgarization and bring it back to its original roots'. What makes Futura unique is 'not the pair of compasses and circle, but rather the reduction of all forms, including the forms of the lower-case letters, back to the simplest, most elementary, basic geometric shapes, and not in the sense that a compass-drawn form should now replace a complicated form.'[42]

DER NEUE GEI
IN
FRANKFU
AM MA

Beilage des Kreifes Frankfurt

Entwurf, Photos (mit Ausnahm

Innenaufnahmen) und Photo

vom Kreisvorftand. Druck d

Druckerei (Volksftimme). Klif

erften und vierten Seite von d

fchen Gießerei (Abtlg. Chem

Klifchees der zweiten und dri

von der Kunftanftalt Guhl &

war die Firma Wellhaufen (

Induftrie-Photographie) an

beteiligt. Jlluftrationsdruck-P

Poensgen & Heyer; alle in F

FRITZ WICHERT

In 1923 the city of Frankfurt appointed the art historian Fritz Wichert founding director of the Frankfurter Kunstschule (School of Art). Under his direction, the Städtische Kunstgewerbeschule (Municipal School of Arts and Crafts) merged with the Städelschule and a reformed educational concept was designed and implemented.

At the time of his appointment, Wichert, who was born in 1878 in Mainz-Kastel, had already occupied various professional positions. He had been Georg Swarzenski's assistant at the Städelsche Kunstinstitut and a culture journalist for the *Frankfurter Zeitung* in Frankfurt before becoming director in 1909 of the Mannheimer Kunsthalle (Mannheim Gallery), where he built up a collection of modern art and gave impetus to a steadily growing art and cultural scene.

Since the school was designed to bring together the fine and applied arts, the lessons at the art school were practice-orientated. Because it became very important from an economic point of view, Wichert invested heavily to expand the faculty of commercial graphic design and typography, which had been established in 1925. As director, Paul Renner had the task of assembling the design programme and the associated studio.[43]

The following excerpt from a letter from Wichert to the Frankfurt municipal authority clearly demonstrates Renner's belief in the importance of maintaining good relations with industry: 'Mr Renner has, through his efforts, and in excellent fashion, with the help of typesetters, type foundries and printing houses, as well as the efforts of his colleagues, reorganized the book industry and book design, and raised it to a higher level of quality. The teaching staff in Frankfurt, a centre of book and type design, will benefit from this change.'[44]

Renner was initially employed for two months as a guest lecturer, during which time he was required to prove his pedagogic abilities. At the end of this trial period, Wichert reported to the city administration that 'Mr Renner has managed to integrate himself well into the school's organization as a teacher and artist.'[45] With the inclusion of a recognized figure such as Renner on his staff, Wichert hoped to compete with the nearby school in Offenbach.

Wichert had originally wanted to contract Renner to remain at the school for five years, but after only one year, Renner switched to Munich, where he took over the direction of the Buchdruckerschule (Master School of German Letterpress Printers).[46] During this brief period in Frankfurt, Renner conceived Futura, a sample of which was presented during the first exhibition of the art school in the autumn of 1925.[47] The name of the typeface originated with Wichert,[48] who had admired its proofs at the Bauersche Druckerei: 'In Paul Renner's new type, I see the formation of what is to come, in the same way that the present-day architecture already contains the seeds of the future, born out of a spiritual necessity. Taken as a whole, this type is the first to truly correspond to the new way of life, and in particular, it is sophisticated and delicate, without detriment to legibility or fluidity. However, the most important thing is that this type is abstract in a true sense, i.e. it heralds a new, severe subservience and the most extreme suppression of individualistic expression.'[49]

In addition to his work as an art-school director, Wichert was the municipal conservator for historical monuments, and the city's director of urban art. He wrote many articles on cultural and political topics and advocated for modern design in Frankfurt. Wichert was also part of the advisory committee for culture for Südwestdeutscher Rundfunk (Southwest German Radio), and editor of the magazine *Das Neue Frankfurt* (New Frankfurt) from 1928 to 1930. His promising cultural and political activities in the Main region during this last period of his career, however, came to an abrupt end. In March 1933 Wichert was stripped of all his offices by the National Socialists. He lived in exile in camps on the island of Sylt until his death in 1951.

19

P.82 – Supplement from the printing trade magazine *Typografische Mitteilungen*, August 1928.

20

Advertisement for Futura with a statement by Fritz Wichert about the typeface, *Typographische Mitteilungen*, June 1928.

21

PP.86–87 – International exhibition 'Musik im Leben der Völker' (Music in the Life of Nations), Frankfurt. View from Platz der Republik (now Ludwig-Erhard-Anlage), south of the exhibition centre's entrance, July or August 1927. Photographer: unknown.

FUTURA

DIE SCHRIFT UNSERER ZEIT

Ganz allein in der neuen Schrift von Paul
Renner sehe ich das Werdende, wie in der
gültigen Baukunst der Zukunft aus geistiger
Notwendigkeit heraus geformt. Als Ganzes
genommen ist diese Schrift die erste, die wirk-
lich dem neuen Lebensgefühl entspricht, und
im einzelnen ist sie, ohne an Lesbarkeit oder
Flüssigkeit einzubüßen, rassig und fein. Das
Wesentliche aber liegt darin, daß diese Type
im wahren Sinne abstrakt ist, das heißt, mit
äußerster Zurückdrängung individualistischer
Expression ein neues hartes Dienen verkündet.

PROFESSOR DR. FRITZ WICHERT · Direktor
der Städtischen Kunstschule in Frankfurt a. M.

mager
halbfett
fett

BAUERSCHE GIESSEREI
FRANKFURT AM MAIN

21

SOMMER DER MUSIK

FRANKFURT AM MAIN 1927
11. JUNI BIS 28. AUGUST

6. WOCHE

6.

IM BACHSAAL
TÄGLICH 16 UHR
ORGELKONZERTE

Tag	Programm	Ort/Zeit
Sonntag 17. Juli	Morgenfeier des Hessischen Sängerbundes Teatro dei Piccoli, Marionettenspiele Gamelan-Orchester und Javanische Tänze Tanz- und Gesangsgruppen aus Rußland	Bachsaal 9 Uhr Bachsaal 20 U. Saxophon 17 U. Opernh. 20 Uhr
Montag 18. Juli	Tanzabend »La Argentina«, Span. Tänze Quartett »Pro Arte«, Belg. Kammermusik Teatro dei Piccoli, Marionettenspiele Gamelan-Orchester und Javanische Tänze	Opernh. 20 Uhr Beethovensaal Bachsaal 20 U. Saxophon 17 U.
Dienstag 19. Juli	Tanzabend »La Argentina«, Span. Tänze Quartett »Pro Arte«, Belg. Kammermusik Teatro dei Piccoli, Marionettenspiele Gamelan-Orchester und Javanische Tänze	Opernh. 20 Uhr Beethovensaal Bachsaal 20 U. Saxophon 17 U.
Mittwoch 20. Juli	Tanz- und Gesangsgruppen aus Rußland Teatro dei Piccoli, Marionettenspiele Gamelan-Orchester und Javanische Tänze Hausfrauen-Nachmittag mit »Küchenmusik«	Opernh. 20 Uhr Bachsaal 20 U. Saxophon 17 U. Unterhalt.-Park
Donnerstag 21. Juli	Tage für mechan. Musik, Leitg. P. Hindemith Teatro dei Piccoli, Marionettenspiele Gamelan-Orchester und Javanische Tänze Streichorchester-Konzert, Leitg. Joh. Strauß	Beethovensaal Bachsaal 20 U. Saxophon 17 U. Unterhalt.-Park
Freitag 22. Juli	Tanz- und Gesangsgruppen aus Rußland Tage für mechan. Musik, Leitg. P. Hindemith Teatro dei Piccoli, Marionettenspiele Gamelan-Orchester und Javanische Tänze	Opernh. 20 Uhr Beethovensaal Bachsaal 20 U. Saxophon 17 U.
Samstag 23. Juli	Tanz- und Gesangsgruppen aus Rußland Teatro dei Piccoli, Marionettenspiele Tage für mechan. Musik, Leitg. P. Hindemith Streichorchester-Konzert, Leitg. Joh. Strauß	Opernh. 20 Uhr Bachsaal 20 U. Beethovensaal Unterhalt.-Park

IM UNTERHALTUNGS PARK: JEDEN TAG KONZERT U. TANZ

TYP: LEISTIKOW

MUSIK IM LEBEN DER VÖLKER
INTERNAT. AUSSTELLUNG

HANS AND GRETE LEISTIKOW

One of the most important figures in the New Frankfurt project was Hans Leistikow, born on 4 May 1892 in Elbing, near Danzig, the nephew of the well-known Secessionist from Berlin, Walter Leistikow. At the age of 15, Hans began his studies at the Breslau Art Academy. Its director, Hans Poelzig, put him in contact with the head of the urban planning authority, Max Berg, who gave the painter and draughtsman commercial jobs, such as the design of colour schemes for architectural purposes, murals, glass windows, lights, carpets and advertising graphics.[50] He also became acquainted in a professional capacity with the Frankfurt-born architect Ernst May in 1922. However, until 1924 Leistikow also continued to make a living as a painter of fine art under the artistic name Hans Hal, in what was at that time Tampadel in Lower Silesia.

When May was appointed head of the urban planning authority in Frankfurt in June 1925, he took Leistikow, as well as other employees, with him to his new place of work, where he would become head of the city's graphic design office. Since the issue at hand in Frankfurt was not just a building project, but an entire political approach to the new city, addressing a new society with a new kind of visual style, the importance of design – and particularly the graphic design in New Frankfurt – cannot be underestimated. In addition to radically objective building designs, such as those by Ferdinand Kramer, Franz Schuster, Margarete Schütte-Lihotzky and Christian Dell, the entire field of visual communication played a prominent role. This initially concerned the municipal corporate design itself, which was strongly influenced by Leistikow as well as other contributors, such as Walter Dexel, Robert Michel, Werner Epstein and Max Bittrof. Leistikow designed business stationery with strong, straight lines and sans serif lettering, and many posters and commercial prints. He also supervised 12 exhibitions (covering music, photography and architecture) and the advertising for the Städtische Bühnen (Municipal Theatres) and Städtische Wirtschaftsbetriebe (Municipal Services), and designed the Constructivist eagle emblem, which had been used in the municipal building administration since 1926 and was expanded to other sections of the city administration in 1930, despite the strong resistance of conservative politicians and the media. FIG.25 P.92

Leistikow was also a teacher at the Städtische Kunstgewerbeschule (Municipal School of Arts and Crafts), and during his time there, formed one of many connections between the school and the municipal building authority, as well as brokering jobs for competent students. There was also an evening course for young letterpress printers. They 'ensured that I would have the influence on the private printing houses that I needed for the city's print materials', he wrote later.[51] Sans serif types, as a symbol of the desired modernity, were intended to become the new standard in Frankfurt.

The magazine *Das Neue Frankfurt*, which had been published by Ernst May since October 1926, was designed by Leistikow as a black-and-white publication, with the close collaboration of his younger sister Grete (1893–1989), until issue no. 9 in 1930. Grete Leistikow was a skilled photographer, and May invited her to Frankfurt, where she worked with Paul Wolff, Hermann Collischonn, Marta Hoepffner and Ilse Bing on the New Frankfurt project.

The medium of photography had a special significance in this respect because attractive advertising, or propaganda, for Frankfurt's modern design was urgently needed. As more of the population was introduced to the advertising material's entirely unfamiliar forms, reactions were initially negative. For all of his work, Leistikow used the typeface Erbar Grotesk, fully justified, and with margin columns, very wide horizontal and vertical lines, and large extra-bold page numbers. In 1928, however, he began to refrain from using the wide vertical lines, and in the late issues, hardly any straight lines can be seen. Initially, on the front and back cover, only the issue number was emphasized, using large, coloured type. This spot colour was later incorporated into the entire title design, which also often made use of photographs or collages by Grete. Many advertisements in the issues also seem to have been produced by Leistikow, or at least influenced by him, given their formal similarities and editorial layout.

A series of pictures entitled *Die Schrift als Ausdruck der Kultur* (Type as an Expression of Culture) was published as early as October/November 1926 in a brochure that was intended to demonstrate the importance of typography within the New Frankfurt project as a whole. It ended with the design of a form by Leistikow for the building administrative authority as a high point of the development. The third issue was dedicated exclusively to advertising design and graphic design. Two major articles by Walter Dexel and Adolf Behne were also published.

The magazine was intended to appeal not only to a professional audience but also to as broad a section of the general public as possible. Text that was easy to understand, a noble typography, lots of white space and a large number of pictures were intended to appeal to many readers, which the specialist critics also commented on: 'the layout [of the text] wastes space, which is curious for a programme that advocates rationalization', was the criticism of the trade association magazine *Die Form* in 1927.[52]

The Frankfurt publishing house Englert & Schlosser, which published *Das Neue Frankfurt*, was also an important private client for Leistikow. The magazine itself became one of the paradigms of modernism in the Weimar Republic in terms of both its content and its design. Its publishers, editors and designers collaborated with one another as equals. Leistikow later offered a very apt description of

22
P. 88 – 'Sommer der Musik' (Summer of Music), type by Hans Leistikow. This poster by Leistikow was reset in Futura and used as a supplement for the first Futura portfolio, in 1927.

23
Hans and Grete Leistikow: cover of the magazine *Das Neue Frankfurt*, vol. 3, no. 2, 1929.

this relationship: 'Long before you begin to design, you must try somehow to think in the same way the client thinks. ... There is actually no such thing as a work of commercial graphic design produced solely by the artist. In reality, there are always two people responsible for the design: the artist and the client. The client is thus the predetermining factor in this process, because he embodies the connection that differentiates this kind of work from works of pure art. By this I mean that it is wrong to label the client as a necessary evil; that the artist's subjugation of him will guarantee the highest quality of work. On the contrary, there is a risk that works created in this way will be neither graphic design nor art.'[53]

After 1945 Leistikow endeavoured to obtain a position in Frankfurt similar to the one he had held in 1930. It seems that he succeeded only in 1947. However, after a year of work the city terminated the new agreement, and in 1950, after a brief period as lecturer of type design at the city's Cultural Institute for Fashion, Leistikow accepted a teaching position at the state Werkakademie (Trade Academy) in Kassel. Frankfurt remained the base for his personal and most of his professional life, however. The attitude towards design in the city administration after 1945 contrasted completely with the euphoric mood of 1925 to 1929. Rational and functional design was now the standard – partly as a reaction against the architecture of National Socialism – although this did not necessarily lead to any impressive aesthetic results. A special graphic style was also of little interest to pragmatic civil servants. On 22 March 1962 Hans Leistikow passed away in Frankfurt.

24

25

24

Newsletter of the Städtischen Bühnen (Municipal Theatres), Frankfurt am Main, 1930, from the collection of Dr Christos N. Vittoratos, Frankfurt a.M.

25

Certificate issued by the city of Frankfurt for the Deutsche Photographische Ausstellung (German Photography Exhibition), Frankfurt am Main, August 1926, from the collection of Dr Christos N. Vittoratos, Frankfurt a.M.

26

Swimming permit issued by the Städtische Bäder Frankfurt (Frankfurt Municipal Baths), with the eagle emblem designed by Hans Leistikow, 1932, from the collection of Dr Christos N. Vittoratos, Frankfurt a.M.

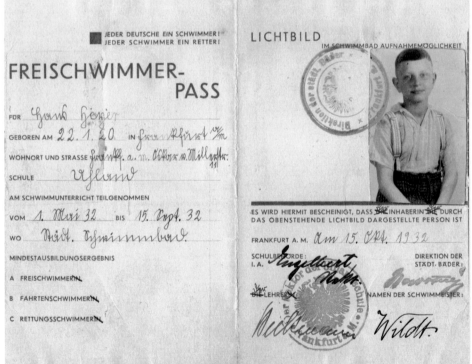

wirke

zum jahreswechsel übermitteln wir allen kollegen und funktionären die herzlichsten

glück- und segenswünsche. zielbewußte arbeit am gemeinsamen werke soll uns

auch im neuen jahre durch alle hemmungen weiter vorwärts und aufwärts führen

ortsgruppe frankfurt am main im bildungsverband der deutschen buchdrucker

CONCEPTIONS AND REACTIONS

'The field of modern type design has recently regained its dynamism, owing to the discussion over the most diverse ideas, and the Bauer Type Foundry, since it has recognized the necessity, must assist this impetus to find its correct type, and has undertaken to release a type by Paul Renner. Designed entirely along the lines of the New Objectivity, it is not intended to be sensational, but rather to truly enrich the field, which would otherwise not always possess good sans serif types. It will be called "Futura".'[54]

In 1926 Futura was further developed and made ready for market release. In November 1927 the geometric sans serif was released by the Bauer Type Foundry in Frankfurt am Main in light and medium weights.[55] Crucially for him, on 18 July that year Renner concluded an agreement with the Bauer Type Foundry that gave him not only the copyright but also payment of 2½ per cent domestically and 1 per cent internationally for the sale of his typeface, providing him with financial security.[56]

The typeface's first release of 1927 also contained special forms. These included the **a**, **g**, **m**, **n** and **ä**, the **&** character and oldstyle figures. Although the moulds for these letters were not manufactured, they were offered as supplementary special characters in addition to the revised letters. In the final revised version of Futura, the **r** was also adjusted.[57]

In a letter from 1927, Christ. Eich, the general representative of the Bauer Type Foundry, writes that Renner was 'on the right track' with his Futura, and that 'there is a close inner relationship between type and architecture from which the forms originate and which is also the foundation for the works of modern architecture, i.e. the basic geometric shapes: circle, square, triangle.'[58]

Futura was much celebrated during its heyday. Although many type designers worked on typefaces that were intended to capture the spirit of the times, in the end Futura was the one that became dominant. The concept of the face was based on simple geometric shapes, and at first glance it seems to consist of circles and straight lines. However, Renner and the Bauersch Giesserei took a more sophisticated approach by means of optical adjustments. This resulted in a type that could be applied in many different ways.

Two specific groups of users were targeted when it came to marketing Futura. Firstly, it was recommended as appropriate for the New Typography that Jan Tschichold, in particular, had advocated since the mid 1920s.[59] The second target group consisted of people who were 'less enamoured of the new method of typesetting', with the note: 'For figures with more extreme designs, we have cut a second form that is similar to the traditional form, but not contrary to the essence of the type. Such double characters were not necessary for the capital letters.'[60]

Debates regarding the advantages and disadvantages of sans serif type became particularly intense following the publication in 1926 of Herbert Bayer's 'Versuch einer neuen Schrift' (Attempt at a New Typeface) [61] and Willi Baumeister's important article on typographic theory, 'Neue Typographie'.[62] In 1927, in response to Renner's reflections on Futura, Konrad Friedrich Bauer remarked on the theories of the Bauhaus regarding a new typeface: 'It is certain that the way to the typeface of the future is ... not via the sans serifs. ... The sans serif types – even the best ones – clearly demonstrate how necessary hatching is in commercial types. The impartial layperson experiences even more strongly than the expert what torture it is to read a sans serif type in which the individual letters do not unite into distinct word pictures and the eye is constantly drawn from one row to the other because all emphasis of the horizontal is absent.'[63]

Criticism was also expressed by moderate professionals, such as Fritz Helmuth Ehmcke in his article 'Wandlung des Schriftgefühls' (Transformations in Type Feeling) of 1930: 'While all type designers have attempted until now to adapt the capitals of Antiqua, which had developed out of stone script, to the later lower-case letters originating from penned script, Paul Renner is trying, with his "Futura", to reject the origin of the lower-case letters and divest them of flowing handwritten characters, and to remodel them in forms that are akin to the still and entirely self-contained forms of the capitals.'[64]

Konrad Bauer had also criticized the one-sided preference for the sans serif, as demanded by the New Typography: 'Constructive is not primitive, but it would be primitive if we were to ... limit ourselves to the use of sans serif types ... as the theorists of constructive advertisements say we should do.'[65]

Towards the end of the 1920s typeface combinations became increasingly popular. The use of Futura for long running text became rarer, but it was increasingly used in the layout of magazines as a display typeface. Thus, at the beginning of the 1930s, Peter Meyer summarized the commonly held view of Futura as follows: 'an extremely respectable, calm "sans serif", but which is not suitable as an "all-purpose type" like other sans serif types.'[66]

28

GEBRAUCHSANWEISUNG

in Anspruch. Dann war Schulschluß. Gottseidank, vier vein Anspruch. Dann le Wochen der Freiheit lagen vor ihm. · Es war ein Tag le Wochen der Freit warm und schön wie selten einer. Er würde Mulchi im Ga warm und schön wie ten finden, sicher, wo es kühl und schattig war. Er dachten finden, sicher, w daran, daß Mulchi nun auch seit Ostern in die Schule gin daran, daß Mulchi n Etwas geringschätzig dachte er an die Kleinen, die erst l Etwas geringschätz sen lernen mußten. Beinahe wäre er lieber zum Schwinsen lernen müssen.

Dr. NESTLES KINDERMEHL

Einladung ▽
zum
Kreistag in Kassel ▽
AM SONNTAG, DEN 8. APRIL 1928
1. OSTERTAG
VOR MITTAGS 9 UHR
IN DER GASTSTÄTTE ZUM
STÄNDEHAUS
AM
STÄNDEPLATZ
Der Vorstand des
Kreises III
Deutscher Faktoren
Bund E·V
W. BIERING
VORSITZENDER

29

Einladung

auf Samstag den 18. Januar 1930

30

27
P.94 – Wirke, New Year's greetings from the Frankfurt group of the Bildungsverband der Deutschen Buchdrucker (Educational Association of German Book Printers), c. 1925/26.

28
'Dr Nestle's Kindermehl' baby food, instructions for use, Albinus Collection, Frankfurt.

29
Invitation to the District Council in Kassel, 1928, Albinus Collection, Frankfurt.

30
Invitation card 'Chaos and Idyll', 1930, Albinus Collection, Frankfurt.

WOLFGANG HARTMANN

THE BAUER TYPE FOUNDRY IN THE CANON OF THE GREAT TYPE FOUNDRIES

Georg Hartmann (1870–1954), my grandfather, was 28 years old when he took over the Bauer Type Foundry in 1898. With hindsight, the acquisition could have been seen as a risk, but it proved to be an extremely fortunate decision.

The type foundry was established in 1837 by Johann Christian Bauer. By the time it was taken over by Hartmann, the company was very engaged in the production of commercial types (types for setting newspapers and books) and it

had over 100 employees. It had opened an office in Barcelona with its own casting machine as early as 1885 – the Neufville company – and the type foundries in Spain had proved to be excellent customers for Antiqua V.

This was sufficient at that time for it to fall victim to technological progress. In 1886 Ottmar Mergenthaler invented the linotype machine, which could set large quantities of type quickly and, therefore, profitably; within just a few years it was introduced at all the newspaper printing presses. In 1896 monotyping was released on to the market and replaced the manual typesetting of books. The number of type foundries fell sharply. While there had been over 100 punchcutting companies and type foundries in the German-speaking lands when the Bauer Type Foundry was founded, by 1903 only 40 companies came together to form the Association of German Type Foundries.

In the years that followed, there were more reasons for the reduction in the number of type foundries, but these were unforeseeable catastrophes: World War I, the international economic crisis and then World War II. The business's offices were partially destroyed in 1945 and production had to be suspended for an extended period of time. Exports to enemy countries had, by this time, already been forbidden, and after World War II deliveries to the east stopped completely.

After the war, Georg Hartmann was able to run the business for another nine years, during which it managed to experience further brief periods of success. Apart from the Bauer foundry,

31

Bauer Type Foundry main entrance, Hamburger Allee, Frankfurt am Main, c. 1927. Cf. the Trajan's Column inscription, p.32.

32

Supplement in *Typographische Mitteilungen* (Typography News). August 1928.

DAS HAUPTGEBÄUD

der Bauerschen Gießerei in Frankfurt a. M., das Zentrum einer weitgreifenden Verkau
organisation, umfaßt zirka 5000 qm Arbeitsfläche. Über 1000 Angestellte und Arbe
werden in dem Betrieb beschäftigt und mehr als 150 Gießmaschinen sind erforderlich,
den Bedarf der Kundschaft decken zu können. Zahlreiche Zweigstellen und Vertretung
in fast allen Kulturstaaten der Welt dienen der Erleichterung des geschäftlichen Verke

BAUERSCHE GIESSEREI · FRANKFURT AM MAI

futura

a

in zeichnung und schnitt gleich vollkommen, besteht vor der strengsten kritik. der typograph läßt sich nicht mehr durch schlagwörter verleiten. seine augen sind geschärft, und mit den künstlern der gegenwart teilt er den sinn für reine, große form. der knappen, ehrlichen gestaltung zuliebe verzichtet er gerne auf jeden dekor. er sucht nach einer schrift von zuchtvoller schönheit, die dem gedanken des typendruckes vollkommenen und reinen ausdruck verleiht. unsere zeit will höchstleistungen. rücksichtslos verwirft sie alles mittelmäßige. sie will eine bessere schrift. schriftkunst und schrifttechnik haben ihr bestes getan. die exakten, edlen formen der futura sind in gewissenhafter arbeit so vollkommen durchgebildet, daß die reinheit der schlichten linie allein überzeugt. die aufgabe war schwer, aber sie wurde gelöst: der typograph verfügt jetzt über eine schrift, die der besten kunst unserer zeit ebenbürtig ist

only seven other type foundries survived these turbulent times: D. Stempel AG, H. Berthold AG, Ludwig & Mayer, Johannes Wagner & Co., Gebrüder Klingspor (until 1956), C. E. Weber and Genzsch & Heyse AG. The ownership of the last was divided into equal thirds, and shared by the Bauer Type Foundry and the first two, Stempel and Berthold.

The Bauer Type Foundry had succeeded in overcoming all adversity, and it continued to flourish under Hartmann's management. So how, exactly, did it succeed?

'Aventur und Kunst' was the name Gutenberg chose when he founded his enterprise for the development of the printing press. Georg Hartmann used these same words for the title of a special publication by the Bauer Type Foundry in 1940, on the occasion of its 70th anniversary. According to the introduction, 'Aventur' stands for 'adventure' – venturing into the unknown, an entrepreneurial undertaking – while 'Kunst' (art) refers to artisanal skills, but in this context primarily indicates a feel for form – in other words, correct judgement when it comes to types.

This suited Hartmann, particularly the use of the second term: art. To be successful in the typesetting business, intuition is required when selecting the right types. The production of a new type was an incredibly difficult task at that time: the engraving of the matrices, the casting of the letters for many languages, the figures and punctures, and all this in multiple sizes and weights. The wrong decisions could have had a profound impact on the company, but Hartmann

maintained firm control. As a typesetter, he felt responsible for the firm's success or failure, and he engaged excellent artists to design the types. His collaboration with Prof. Emil Rudolf Weiss, for example, had begun as far back as 1905, and Weiss Antiqua in a medium weight, italics with and without swash capitals, a bold weight, and Kapitale Light and Bold, had been a success. Weiss's influence was also felt in the work of other type designers, such as Elisabeth Friedländer, who had studied under Weiss; the Czechoslovakian designer Oldrich Menhart, who worked with Weiss's creations; and Imre Reiner in Hungary. Another designer, Prof. Friedrich Hermann Ernst Schneidler, later designed Schneidler Antiqua for Bauer, as well as a very successful display typeface, Legende. These types were full of personality, and suitable for printing celebratory publications and advertising material, where they sat apart from the types produced by the single-tone typesetting machines of the time.

The appointment of Heinrich Jost in 1922 was a decisive one for the success of Bauer. Jost was appointed artistic director and he became responsible for the technical execution of newspaper printing, as well as the typographic design of advertising and private publications. He was also the broker in the fortunate selection of the most successful typeface of all time: Futura. In 1924 Paul Renner had turned to Jost, his former pupil, when looking for a type foundry to manufacture the first sketches of the 'typeface of our time' that would become Futura. Jost himself designed two typefaces: Beton and Bodoni. The latter found greatest success in the USA, where it is known as 'Bauer' Bodoni.

Jost was succeeded as artistic director in 1948 by Dr Konrad Friedrich Bauer, an art historian who had been responsible since 1928 for the text of special prints

and advertisements. His commissions resulted in the typefaces Folio, Imprimatur, Volta, Alpha and Beta.

Hartmann greatly enjoyed interacting with artists. They also played an important part in his private life as a serious art collector, with one of the most important collections of medieval pictures and sculptures in Germany, alongside masterpieces by French Impressionists. In particular, Hartmann maintained friendly relations with painters including Max Beckmann, Gunter Böhmer and Fritz Kredel, who supplied illustrations for Bauer's special publications.

Hartmann also knew how to make the right business decisions. The size of the company was partly due to his acquisition of several other type foundries, including A. Numrich & Co in Leipzig (in about 1912), which had a division for the manufacture of brass rules. This enabled

Bauer to offer the complete production of manual setting materials. In 1916 the company's prestige grew with the acquisition of the Flinsch Tye Foundry in Frankfurt, whose portfolio included the types of such famous artists as Fritz Helmuth Ehmcke and Prof. Lucian Bernhard.

As for the selection of representatives for the company's network abroad, Hartmann made a point of choosing companies that owned well-known book-printing machines – particularly those manufactured by Schnellpressenfabrik Heidelberg. This ensured that types were released in optimum conditions and could be reliably produced to supply the market. In 1927 Hartmann opened an office in the USA in order to be able to sell typefaces there directly.

A few years after Hartmann's death, the Bauer Type Foundry entered its golden age. By about 1960 the type foundry was receiving a huge number of orders, but it lacked the in-house production capacity to supply this quantity of types to its customers on time. The English type foundry Stephenson Blake provided assistance and was contracted by Bauer to mould the English metal sorts for Futura.

33

PP.100-1 – Advertisement for Futura in *Graphische Nachrichten*, 1931. The man in the white coat holding the drawing is, according to Christopher Burke, Adolf Bernd, who worked under Heinrich Jost at Bauer. The man in the middle is the Spanish printer Francisco P. Custodio. The third man could not be identified. This advertisement also appeared in red as early as 1929, in the magazine *Gebrauchsgraphik*.

34

Specimen brochure for Heinrich Jost's Beton typeface.

FRANKFURT AM MAIN

DIE
SCHRIFT
UNSERER
ZEIT

FUTURA

NIEDERLASSUNGEN IN ALLEN TEILEN DER WELT

Nicht die Anpassung der Letter an die maschinelle Arbeitsweise ist das Entscheidende, sondern daß die Schrift selber den klaren und sauberen Stil der Maschine trägt. – Um das Prinzip allein willen wäre sie höchstens ein interessanter Versuch. Aber in Wahrheit ist sie mehr, nämlich ein sehr geglückter Versuch; sie ist in Wahrheit auch mehr als ein neues und ausdrucksloses Maschinen-produkt, nämlich eine Schrift von bestimmtem Ausdruckswert. Es gibt viele Antiqua-Grotesk-schriften, die an technischer Vereinfachung der Futuraschrift kaum nachstehen, dagegen keine, die ihr an klassischer Reinheit des Satzbildes gleichkommt. – Das Bemerkenswerte an dieser Schrift ist nicht der Versuch der Reduktion der Buchstaben auf abstrakte Formelemente, son-dern daß das Schriftbild im Ganzen trotz den abstrakten Formen im Einzelnen einen harmo-nischen und doch nicht langweiligen Charakter trägt. / Hermann Herrigel im »Kunstwart«

mager
halbfett
und fett

BAUERSCHE
GIESSEREI

However, the situation soon changed dramatically. Printing presses switched their production to offset machines. Typesetting was superseded by the much cheaper photosetting, and later, metal type in particular was replaced entirely by digital fonts. In 1972, some 18 years after the death of Georg Hartmann, the Bauer Type Foundry was forced into liquidation. Production was taken over by its associate company in Spain, Fundición Tipográfica Neufville, SA, which was later renamed Bauer Types, SL, and which also acquired the international rights to the types. Metal types continued to be cast there until 2008, when production was finally stopped. Some steel stamps and matrices are now held by the Museum für Druckkunst (Museum of Printing Arts) in Leipzig, but most are kept at the University of Barcelona on loan; the matrices from the casting course of the final years were eventually acquired by the Imprenta Municipal – Artes del Libro in Madrid.

All the Bauer typefaces remain highly contemporary, even in today's digital age, and Futura is still one of the best-selling types online in the whole world. It can be found everywhere – as a font for desktop use, for web applications and on tablets and mobile phones. As a successful publisher of types, Georg Hartmann made himself immortal.

36

35
Advertisement for Futura in the magazine *Gebrauchsgraphik*, 1929.

36
Futura. Die Schrift unserer Zeit im Urteil des Fachmanns. Tatsachen sprechen für die Futura; the Bauer prospectus, with statements and information regarding Futura, Frankfurt am Main, 1930.

HEINRICH JOST

Heinrich Jost (1889–1948) is credited with having a decisive influence on the success of Futura. He was a pupil at the Schule für Illustration und Buchgewerbe (School of Illustration and Publishing) founded by Paul Renner and Emil Preetorius, and later at the Debschitzschule, and he maintained a friendship with his former teacher throughout his life. Jost, who was the artistic director of various publishing houses, and was already working as a book and type designer, became artistic director of the Bauer Type Foundry in 1922. There, he supervised the 'types that had recently been recast', collected type specimens and presented 'the new types in all their various possible applications'.[67] He supervised the work of the Bauer Type Foundry in great detail: 'where artistic creation was turned by machines into a reality, he was responsible for the typographic design of all the print materials used in the marketing of the Bauer Type Foundry: type specimens, advertising prints, announcements and private publications.'[68]

To achieve this, Jost kept a highly experienced team of staff by his side: 'The employees know his intentions, and how, on a well-directed stage, the individual can execute the director's idea without the need for painstaking instructions.'[69] The same source went on to describe Jost's role in the design of types: 'And during the cutting, too, the resulting type remains under the constant watch of the artistic director, who must manage and monitor each of the countless number of attempts through which the sketch of the design is made into a printable type. It pained Jost to know that this laborious work would ultimately be credited by the general public to the person whose name is borne by the type. The same fate befell the much-admired specimen brochures for the new types, the creation of which was usually determined and monitored by the artistic directors of the Bauer Type Foundry rather than the type artists.'[70]

37–39

P. 107 et seq. – Heinrich Jost (design): *Futura: Für Fotomontage*, supplementary leaflet in the first Futura portfolio, 1927, and advertisements in the magazine *Gebrauchsgraphik*, 1929.

—

'i came to the bauhaus through "die neue typographie" of jan tschichold. i ordered a prospectus, talked to mr beyer and mr grün ... and both recommended dessau. they said dessau was the only school that was keeping up with the times. that was exactly what i was looking for. [...] on 24 April 1930, i became a bauhäusler.'[*]

* (Rose to Noack, 9 March 1930, inv. no. 12762/33, Bauhaus Archive Berlin)

(UB) This Bauhäusler who wanted to keep up with the times was Hajo Rose, a photographer and commercial graphic designer who took these two Futura specimens with him when he emigrated to the Netherlands. He clearly considered them so exemplary that he brought them back with him to Germany, where they were found among his possessions after his death.

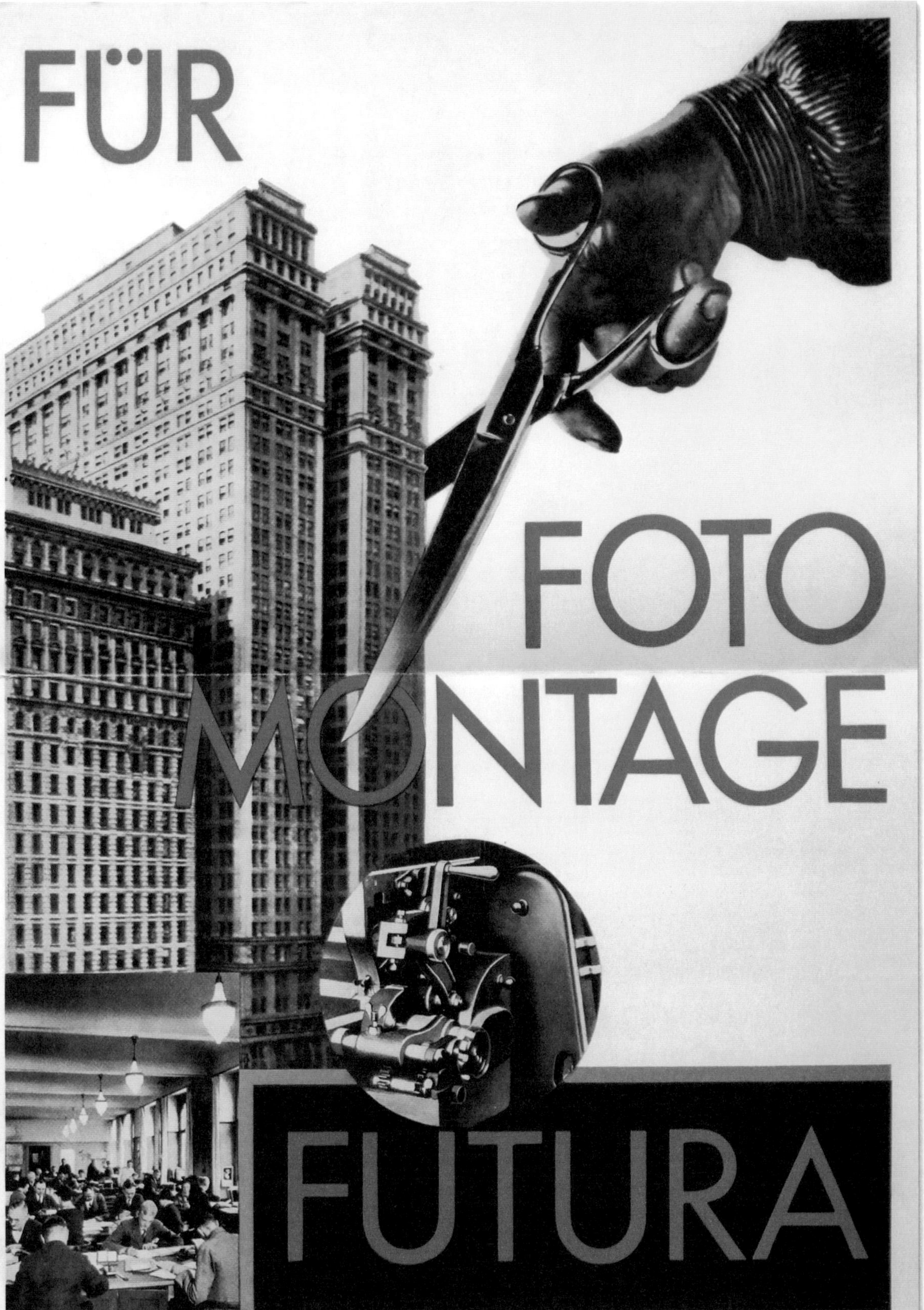
FÜR
FOTO
MONTAGE
FUTURA

BAUERSCHE
GIESSEREI

FRANKFURT A · M

Fotomontage

ist ein neues Ausdrucksmittel, das die Präzision der fotografischen Aufnahme mit den optischen Reizen freier Raumgestaltung vereinigt. In EINEM Bildzentrum faßt die Fotomontage Eindrücke zusammen, die das menschliche Auge vor den Gegenständen nur in räumlicher Trennung aufnehmen kann. Aneinanderreihung von Teilbildern wirkt leicht ermüdend. Fotomontage packt den Beschauer mit einem Blick. Es gibt kein Mittel, Wesentliches in überzeugenderer Weise bildhaft zu konzentrieren. Wenn Sie auf einem Plakat, in einer Anzeige, in einem Prospekt die Größe, das Wesen und das vielseitige Getriebe Ihres Unternehmens packend und eindringlich darstellen wollen, so ist

Fotomontage das Ausdrucksmittel unserer Zeit

Zur Fotomontage gehört ein knapper Text, oft genügt ein Schlagwort, das die Bedeutung des Ganzen blitzartig erhellt oder dem Sinn eine überraschende Wendung gibt. Dieser Text muß zur Komposition gehören. Wort und Bild müssen sich in der Gestaltung durchdringen, wie sie im Sinn eine neue Einheit schaffen. Deshalb brauchen Sie zur Beschriftung der Fotomontage eine Type, die dem Wesen dieses neuen Ausdrucksmittels gewachsen ist. Eine Schrift, exakt und unpersönlich wie die fotografische Aufnahme. Eine Schrift, die das Bedeutungsvolle der Drucktype knapp und überzeugend zusammenfaßt, wie Fotomontage das Wesentliche der Dinge zu neuer, sinnvoller Einheit gestaltet. Diese Schrift ist die

Futura · die Schrift unserer Zeit

40

First Futura portfolio, Bauer Type Foundry, Frankfurt am Main, 1927.

41

Persil, das ideale Waschmittel (Persil, the Ideal Laundry Detergent), supplementary leaflet in the first Futura portfolio, 1927.

40

41

Renner found his way to the Bauer Type Foundry through his former pupil Jost. Jost supervised the development of Futura professionally at the foundry by reconciling the design ideas of the type artist and the technical aspects involved in casting the type, so that the design would 'achieve the desired degree of legibility without losing character'.[71]

In an article in 1933 entitled 'Zweifel' (Doubt), Jost also expressed a negative view of the 'attempts at a new type', as it was presented by advocates of the New Typography. 'An attempt is being made here, with childish naivety, to apply a supposedly logical reasoning to practice, where there are naturally no rules: a new kind of visual training in schools, an entirely different way of training the eye and, consequently, an entirely new language.'[72] In accordance with this criticism, Jost made the following artistic decisions regarding the conception of Futura: 'While the "Futura" typeface was based on simple basic shapes, the circle, triangle and square, to become a usable, legible and even very legible type, it often had to give up the constructed form for the sake of optical clarity, and Renner was tolerant enough, given his experience in book design, not to sacrifice the knowledge gained from tradition for the sake of the new dogma.'[73]

42

42
Liselotte Müller, advertisement, Bauer Type Foundry, 1929/31.

s-t ligature, Futura Medium.

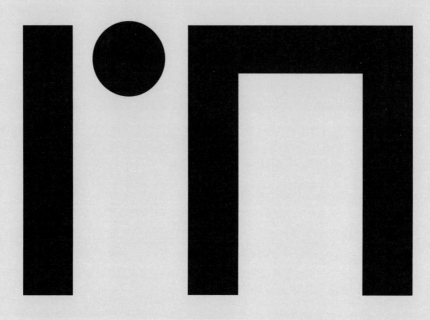

r and n alternates, Futura Medium.

FUTURA AND THE NEW TYPOGRAPHY

'It is economically irrelevant [sic] whether the typesetter has to deal with only half of the letters, whether the cast of the letters is encumbered by the capital letters, whether letter metal remains unused, whether the storage of the letters will require a lot of space, be less labour-intensive to use or use fewer storage containers, and finally, whether there is a recurring error in a source, and how much it will all cost! How much energy could be spared if the capital letters were removed from the type machine?'[74]

THE LOWER-CASE ALPHABET AND SANS SERIF TYPE

The decisive impetus for the discussion of the use of lower-case letters that took place in the context of the New Typography came from a mathematician and engineer from Berlin by the name of Walter Porstmann. In 1920 Porstmann had published his book *Sprache und Schrift*, in which he had advocated for a spelling reform that would lead to an international language. This would require the application of Taylorism as a way for typesetters to save time, materials and money. It is well known that Porstmann gave lectures at the Bauhaus, probably at the invitation of László Moholy-Nagy in 1925, because in that year a decisive shift towards economy and rationalization occurred at the Bauhaus school.[75]

In an article in September 1925 entitled 'Bauhaus und Typografie' (Bauhaus and Typography), Moholy-Nagy refers explicitly to Porstmann's book, from which he even cites excerpts.[76] The following month, Jan Tschichold, who was only 23 at the time, published his 'elementare typografie' as a special issue of *Typographische Mitteilungen* (Typography News) – a magazine that was published by the Bildungsverband der Deutschen Buchdrucker (Educational Association of German Letterpress Printers) and aimed primarily at members of the printing industry. Tschichold's publication constitutes a first attempt to present the ideas of the design avant-garde to professional typographers.[77] It also contains a reference to Porstmann: 'Enormous savings would be achieved by eliminating all the capitals and making exclusive use of the lower-case alphabet, an orthography that is recommended by the innovators of type as our future type. ... our type loses nothing in lower case, but it becomes easier to read, easier to learn, and much more economical. Why two alphabets for one word, why double the number of characters when the same result can be achieved with half?' [78] FIG.45 P.120

Tschichold also pleaded for the use of sans serif types: 'The elementary form of type is the sans serif type in all its variations: light – medium – bold – condensed to wide.'[79]

In the summer of 1926 the Bauhaus master complained in the so-called

Bauhaus issue of *Offset, Buch und Werbekunst* compiled by Moholy-Nagy: 'We currently do not have a very clearly legible commercial type in the right size without idiosyncratic characteristics and designed to have a functional, optical appearance without distortions and embellishments.'[80] For display and title types, there was Venus-Grotesk and Lapidar, which were 'more or less usable and good types, whose basic geometric and phonetic form, such as the square or circle, are used to full effect without distortion'.[81] However, Tschichold observed that 'when used in large quantities, they flicker.'[82]

Moholy-Nagy also declared that 'the use of basic shapes such as the circle, square and triangle is currently taking type design firmly in the direction of interesting formal, even essential and practical results.'[83] With this, he was clearly alluding to the type designs of both the young Bauhaus masters – Herbert Bayer and Josef Albers – who were presented in the same issue: FIG.44 P.119 'Time is money: being is economically determined.'[84] In his typeface designs, Albers was concerned with the need to save time and the effect of this on speaking and writing. To minimize the typesetting equipment used and to save on materials and time, he published Schablonenschrift in 1926. This typeface concentrated on three basic geometric shapes, with which, in his view, every letter could be constructed: 'the square, the triangle, as one half, and the quarter circle, the radius of which corresponds to one side of the square'.[85]

Bayer took a similar approach with the design of Universal. FIG.43 P.118 To achieve unity between the characters, he focused on the primary shapes of the circle and the square, in even stroke weights, with no optical corrections. He conceived his typeface as a lower-case alphabet: 'There is an upper-case and a lower-case alphabet. It is not necessary for a sound to have an upper-case and a lower-case character.'[86] His argument culminated in the following statement: 'The typeface that corresponds most closely to the requirements of the present day is the so-called sans serif. It is also used internationally, although it is still imperfect and complex, on account of having been developed arbitrarily, but it is the type that is being used as a basis here. Today, it consists of two alphabets, namely, the upper-case letters, which are purely classical in form, and the lower-case letters. These letterforms are thus the ones that require further development.'[87]

Bayer's primary goal, again along the same lines as Porstmann's, was the idea of an international script, consisting of simple and clear characters that would facilitate understanding between nations. This single script should be universally applicable in print, manual, machine and stencil setting.[88] To achieve 'unity in the construction of the letters', it should be 'constructed from the primary forms, circle and square', with an even stroke weight. Like Renner, Bayer strove for 'the greatest possible degree of concentration' – in other words, the greatest possible degree of formal reduction, based on the idea that 'to print handwriting with a machine is a false romanticism.'[89]

From the perspective of the New Typography, the demand for lower-case

'In the same way
that modern machines,
architecture and cinema
are an expression of
our specific times, so
must typography
be as well.'

HERBERT BAYER
'Versuch einer neuen Schrift' (Attempt at a New Typeface), 1926.

abcdefghi
jklmnopqr
stuvwxyz

HERBERT BAYER: Abb. 1. Alfabet
„g" und „k" sind noch als
unfertig zu betrachten

Beispiel eines Zeichens
in größerem Maßstab
Präzise optische Wirkung

sturm blond

Abb. 2. Anwendung

399

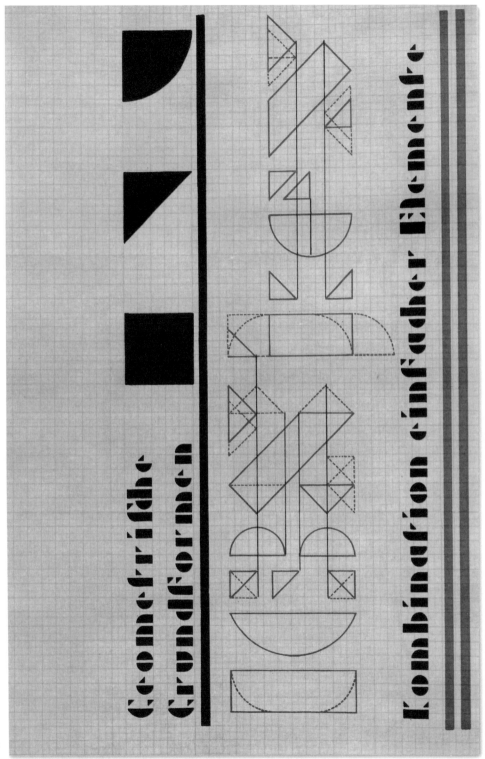

𝔄 + a + A + a

a

warum 4 alphabete, wenn sie alle gleich ausgesprochen werden (großes lateinisches, kleines lateinisches, großes deutsches, kleines deutsches)? warum 4
verschiedene klaviaturen einbauen, wenn jede genau dieselben töne hervorbringt?
welche verschwendung an energie, geduld, zeit, geld! welche verkomplizie-
rung in schreibmaschinen, schriftguß, setzerkästen, setzmaschinen, korrekturen
usw.! warum hauptwörter groß schreiben, wenn es in england, amerika, frankreich ohne das geht? warum satzanfänge zweimal signalisieren (punkt und großer
anfang), statt die punkte fetter zu nehmen? warum überhaupt groß schreiben,
wenn man nicht groß sprechen kann? warum die überlasteten kinder mit 4 alpha-
beten quälen, während für lebenswichtige stoffe in den schulen die zeit fehlt?

die kleine schrift ist „schwerer lesbar" nur, solange sie noch ungewohnt. „ästhe-
tischer" ist sie nur für die verflossene zeit, die in der architektur das auf und
ab von dächern und türmchen wollte.

unser vorschlag wäre puristisch? im gegenteil: wir sind für bereicherung aller
wirklichen lebensregungen. aber alle 4 klaviaturen drücken ja dieselben lebensregungen aus.

und das „deutsche lebensgefühl"? hatte unser eigenstes gut, die deutsche
musik etwa nötig, eine deutsche (und vierfache) notation hervorzubringen?

franz roh

45

43

P.118 – Herbert Bayer: 'Versuch
einer neuen Schrift', in Offset, Buch- und
Werbekunst, 1926 (special Bauhaus issue).

44

P.119 – Josef Albers: 'Schablonenschrift,
1923–26', in Offset, Buch- und
Werbekunst, 1926 (special Bauhaus issue).

45

Leaflet on lower-case lettering and
sans serif type, supplement in Franz
Roh and Jan Tschichold's publication
Foto-Auge, 1929.

lettering and a formal, aesthetic reduction
in type design to as few primary shapes
as possible would give rise to a consistent
('universal') and internationally legible,
unified type: 'a unified type, without lower-
case and upper-case letters; only single
letters – not in terms of size, but in terms
of form', as described by Moholy-Nagy.[90]

Since the beginning of the 1920s, Paul
Renner had studied the history as well
as the advantages and disadvantages of
typefaces and expressed his opposition
to black letter types.[91] For Futura, he
used as his foundation the 'Roman
capitals', consisting of 'the most simple
forms conceivable, standing next to one
another: circle, triangle, square', which he
described as 'easily understandable' and
'crystal clear'.[92]

While advocates of the New
Typography increased their demand for
sans serif types, Renner was intensively engaged with the classical Antiqua, which he
considered unsuitable for the German language because of the 'difference between
the upper-case and lower-case letters', and
therefore open for development.[93] Renner
saw a new 'Antiquatypus' in the so-called
Grotesk types, and hoped that the attempt
'to subject the upper-case and lower-case
letters to a single formal principle' would be
successful.[94] He stated something similar in
the 1925 edition of a Gutenberg commemorative publication: the task was to develop a
book type that was suitable for the German
language. Fraktur was not suited to this task,
and Antiqua, too, looked 'out of place and
foreign' in German texts.[95] The lower-case
letters must become akin to the self-sufficient
Roman capitals, which were 'derived from

the most elementary planes: circle, square, triangle',[96] stripped of movement and brought 'back to the formal principle of the simplest and most contrasting planes'.[97]

As mentioned, Bayer had incorporated radical lower-case spelling into the Bauhaus's printed materials in 1925. In particular, the lower-case letters that appeared at the bottom of the school's official notepaper, which carried the name of the Bauhaus around the world, were revised by him over the years into increasingly conciser forms.[98]

In 1928 Renner responded to the statement from the Bauhaus that 'we write everything in lower case because it saves us time. also, why have two alphabets when one can achieve the same result? why write in capitals when we cannot speak in capitals?'[99] Renner was not opposed to lower-case lettering, but rather to what he viewed as an 'illogical basis': 'We would like to thank the Bauhäusler in Dessau from the bottom of our hearts for how they turn their demands, so often based in theory, into actual reality. However, we merely ask that they do not damage their good work with arguments that are invalid and prone to misinterpretation.'[100]

With regard to contemporary demands for radical lower-case spelling, Renner revealed himself to be moderately modern: 'Even if a true democracy were to ... do away with the intolerable and obsequious frequency of capital letters, and even if the capital letters were restricted to the beginning of sentences and proper names, in accordance with Jacob Grimm's rules, German text would still not look as good in Antiqua as Latin does because the German language lacks many n's, m's and u's, and because it has more arcs, ascenders and descenders than the Latin alphabet. Nor is the finest classical Antiqua a type suited to our language.'[101] In the Gutenberg commemorative publication of 1925, Renner wrote: 'We Germans have unfortunately insisted on gracing every noun with a capital letter since the end of the 17th century. We must urgently do away with this obsequious habit and instil a true democracy.'[102] Until then, however, there was still the need to contend with the old spelling, wherein 'every noun begins with a capital letter'. Therefore, Renner stressed, either 'the capitals must be made less distinctive by making them more modest and inconspicuous', or an attempt was necessary to 'make the lower-case letters more akin to the Roman capitals, strip them of movement and bring them back to the formal principle of the simplest and most contrasting planes'.[103]

Renner supported the use of lower-case letters, but called for their moderate application; he was also very realistic about the fact that capital letters in German texts would probably remain.[104] Futura, therefore, should be viewed in the context of these discussions. Renner designed his typeface to account for the fact that German text is characterized by the rhythm of lower-case and upper-case letters, by harmonizing the lower-case letters with the upper-case letters.

In terms of type design, much more radical solutions were demanded by the design avant-garde. For example,

Jan Tschichold made this sharp judgement in his publication *Die Neue Typographie* (The New Typography) in 1928: 'There is no doubt that the sans serif types available today do not yet fulfil the requirements of an entirely satisfactory typeface. The specific characteristics of this type have not been fully worked out: the lower-case letters, in particular, are still too much like the Humanist lower-case alphabet. The majority, as well as the most recent artistic Grotesk types (such as Erbar-Grotesk and Kabel) show, to their detriment in comparison with the nameless older Grotesks, individually modified movements that essentially place them on a par with other artistic scripts. As all-purpose types, they are inferior to the old Grotesks. Paul Renner's Futura is making a significant step in the right direction.'[105]

Despite the praise, there was also criticism. Tschichold implied that with Futura, the optimum had still not been achieved: 'all previous efforts to create the type of the new era are merely attempts to "improve" the previous grotesques; what is missing from all these attempts, which are still much too artistic, or "artificial" in the older sense of the word, is the fundamental approach required. I personally believe that no one can be asked to create the typeface of our time because every individual must have the freedom to determine this according to his personal preferences. It should be the work of many people, one of whom must be an engineer.'[106]

MOVEMENTS FOR OPTOPHONETIC REFORM

When it came to the possible optophonetic reform of type design, Porstmann's *Sprache und Schrift* again became a driver of debate. Porstmann had pleaded not only for a radical reduction in the number of letters, but also that type characters should be better reflections of the sounds they represented.[107] He also wanted an international language. Moholy-Nagy's thoughts on the future of *Typografische Mitteilungen* were also a subject of controversy among specialists. The Bauhaus master had predicted that the spread of film, the gramophone and radio would lead to fundamental changes: 'With the perfection of the gramophone process and amplifier tubes, and with the development of a mechanical language that is phonetically best suited to these kinds of tools, what will probably happen is that future authors will no longer publish their literary works using an optical typography, but rather a phonetic-mechanical ... or possibly also an optical phonetic ... one.'[108]

Renner also seems to have been concerned with the question of whether spoken language could have an impact

46

Max Burger (design): cover of the magazine *Typographische Mitteilungen*, August 1928. The cover, with its consistent use of lower-case letters and setting in Futura alternates, was awarded third prize at the international 'Pressa' competition.

typographische mitteilungen

zeitschrift des bildungsverbandes
der deutschen buchdrucker
heft 8 · august 1928 · 25. jahrgang

8

'I personally believe that no one can be asked to create the typeface of our time because every individual must have the freedom to determine this according to his personal preferences. It should be the work of many people, one of whom must be an engineer.'

JAN TSCHICHOLD
Die Neue Typographie (The New Typography), 1928.

on the design of letters: 'The rich variety of sounds in our language, which correspond to the round forms in Antiqua, justify the effort of making the arcs more vertical. This results in a stronger delineation of the upper and lower limit of the row (the M height), as can be seen in the Roman Rustica and the later Gothic lower-case alphabet.' [109]

After Futura was released, further urgent calls for phonetic alphabets were published but not implemented. In 1927 Kurt Schwitters published 'Anregungen zur Erlangung einer Systemschrift' (Suggestions Why a System Type Is Needed), and in 1930 Tschichold presented a phonetic alphabet.[110]

Renner's views on the theory and history of typography therefore differed from the radical demands of the New Typography; he thus chose to design a new sans serif type. However, he did not develop this type using purely geometric forms, as Bayer had attempted to do with Universal, but instead used classical models. Renner also demonstrated a moderate approach to modernism with regard to the lower-case alphabet, expressed in his plea for its use in moderation – a conviction that he remained faithful to, despite political resistance. In 1946 he wrote: 'We should ... limit the use of capitals to the beginning of sentences and proper nouns, as we used to do in the past and as is the custom everywhere else in the world.' [111] Futura met this demand through its harmonization of lower-case letters with capitals, thereby achieving a more balanced optical effect.

FUTURA – THE TYPEFACE OF MODERNITY

The semantic impetus behind the sans serif types of the 1920s was strongly influenced by a mechanical and functional view of the world, which expressed a rational way of thinking through the geometrical construction of a type by means of lines and circles. With Futura, Renner created a geometrically constructed sans serif type that expressed that spirit of the machine and the engineer in an almost ideal fashion. As a result, this first geometric sans serif type, based on clarity of construction and a rational technical approach, received a largely warm welcome among the typographic avant-garde.

By constructing the lower-case letters geometrically, like Roman capitals, Renner clearly distinguished Futura from the handwritten style of individual artistic types. Liberated from any individual style, Futura indeed became the supra-individual 'typeface of its time'. In its timeless and perfect geometry, it symbolized mechanization and industrialization, the division of labour and Taylorism.

However, the construction of the type was also based on models from antiquity and guided by the rules of perception of type design, enabling it – much more so than the type experiments at the Bauhaus – to join the canon and become part of the self-identity of professional type designers. In this way, Futura was able to kill two birds with one stone: it visualized concepts of the New Typography but was also acceptable to typographers who were open to a more moderate form of modernism.

Precisely because it brought the avant-garde together with the quality requirements of practice, Futura grew to become *the* typeface of modernism. It is not absolutely geometric, like Bayer's Universal, but it combines abstract forms with classical models to create a modern type with a noble appearance.

FUTURA
EIN WELTERFOLG

mager

halbfett

dreiviertelfett

fett

schmalfett

schräg mager

schräg halbfett

black

Die Futura hat im Laufe weniger Jahre in Europa wie in Amerika eine überraschend weite Verbreitung gefunden, und die Zahl ihrer Freunde mehrt sich stetig. Die uneingeschränkte Anerkennung, die diese Schrift fand, war nicht vorauszusehen, denn man weiß, wie sehr in Dingen der Typographie die Anschauungsweise der Völker und Kontinente auseinandergeht. Worin beruht das Geheimnis dieses Erfolges? Soviel ist gewiß: die Futura ist keine modische Schrift, weder im besseren noch im minderen Sinne des Wortes. Sie erzwang nicht durch verblüffende Formen Beachtung, sie dient nicht nur dem Augenblick, und sie deckt mehr als die Absichten des Tages. In der Futura gelang die vollendete Sichtbarmachung eines großen Formgedankens. Ihre Schönheit gründet sich auf die Reinheit ihrer Gesinnung, und sie überzeugt mit der Kraft, mit der ein vollkommenes Werk überzeugt.

BAUERSCHE GIESSEREI
FRANKFURT AM MAIN · NEW YORK

47

47

Advertisement for the Bauer Type Foundry, in *Gebrauchsgraphik*, vol. 7, no. 8, 1930.

48

'Futura: ein Welterfolg' (Futura: An International Success), advertisement by the Bauer Type Foundry, set in consistent lower-case letters, for Jan Tschichold's supplement in *Typografische Mitteilungen*: 'noch eine neue schrift. beitrag zur frage der ökonomie der schrift' (yet another new typeface. supplement on the question of economy in type), 1930.

FUTURA
ein welterfolg

mager

halbfett

fett

schräg mager

halbfett

black

die futura hat im laufe weniger jahre in europa wie in amerika eine überraschend weite verbreitung gefunden, und die zahl ihrer freunde mehrt sich stetig. die uneingeschränkte anerkennung, die diese schrift fand, war nicht vorauszusehen, denn man weiß, wie sehr in dingen der typografie die anschauungsweise der völker und kontinente auseinandergeht. worin beruht das geheimnis dieses erfolges? soviel ist gewiß: die futura ist keine modische schrift, weder im besseren noch im minderen sinne des wortes. sie erzwang nicht durch verblüffende formen beachtung, sie dient nicht nur dem augenblick, und sie deckt mehr als die absichten des tages. in der futura gelang die vollendete sichtbarmachung eines großen formgedankens. ihre schönheit gründet sich auf die reinheit ihrer gesinnung, und sie überzeugt mit der kraft, mit der ein vollkommenes werk überzeugt.

bauersche giesserei
frankfurt am main

ANNETTE LUDWIG

WILLI BAUMEISTER

THE AVANT-GARDIST FROM SWABIA IN THE CITY OF TYPE FOUNDRIES (1928–1933)

'In Frankfurt, I not only witnessed the emergence of a new style of architecture, but also, as a teacher, worked at an art school that set itself the task of providing instruction in the forms and styles of the New Era. Art schools are not regarded highly among professionals. And yet they have been of invaluable service to typography because they produce commercial graphic designers who are trained in typographic sketching and skilled in lettering.'[112]

With these words, Paul Renner described the one year he worked at the Städtische Kunstgewerbeschule (Municipal School of Arts and Crafts). This was two years before his nomination, which had been a result of the merger of the Städelsche Kunstinstitut with the Kunstgewerbeschule, supported by the Kunstgewerbeverein (Arts and Crafts Association). Under the director of the 'Stadtkunstwart' (the city's culture and heritage authority), Fritz Wichert, and at a time when design was undergoing an unprecedented level of modernization as a result of the 'New Frankfurt' project, teaching was interdisciplinary and squarely focused on the requirements of practice. The faculty of commercial graphic design and typography, directed by Renner, therefore acquired a particular importance, which it owed partly to the great type foundries based in the area and their economic potential.[113] The faculty's programme was suspended after Renner's departure, until the artist Willi Baumeister (1889–1955), from Stuttgart, was appointed his successor on 1 April 1928.

The 39-year-old was renowned both nationally and internationally as an artist, reflected in a number of much-admired exhibitions and sold works. In the previous decade, however, he had become equally successful in the field of applied art. His outstanding design solutions included prints and space design for the Stuttgart Architecture Exhibition in 1924, and the Werkbund exhibition 'Die Wohnung' (The Apartment), which was held in 1927 in connection with the opening of the Weissenhof housing estate.

This work, which was referred to by Baumeister himself as 'commercial art',[114] continued in Frankfurt, and he was honoured with the title of professor after just six months of teaching in the commercial graphics, typography and textile printing classes offered by the faculty.[115] When a painter attached to Constructivism and abstraction had questioned Baumeister about the 'pictoriality' of the New Typography in the design maxims he was prescribing, he received the following response: 'The typographer is faced with the same task as the painter when he finds

49
Willi Baumeister: exhibition poster 'Vom Abbild zum Sinnbild', Städelsche Kunstinstitut, Frankfurt am Main, 1931.

himself at the beginning of his creative and conscious work. [but] The rules governing the distribution of planes are different. The printed page contains pictures and informational messages. ... In typography, the message is presented pictorially.'[116] Baumeister's many students were taught how to implement this aesthetic by studying various examples of its application, such as the commercial prints produced by the company Hartmann & Braun, designed by Baumeister during his time in Frankfurt in accordance with 'modern requirements'.[117]

In October 1930 Baumeister was entrusted with improving the typography of the magazine *Das Neue Frankfurt/die neue stadt*, which had been founded in 1926 by the head of the urban planning authority, Ernst May, and had, from its second volume, been jointly published with Wichert. Baumeister applied his usual standards to the task:

'Many "modern" advertisements, letterheads, etc., are designed according to the compositional principles of painting, even when Constructivist in style. ... Paintings are looked at, but advertisements, lines of texts, etc., must be read. We know that reading is a type of movement. Every movement, i.e. everything that moves in a certain direction, has no balance. Unlike the still point of the composition of a painting, the arrangement of a print has a very particular direction. Thus, the primary concern in typesetting is not the fine adjustment of free balance. Rather, everything must be sacrificed to the graphic line in this case.'[118]

Baumeister 'calmed' the layout of the design for the monthly magazine, which until then had been the responsibility of Hans Leistikow, head of the city's urban planning authority, who had gone to Moscow with the 'May Brigade'. FIG.23 P.91 For the inside title page of issue no. 4/11, Baumeister developed the new 'dnf' emblem using Futura Inline; an approach was applied until December 1932 – particularly in the title pages, in which 'the issue's content is condensed into succinct signals' – which aimed at international levels of distinction.[119] Here, he refrained from using the repeatedly criticized capital set, and combined planes of colour and photographs with bold, right-justified Futura.

Baumeister had expressed his 'preference for grotesque types' as early as 1926, and his preference now – based on the newly released Erbar-Grotesk – led him to declare that 'the precise face gives the word's appearance a clarity that brush scripts, decorative scripts and Fraktur never managed to achieve. The block of type is clearly delineated, which, unlike other types, makes it possible to execute an excellent design.'[120] As an advocate of artistic individuality, he did not, like Kurt Schwitters – to whom he was also connected as a member of the ring neue werbegestalter CF. P.157 – commit to Futura. He simply used it where he saw fit – for example, in a poster for an art exhibition designed by Wichert entitled 'Vom Abbild zum Sinnbild' (From Likeness to Symbol) in 1931. FIG.49 P.128 He also used it when, having been ostracized by the National Socialists, stripped of his professorship and banned from organizing exhibitions, he was forced to earn a living as a graphic designer for Dr Kurt Herbert's paint factory in Wuppertal.[121]

Lower-case **o**s in Futura Light, Medium and Bold. Shown here: type specimens, 1927/28.

1

[Lecture given by] Paul Renner, in: *Kampf um München als Kulturzentrum. Sechs Vorträge von Thomas Mann, Heinrich Mann, Leo Weismantel, Willi Geiger, Walter Courvoisier und Paul Renner*, Munich, year not specified [1926], p. 49.

2

Cf. Grete Lihotzky: 'Rationalisierung im Haushalt'. In: *Das Neue Frankfurt* (Frankfurt am Main), vol. 1, April/June 1927, no. 5, pp. 120–23.

3

Four different apartments were displayed inside the exhibition hall. Two corresponded to the types that had been built in Praunheim. Cf. abridged: 'Eine Bauausstellung auf der Frankfurter Frühjahrsmesse'. In: *Das Neue Frankfurt* (Frankfurt am Main), vol. 1, February/March 1927, no. 4, pp. 90–91; Werner Nosbisch: 'Die neue Wohnung und ihr Innenausbau: Der neuzeitliche Haushalt'. In: *Das Neue Frankfurt* (Frankfurt am Main), vol. 1, 1927, no. 6, pp. 129–33.

4

Paul Renner: 'Entbehrliche Künste, notwendige Kunst'. In: *Die Bücherstube* (Munich), vol. 4, 1925, p. 244.

5

Paul Renner: 'Die Schrift unserer Zeit'. In: *Die Form* (Berlin), vol. 2, 1927, no. 4, p. 110.

6

[Paul Renner]: 'Aus der Geschichte der neuen deutschen Typografie'. Lecture given at the annual assembly of Grafisches Gewerbe in Freiburg im Breisgau, 1947, typewritten copy, p. 8.

7

[Paul Renner]: 'Vom Georg-Müller-Buch bis zur Futura und Meisterschule. Erinnerungen Paul Renners aus dem Jahrzehnt 1918 bis 1927'. In: *Imprimatur* (Munich), vol. IX, 1940, p. 7.

8

[Paul Renner]: 'Aus der Geschichte, p. 9.

9

Albinus' estate at the MAK contains two invitation cards and many commercial prints, which were printed using the same typesetting equipment.

10

The afterword dates the publication as 3 July 1925; the sample can be found in: Fritz Helmuth Ehmcke: *Schrift. Ihre Gestaltung und Entwicklung in neuerer Zeit*, Munich 1925, p. 66.

11

Wichert felt the new school should have been given an appropriate name when the two institutions merged. The names 'Kunstgewerbeschule', 'Städtische Kunstschule' and 'Hochschule für freie und angewandte Kunst' were used interchangeably. Cf. Hans M. Wingler (ed.): *Kunstschulreform 1900–1933*, Berlin 1977, p. 146, and Heike Drummer: 'Reform und Destruktion – die Geschichte der Städelschule während Weimarer Zeit und Nationalsozialismus'. In: Hubert Salden (ed.): *Die Städelschule Frankfurt am Main von 1817 bis 1995*, Mainz 1995, p. 139.

12

Led from 1927 by Franz Schuster, originally from Vienna, cf. Klaus Klemp: *Design in Frankfurt 1920–1990*, ed. Matthias Wagner K. (exhibition catalogue, Museum of Applied Arts, Frankfurt am Main), Stuttgart 2014, p. 34.

13

Ibid.

14

Drummer: 'Reform und Destruktion', p. 143.

15

The department was created in 1924 under the name 'Typography and Book Binding' and was initially led by Albert Windisch, Albinus and Ernst Rehbein. Renner was also employed so that he could combat the competition from Offenbach. Cf. Hans M. Wingler (ed.): *Kunstschulreform 1900–1933*, Berlin 1977, pp. 157–58. The master typesetter Philipp Albinus played an important role at the Frankfurt School, where he taught in the faculty of commercial graphic design, which was led by Renner and later Willi Baumeister, and collected examples of commercial prints. He was also chairman of the Frankfurt group of the Bildungsverbandes der Deutschen Buchdrucker (Educational Association of German Book Printers), the institution that published Jan Tschichold's 'elementare typografie' special issue in 1925, thereby playing a decisive role in the popularization of the 'New Typography' among professional groups in the industry. Albinus also summarized the developments of the previous five years in *Grundsätzliches zur Neuen Typographie*

(Essential Guide to the New Typography), published in January 1929. Cf. Philipp Albinus: *Grundsätzliches zur Neuen Typographie*, Berlin 1929; also cf. Paul Renner: *Aus meinem Leben*, Frankfurt am Main, year not specified [c. 1945], p. 5, and *Alles neu! 100 Jahre neue Typografie und neue Grafik in Frankfurt am Main*, ed. Klaus Klemp, Matthias Wagner K. et al. (catalogue of the Museum of Applied Arts, Frankfurt am Main), Stuttgart 2016.

16

A sample of Renner-Futura was displayed during an exhibition at the art school in November 1925. Unfortunately, it has not been preserved. Cf. Städtische Kunstgewerbeschule Frankfurt am Main: first exhibition. *Grafische, malerische, plastische Kräfte* (no. 23) (exhibition catalogue, Kunstgewerbemuseum/49 Neue Mainzer Strasse, Frankfurt am Main), Frankfurt am Main 1925.

17

Wingler (ed.): *Kunstschulreform 1900–1933*, pp. 158–59.

18

DNF, 1929, no. 5, cit. in ibid., p. 157.

19

Paul Renner: 'Vom Georg-Müller-Buch bis zur Futura und Meisterschule'. In: *Gebrauchsgraphik* (Berlin), vol. 20, May 1943, no. 5, page not specified; Renner: *Aus meinem Leben*, p. 5; [Renner]: 'Aus der Geschichte', p. 9.

20

Regarding the term 'typotechture', cf. Harald Wanetzky: *Typotektur. Architektur und Typografie im 20. Jahrhundert – der Modellfall einer Zusammenführung*. Dissertation. Freiburg im Breisgau 1995.

21

E[rnst] M[ay]: 'Reklamereform'. In: *Das Neue Frankfurt* (Frankfurt am Main), vol. 1, 1927, no. 3, p. 64.

22

Walter Dexel: 'Reklame im Stadtbilde'. In: *Das Neue Frankfurt* (Frankfurt am Main), vol. 1, 1927, no. 3, p. 45 et seq.

23

During his time at the Frankfurt urban planning authority, Dexel published his article 'Was ist neue Typographie?' (What is New Typography?) in the *Frankfurter Zeitung*, 1 February 1927.

24

Dexel: 'Reklame im Stadtbilde', p. 46.

25

Ibid, p. 45 et seq.

26

Ibid.

27

Ibid.

28

Paul Renner: 'Vom Georg-Müller-Buch bis zur Futura und Meisterschule' (Gebrauchsgraphik), page not specified; Renner, Aus meinem Leben, p. 5; [Renner]: 'Aus der Geschichte', p. 9. Christopher Burke also stresses that Renner drew samples for city signs in 1925/26, so Futura was present not only at the Frankfurt urban planning authority but also in public spaces, particularly New Frankfurt. Cf. Christopher Burke: Paul Renner: The Art of Typography, London 1998, p. 88, note 39.

29

Cf. copy in the Bauhaus Archive with the description 'Typeface "Kramer Grotesk", 1925, for the city of Frankfurt am Main, further developed by Paul Renner, two sheets, portfolio of copies Ferdinand Kramer (BHA)', and Andreas Hansert: Georg Hartmann (1870-1954). Biografie eines Frankfurter Schriftgiessers, Bibliophilen und Kunstmäzens, Vienna/Cologne/Weimar 2009, p. 88. See also Pennoyer, Katharina: To Ferdinand Kramer and Paul Renner – hitherto unobserved facts and details. In: Klaus Klemp, Matthias Wagner K., Friedrich Friedl, Peter Zizka: Alles Neu! 100 Jahre Neue Typografie und Neue Grafik in Frankfurt am Main, Kat. Museum für Angewandte Kunst Frankfurt/M. Stuttgart: av edition, 2016, pp. 99–111.

30

This was an important topic in older research: Eckhard Neumann writes that Kramer had mentioned in conversation that 'he too, sees himself as one of the "fathers" of Futura', but points out that this was not to be taken literally as a challenge to Renner's authorship. Significant deviations in form had occurred between the first studies and the final packaging of the typeface, which may 'very well have been a result of the dialogue between Kramer and Renner'. He reports that Kramer's estate contains 'a sheet showing studies of type designs for capitals that meet all the aesthetic specifications of Futura capitals'. It has been dated back to 1925, prior to the design for the hat shop.

31

According to Stresow, a brochure from the Bauer Type Foundry includes the note 'one of the first drawings of Futura by Paul Renner (1925)'. Cf. Gustav Stresow: 'Paul Renner und die Konzeption der Futura'. In: Buchhandelsgeschichte (Frankfurt am Main), 2/1995 (supplement in Börsenblatt für den Deutschen Buchhandel, no. 51, 27 June 1995, B 44).

32

'Neue Reklame in Frankfurt am Main'. In: Das Neue Frankfurt (Frankfurt am Main), vol. 1, 1927, no. 3, p. 61.

33

The picture of the hat shop can be found in the special issue of the magazine Das Neue Frankfurt entitled 'Reklame im Stadtbilde'. Neumann remarks that there is another picture on the same page of the facade of a bakery/pastry shop bearing the same typographic characteristics, for which Renner is also credited. Cf. 'Neue Reklame in Frankfurt am Main', p. 61, and Neumann: 'Frankfurter Typografie', p. 33.

34

Ibid. Burke also refers to the logical argument that the naming of Renner as the designer of the 'AUSSEN-REKLAME der Firma G. Kramer' would certainly not have happened if Kramer himself had designed the typeface. Cf. Burke: Paul Renner.

35

[Rudolf] Conrad: [Report on statements by Paul Renner]. In: Klimschs, no. 12, cit. in Hermann Hoffmann, 'Reform und Bolschewismus'. In: Zeitschrift für Deutschlands Buchdrucker und verwandte Gewerbe (Leipzig), vol. 38, 1926, no. 23, p. 191.

36

Paul Renner: 'Zu den Arbeiten von Ferdinand Kramer'. In: Die Form (Berlin), vol. 2, 1927, no. 10, pp. 320–22.

37

Ibid, p. 320.

38

Ibid, p. 322.

39

Ibid.

40

Gerda Breuer (ed.): Kramer, Ferdinand. Design für variablen Gebrauch, Tübingen/Berlin 2014, pp. 194–95.

41

Paul Renner: Futura. Die Schrift unserer Zeit. Specimen der Bauerschen Giesserei Frankfurt am Main, year not specified [1927], p. 4.

42

Letter from Renner to the Bauer Type Foundry on 14 March 1940. Archive of Andrea Haushofer, Munich.

43

Wingler (ed.): Kunstschulreform 1900–1933, Bauhaus Weimar, Dessau, Berlin, Debschitz Art School, Munich, Frankfurt Art School, Breslau Academy, Reimann School Berlin (exhibition catalogue, Bauhaus Archive), Berlin 1977, p. 157 et seq.

44

Wichert to the municipal head of staff on 15 July 1925. Institut für Stadtgeschichte Frankfurt (ISG), municipal records, p. 1753 I, sheet 47 b.

45

Ibid.

46

Wingler (ed.): Kunstschulreform, p. 157 et seq.

47

See list of displayed works in the catalogue of the school's first exhibition in 1925. Grafische, malerische, plastische Kräfte.

48

Burke: Paul Renner, p. 88, note 38.

49

Futura. Bauer Type Foundry. Frankfurt. Barcelona. New York, year not specified. Bauhaus Archive Berlin, NL Paul Renner, inv. no. 10364/1.

Cf. Eckhard Neumann: 'Frankfurter Typografie. Bemerkungen zur Futura und zur angeblichen Kramer-Grotesk'. In: Claude Lichtenstein (ed.): Ferdinand Kramer. Der Charme des Systematischen. Architektur, Einrichtung, Design, Giessen 1991, pp. 32–33. This very sheet of corrections on graph paper is referred to in Willberg's work as a design by Kramer. Cf. Hans Peter Willberg: Ungedruckte Illustrationen von Willi Baumeister. Schrift im Bauhaus. Die Futura von Paul Renner (Monographien und Materialien zur Buchkunst II), Neu-Isenburg 1969, fig. 15.

50

Cf. Tobias Picard: 'Durch den Kopf des Auftraggebers denken. Der Gestalter Hans Leistikow'. In *Archiv für Frankfurts Geschichte und Kunst* (vol. 69), ed. Dieter Rebentisch and Evelyn Hills, Frankfurt am Main 2003, pp. 99–126, here p. 102.

51

Institut für Stadtgeschichte Frankfurt (ISG), employee records (PA 205.749) Leistikow, no. 8.

52

Die Form (Berlin), vol. 2, 1927, no. 1, p. 32.

53

Quoted in Heinz and Bodo Rasch (eds): *Gefesselter Blick*. 25 short monographs and contributions on modern advertising design, with the support of the 'Ring d. Werbegestalter d. Schweizer Werkbundes' et al., Stuttgart 1930, Reprint Baden (Switzerland) 1996, p. 61 et seq.

54

Rudolf Conrad: 'Frankfurt-Offenbach und die Deutsche Schriftentwicklung seit der Jahrhundertwende/Frankfurt-Offenbach and the Development of German Type since the Beginning of the New Century'. In: *Gebrauchsgraphik* (Berlin), vol. 3, March 1926, no. 3, p. 41.

55

Cf. Justina Schreiber: 'Die Avantgarde der Buchstaben. Vor 80 Jahren erfand Paul Renner die Futura. Nach einer steilen Karriere treibt die Schrift ihren Fans noch heute Tränen in die Augen'. In: *Süddeutsche Zeitung* (Munich), 16 March 2006 (weekend supplement). Bauhaus Archive Berlin.

56

Archive of Andrea Haushofer, Munich.

57

Schreiber: 'Die Avantgarde der Buchstaben; Hansert: *Georg Hartmann*, p. 91.

58

Letter from the Bauer Type Foundry on 16 November 1927 to the company G. Kreysing, Leipzig. Gutenberg Museum, Mainz.

59

Ibid.

60

Ibid.

61

Herbert Bayer: 'Versuch einer neuen Schrift'. In: *Offset, Buch- und Werbekunst* (Leipzig), 1926, no. 7 (the so-called Bauhaus issue), p. 398 et seq.

62

Willi Baumeister: 'Neue Typographie'. In: *Die Form* (Berlin), vol. 1, July 1926, no. 10, pp. 215–17.

63

Konrad Friedrich Bauer: 'Zukunft der Schrift'. In: *Klimschs Druckereianzeiger* (Frankfurt am Main), vol. 54, 1927, no. 56, pp. 1329–30.

64

Fritz Helmuth Ehmcke: 'Wandlung des Schriftgefühls'. In: Hans H. Bockwitz (ed.): *Buch und Schrift – Schriftprobleme. Jahrbuch des Deutschen Vereins für Buchwesen und Schrifttum zu Leipzig*, vol. 4, Leipzig 1930, p. 13.

65

Konrad Friedrich Bauer: 'Elementare Typographie'. In: *Klimschs allgemeiner Anzeiger für Druckereien* (Frankfurt am Main), vol. 52, 1925, no. 8, p. 3.

66

[Peter Meyer:] 'Mechanisierte Grafik'. In: *Das Werk* (Zurich), vol. 19, April 1932, pp. 118–20.

67

Rudolf Conrad: 'Heinrich Jost als Typograph'. In: *Klimschs Jahrbuch des graphischen Gewerbes* (Frankfurt am Main), vol. 26, 1933, p. 39.

68

Konrad Friedrich Bauer: *Werden und Wachsen einer deutschen Schriftgiesserei*. On 100 years of existence of the Bauer Type Foundry, Frankfurt am Main 1837–1937, pub. in the anniversary year 1937, Frankfurt am Main, p. 49.

69

Konrad Bauer: 'Heinrich Jost'. In: *Gebrauchsgraphik* (Berlin), vol. 7, April 1930, no. 4, p. 47.

70

Ibid, p. 46.

71

Gustav Stresow: 'Gedenkblatt für Heinrich Jost'. In: *Philobiblon* (Stuttgart), vol. 33, 1989, p. 219.

72

Heinrich Jost: 'Zweifel'. In: *Klimschs Jahrbuch des graphischen Gewerbes* (Frankfurt am Main), 1933, p. 9.

73

Ibid, p. 10. Jost was employed as an artistic advisor on graphic design at the newspaper *Münchner Neueste Nachrichten* during World War I. He was therefore charged with the design of advertisements and public relations activities.

74

Walter Porstmann: *Sprache und Schrift*, Berlin 1920, page not specified [p. 70].

75

In addition, a letter exists from Herbert Bayer to Walter Porstmann, dated 26 July 1925, in which he describes an idea for a 'unified type' in which 'there are no lower-case and upper-case letters at all'. Bernd Freese collection, Frankfurt am Main.

76

László Moholy-Nagy: 'Bauhaus und Typographie'. In: *Anhaltische Rundschau*, 14 September 1925. Reprinted in: Hans M. Wingler: *Das Bauhaus 1919–1933. Weimar, Dessau, Berlin und die Nachfolge in Chicago seit 1937*. 6th ed., Cologne 2009, p. 124.

77

The 'elementare typografie' special issue at first triggered an intense 'storm of indignation', and was also frequently discussed in subsequent issues of the magazine. Cf. Albinus: *Grundsätzliches zur Neuen Typographie*, p. 5; Friedrich Friedl: 'Echo and Reactions to the Special Issue Elementare Typographie'. In Iwan [Jan] Tschichold: *Elementare Typographie*, facsimile edition of the 1925 edition, Mainz 1968, pp. 8–12.

78

Iwan [Jan] Tschichold: 'elementare typographie'. In: *Typographische Mitteilungen* (Leipzig), vol. 122, October 1925, no. 10, p. 198.

79

Ibid, p. 198. Tschichold remarked, however, that no type of a satisfactory quality had yet been designed: 'Until an easily legible, elementary form has been created in commercial type, an impersonal, objective, and the least unobtrusive form possible of oldstyle Antiqua ... is to be preferred over the grotesque for practical purposes.'

80

László Moholy-Nagy: 'Zeitgemässe Typographie (Ziele, Praxis, Kritik)'. In: Offset-, Buch und Werbekunst (Leipzig), 1926, no. 7 (the so-called Bauhaus issue), p. 380. The text is dated 1924. It had already been published in 1925 in the Gutenberg commemorative publication. Cf. Ladislaus Moholy-Nagy: 'Zeitgemässe Typographie – Ziele, Praxis, Kritik'. In: Gutenberg commemorative publication to celebrate the 25th anniversary of the Gutenberg Museum in Mainz 1925, ed. by A[loys] Ruppel. Mainz 1925, pp. 307–17.

81

Ibid.

82

Ibid, pp. 380, 382.

83

Ibid, p. 380.

84

Josef Albers: 'Zur Ökonomie der Schrift-form'. In: Offset, Buch- und Werbekunst (Leipzig), 1926, no. 7 (the so-called Bauhaus issue), p. 395.

85

The length of every edge corresponds to the square. If a letter consists of two combined surfaces, they stand uncon-nected next to each other. The ratio of the spacing was set at 1:3, i.e. optical adjust-ments were not provided for. To remedy the poor legibility, which is a fault of many types, Albers' Schablonenschrift was set in large point sizes only and used as let-tering for posters and advertisements. Cf. ibid, p. 397.

86

Bayer: 'Versuch einer neuen Schrift', p. 400.

87

Ibid. It seems even more astounding that Bayer used capital letters for the vertical lettering on the Dessau Bauhaus building, for which the individual letters, e.g. the **S**, were modified.

88

Ibid, p. 398.

89

Ibid, p. 400.

90

Moholy-Nagy: 'Zeitgemässe Typographie, p. 379.

91

Cf. Paul Renner: Typographie als Kunst, Munich 1922, p. 39 et seq.; Paul Renner: 'Neue Ziele des Schriftschaffens'. In: Die Bücherstube (Munich), vol. 4, 1925, no. 1, pp. 21–23.

92

Paul Renner: 'Die Zukunft unserer Druck-schrift'. In: Typographische Mitteilungen (Leipzig), vol. 22, 1925, no. 5, p. 86.

93

Renner: 'Neue Ziele des Schriftschaffens', pp. 18–19. While the Roman capitals are constructed from the simplest forms imagi-nable – the circle, square and triangle – the lower-case letters originate from the Roman cursive, as well as its alterations in the uncial, semi-uncial, Carolingian and, lastly, the humanist lower-case alphabet.

94

Cf. Renner: 'Die Zukunft unserer Druck-schrift', p. 87.

95

Paul Renner: 'Revolution der Buchschrift'. In the Gutenberg commemorative publica-tion to celebrate the 25th anniversary of the Gutenberg Museum in Mainz, ed. by A[loys] Ruppel. Mainz 1925, p. 280.

96

Ibid.

97

Ibid, p. 281.

98

At first, lengthy explanations were required: 'try to write in a simpler way: 1. this type of script is recommended by all innovators of script as our future script. compare the book "sprache der schrift" by dr. porstmann, verlag des vereins deutscher ingenieure, berlin 1920. 2. our script loses nothing in lower case, but it be-comes easier to read, easier to learn, and much more economic. 3. why does one sound, for example, a, require two charac-ters: A and a? one sound, one character. why two alphabets for one word, why double the number of characters when the same result can be achieved with half?', cit. in Magdalena Droste: 'Herbert Bayers künstlerische Entwicklung 1918–1938'. In: Hans Maria Wingler/Magdalena Droste: Herbert Bayer. Das künstlerische Werk 1918–1938 (exhibition catalogue, Bauhaus Archive Berlin), Berlin 1982, p. 40; around 1927, the following was added: 'we write everything in lower case because it saves us time.'

99

From 1927 this statement was included on the letterhead designed by Herbert Bayer for the Bauhaus.

100

Paul Renner: 'Gegen den Dogmatismus in der Kunst'. In: Die Form (Berlin), vol. 3, 1928, no. 11, p. 313.

101

Renner: 'Neue Ziele des Schriftschaffens', p. 19.

102

Renner: 'Revolution der Buchschrift', p. 280. In: Gutenberg commemora-tive publication, Gutenberg-Jahrbuch (Almanac)

103

Ibid, p. 281.

104

Paul Renner: Kunst und Technik im Buch-gewerbe. Series of lectures presented to the German Book Industry Association in the winter of 1928. Second lecture, 'Type and Typography'. In: Archiv für Buchgew-erbe und Gebrauchsgraphik (Leipzig), vol. 65, 1928, no. 6, p. 462.

105

Jan Tschichold: Die neue Typografie. Ein Handbuch für zeitgemäss Schaffende. (Berlin 1928), 2nd ed., Berlin 1987, pp. 75–76.

106

Ibid, p. 76.

107

'ain laut – ain zeichen', in: Porstmann: Sprache und Schrift, page not specified [p. 74].

108

Moholy-Nagy: 'Zeitgemässe Typographie, p. 375.

109

Renner: 'Die Zukunft unserer Druckschrift', p. 87.

110

Kurt Schwitters: 'Anregungen zur Erlan-gung einer Systemschrift'. In: i 10. Interna-tionale Revue (Amsterdam), vol. 1, August/September 1927, no. 8/9, pp. 312–16; Jan Tschichold: 'Noch eine neue Schrift. Bei-trag zur Frage der Ökonomie der Schrift'. In: Typographische Mitteilungen (Berlin), vol. 27, March 1930, no. 3, supplement.

111
Paul Renner: 'Schrift und Rechtschreibung'.
In: *Pandora* (Ulm), 1946, p. 34.

112
[Renner]: 'Aus der Geschichte der
deutschen Typografie', p. 9.

113
The Bauer Type Foundry in particular,
where over 1,300 people worked, as well
as Stempel AG and Ludwig & Mayer,
should be mentioned in this context. Cf.
the recent publication on New Typography in Frankfurt: *Alles neu!*; and the
exhibition catalogue *Willi Baumeister. Die
Frankfurter Jahre 1928-1933*, to mark the
50th anniversary of his death, published
by Museum Giersch, Frankfurt am Main
2005.

114
Cited in: Wolfgang Kermer: *Zur Kunst-
lehre Willi Baumeisters*. A suggestion
by Willi Baumeister for the reform of
the foundation course in art from 1949.
The students of Willi Baumeister at the
Staatlichen Akademie der Bildenden
Künste Stuttgart (Stuttgart State
Academy of Fine Arts),1946-1955. In:
Willi Baumeister 1945-1955, (exhibition
catalogue, Württembergischer Kunstverein
(Württemberg Art Association)), Stuttgart
1979, pp. 129-34.

115
Here, the typographer and printer Philipp
Albinus, the typesetter and photographer
Friedrich Wilhelm Biering, and the book
binder Ernst Rehbein should be mentioned
in particular.

116
Cited in: Baumeister: 'Neue Typographie',
p. 215.

117
Cited in: *Willi Baumeister. Typografie
und Reklamegestaltung*, ed. by Wolfgang
Kermer, (exhibition catalogue, Staatliche
Akademie der Bildenden Künste Stuttgart
(Stuttgart State Academy of Fine Arts)),
Stuttgart 1989, p. 93.

118
Baumeister: 'Neue Typographie', p. 216
et seq.

119
*Willi Baumeister. Typografie und Re-
klamegestaltung*, p. 34.

120
Baumeister: 'Neue Typographie', p. 217.

121
*Willi Baumeister. Typografie und Re-
klamegestaltung*, p. 124 et seq.

LICHTSPIELE
ALAST
AUTOMOBILE
ADLER
Jack Trevor
Arthur Kraussneck

HANO VER

'The people of Hanover are the inhabitants of a city, a large city. Their dogs never succumb to disease. Hanover's town hall belongs to the people of Hanover, which is a justifiable demand. The difference between Hanover and Anna Blume is that Anna can be read from left to right and from right to left, while Hanover can only be read properly from left to right. However, if Hanover is read backwards, three words are formed: "re von nah". The word "re" can be translated in different ways: "backwards" or "return". I recommend translating it as "backwards". Then, the word Hanover, when translated backwards, would be: "backwards from up close". This is correct if the translation of the word "Hanover" were to read: "Forward into the distance". This means: Hanover strives forward, into the immense. Anna Blume, however, is the same back to front as it is front to back:

A-N-N-A. (Please keep dogs on a leash.)'[1]

    With this piece of prose, composed in about 1920, Kurt Schwitters (1887–1948) captured the ambivalence prevalent at the time towards the mood of euphoria in his native city, which in the 1920s, with over 400,000 inhabitants, was not only the twelfth largest German city, but was also growing as a centre of 'Merz' art and thereby into one of the most important 'cultural capitals' of Germany. There, the painter, graphic designer, poet, typographer and advertising specialist had – with his Dadaist parody of a love poem 'An Anna Blume' (To Anna Blume), composed the previous year – conquered the public spaces of the provincial Lower Saxony town with a spectacular (figuratively and literally) promotional poster campaign that clearly portrayed the unity of art and life. The time was ripe for artistic experimentation, but Schwitters felt that 'in such a remarkable city as Hanover, where Steegemann, Haarmann, Gleichmann, Wilhelm Gross, Behrens, Dorner, v. Garvens and many others'[2] worked, there should 'also arise a homegrown art'.[3]

Advocates of this new beginning, which rejected traditional views in all fields of design, included the advertising executive and art critic Christof Spengemann, who between 1919 and 1920 co-published ten issues of the magazine *Der Zweemann*; the small publishers of the magazines that followed, *Die Pille* and *Das hohe Ufer*; and Paul Steegemann, editor of the radical book series *Die Silbergäule*, in which Schwitters' first volume of poetry was published. Schwitters co-founded the 'Aposs' publishing house with Käte (Kate) T. Steinitz, and set up the 'Merz' publishing house, which from 1923 published Schwitters' magazine of the same name.

Merz featured articles by internationally leading Dadaists, Constructivists, Suprematists, and De Stijl and Bauhaus representatives such as Hans Arp, Theo van Doesburg, Hannah Höch, Raoul Hausmann, El Lissitzky and László Moholy-Nagy – an overview of the latest artistic discussions and a contemporary 'Topography of Typography' that ran until 1932.[4]

One issue of the magazine was dedicated exclusively to typography in advertising. It featured products by Pelikanwerke Günther Wagner in an attempt to make other companies aware of its visual style.[5] By 1924, when his Merz-Werbezentrale design business was founded in Hanover, 'advertisements and design of print materials in general'[6] had become Schwitters' main source of income, and his clients included the Bahlsen biscuit factory, the wallpaper manufacturer Norta, the pump factory

Weise Söhne and Hanover's city administration. As the 'artistic advisory committee' for the city administration, the typographer developed, from 1929, a pioneering 'style of print' in which Futura was frequently used, owing to its 'benefits' in terms of 'design', 'richness' and 'exactitude'.[7] In this way, Paul Renner's type not only proved to be not only a synonym for the visuals of modern organizations, but also had a key impact on style and the formation of identity.

The members of the new Hanover, who were almost identical to Schwitters' circle of friends, included the art historian Alexander Dorner, who had established the Provinzial-Museum as a forum for abstract art. Together with the Kestnergesellschaft (Kestner Society) – one of the co-founders of which was the gallery owner Herbert von Garven-Garvensburg – it developed into one of the leading German institutions for the promotion and distribution of contemporary art. As a guest of the Kestnergesellschaft, El Lissitzky created the museum's *Kabinett der Abstrakten* (Abstract Cabinet) in 1927, and in the same year the Abstractionists of Hanover formed a local subgroup of the Internationale Vereinigung der Expressionisten, Kubisten und Konstruktivisten (International Association of Expressionists, Cubists and Constructivists) in Schwitters' apartment. The Hanover members Carl Buchheister, Hans Nitzschke and Friedrich Vordemberge-Gildewart were engaged in a social and political rejuvenation through art, and so the last also joined the 'ring neue werbegestalter' (Circle of Contemporary Advertising Designers) in 1927, which organized travelling exhibitions of its members' latest typographic works. This largely self-taught group of typographers, but which included Jan Tschichold and Georg Trump, shared Schwitters' view 'that typography and architecture [are] phenomena which run in parallel with [sic!] abstract art.'[8] In this sense, the bourgeois disdain for the 'Hanover habitus'[9] was caused by the intensely progressive artistic and typographic activity that had existed in the city since 1926: 'Unlike the critics, I think Hanover is the most important city for art in Germany.'[10]

AL

MR ANNA BLUME FROM REVON AND THE FUTURISTS

'My dearest! I'm working on a typeface. I learned many things from my visit to the Bauer Type Foundry, e.g. that one should have a pleasing replacement for the difficult letters', reported Kurt Schwitters, writing from Bad Ems on 14 August 1927 to his wife, Helma, who had remained in Hanover.[11] This note, in connection with his work on an 'optophonetic script', presumably refers to the genesis of Futura, which was cast and sold in the light and medium weights, beginning in November that year, by the Bauer Type Foundry in Frankfurt am Main.[12] In 1925 Fritz Helmuth Ehmcke had received 'sample lines of Paul Renner's new type through the goodwill of the foundry',and it was published by Günther Wagner together with an explanatory commentary for the Hanover-based paint factory.[13] The comparison of the radically sharp basic shapes, derived from Capitalis Monumentalis, with the lead type that was ready for market, demonstrated to Schwitters – who was also working for Wagner's advertising department – that the sans serif type Fritz Wichert had referred to as 'futuristic', in the sense that it was paving the way for the current times, had not simply undergone

modifications; unusual special characters and 'more pleasant' variants offered design options[FIG.5 P.67] that interested the rational 'builder' of geometrically based (system) types, primarily in relation to advertisement design.[14]

The early development of the Dadaist movement manifested itself in Schwitters' tendency towards constructive, geometric shapes and clear typographic structures. During the period of hyperinflation experienced in Germany in 1924, Schwitters began working professionally as a commercial graphic designer, founding the Merz Werbezentrale (Merz Advertising Centre) from his apartment at 5 Waldhausenstrasse. Given his lifelong theoretical bent, he summarized his typographic design approach in ten principles and continued to develop those principles over the years, with the values of aestheticism acquiring increasingly primary importance. The oft-quoted dictum 'Typography can also be art'[15] does not, therefore, refer to his view of himself as an artist-typographer, but rather was intended to highlight the fact that the use of 'simple' typefaces had, under artistic auspices, developed into one of the 'main advertising tools' of leading contemporary magazines.[16] At the end of the 1920s, magazines such as *Gebrauchsgraphik*, *Graphische Nachrichten*, *Die Form* and *neue stadt* began to make increasing use of Futura. Schwitters, for whom the years 1927/28 marked a kind of turning point in 'the development of typography',[17] also recommended Futura to the advocates of the 'New', 'Elementary Typography' as 'the appropriate type'.[18] In his own

FUTURA

in allen Größen

und allen Schnitten, für alle Zwecke.

mager	4 - 84 Punkt
halbfett	4 - 84 Punkt
dreiviertelfett	6 - 84 Punkt
fett	6 - 84 Punkt
black	20 - 84 Punkt
schräg mager	6 - 48 Punkt
schräg halbfett	6 - 48 Punkt
schmalfett	6 - 84 Punkt
PLAKAT halbfett	8 - 60 Cicero
PLAKAT **fett**	8 - 60 Cicero
PLAKAT schmalfett	8 - 60 Cicero
PLAKAT **black**	8 - 60 Cicero

Bauersche Gießerei · Frankfurt am Main

Gezeichnet von Paul Renner, München

12

FUTURA

ihre Vorzüge:

konstruktiv **und bestimmt im Ausdruck,**

klar, exakte Formen, gleichmäßiger Lauf, schmucklos,

elegant, rassig, klassisch rein, edel, ebenmäßig in den Verhältnissen, abstrakte Strenge,

neutral, große Ruhe des Satzbildes, lebendig im Versalsatz, vielseitig,

leicht lesbar, Betonung formaler Gegensätze der einzelnen Buchstaben, knapp, präzis,

gespannt, bewegt charaktervoll, technisch,

geistreich, trotz des sauberen Stils der Maschine; daher suggestiv.

NICHT DAS KLEINE a

unterscheidet die Futura wesentlich,

sondern ihre Gestalt, ihr Reichtum, ihre Durcharbeit.

13

deutliche Begriffsgruppen, Heftrand, Zeichen oben rechts, Anschrift absichtlich klein, trennende Linien.
Briefkopf für das Fürsorgeamt Karlsruhe, Entwurf Kurt Schwitters

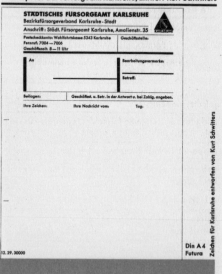

Zeichen für Karlsruhe entworfen von Kurt Schwitters

Din A 4
Futura

14

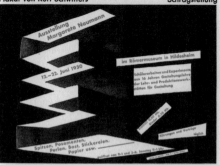

Funktion des ausfließenden Wassers

zentrische Bewegung ausstrahlend, aktiv

Schutzmarke für Weise Söhne

Entwurf Kurt Schwitters

Plakat von Kurt Schwitters   Schrägstellung

15

promotional brochures, set in Futura and containing sample prints for public and private customers, he described the sans serif using adjectives such as 'constructive', 'clear', 'sparse', 'elegant', 'classic', 'pure', 'noble', 'neutral', 'versatile', 'easily legible', 'concise', 'precise' and 'technical', and observed with regard to the strict forms of the special characters: 'It is not the lower-case a that essentially makes Futura distinctive, but rather its form, its richness, its exactitude.'[19] Schwitters brought out these qualities of the typeface in many innovative ways. He drew ironic similarities between Futura's innate future potential and the product of his client H. Bahlsen, when in about 1929 he designed a leaflet with type set obliquely, bearing the slogan 'Biscuits are progress'. Schwitters favoured type combinations and referred back to 'the Universal food' as well as Futura for his Balkenschrift, which he probably designed jointly with Robert Michel. FIG.4 P.150 In *Erstes Veilchenheft*, a collection of Merz poetry published in 1931, which also contains an artistic-typographic credo,[20] the severe cover image, constructed out of purely geometric elements, is reflected in the conspicuously typographically clean inner pages; the two-columned text was consistently set in varying sizes of Futura. FIG.5 P.150 In terms of form, it is reminiscent of the state's official catalogue that was issued for the opening of the Dammerstock housing estate in Karlsruhe. FIG.6 P.150 Schwitters' one-man agency was responsible for the design of all the print materials for this 'most modern settlement of row houses', built in 1929 under the artistic direction of Walter

3

1–2

Kurt Schwitters: Werbe-Gestaltung: *Die neue Gestaltung in der Typographie*, brochure, 1930. 'Praise for Futura' and sample applications in modern advertising.

3

Kurt Schwitters: Werbe-Gestaltung: *Die neue Gestaltung in der Typographie*, 1930.

Gropius and Otto Haesler. Dammerstock embodied the ideal of modernism in white and promoted the minimalist 'utility apartment', as described in the exhibition organized to mark the preparations for the first phase of construction. Schwitters developed a comprehensive design concept, easily recognizable on account of its '**d**' emblem. Also decisive was the consistent use of 'geometric' Futura, which was seen as a suitable typeface in the context of the New Architecture.[21] In tune with the contemporary debate regarding economization, it consisted entirely of simple forms and strongly influenced the brochure – published in 1932, in tried-and-tested landscape format – of Heimtyp A. G. Celle,[22] and in an innovative commission from the Berlin architectural publishing house W. & S. Loewenthal of 1931. For the commission Schwitters assembled stickers, letters, numbers and signs in various sets, which were intended for use as text on planning documents for public housing.FIG.9 P.152 The typographers used 'Futura weights with a palette from the most delicate grey to the most power-ful black'.[23] By using the *KLEB* cut-out book, architects attempting unification, sys-tematization and internationalization were expected to apply the 'neutral elements' quickly, shaping them 'into a building'.[24]

In connection with his work for the Dammerstock housing estate, Schwitters also completed work for the administration of the capital city of the state of Baden, which was notable for the design of a form for the city's social security office.FIG.2 P.148 At almost the same time, he was appointed to the artistic advisory committee of the

4

Kurt Schwitters: 'Keks ist Fortschritt'
(Biscuits are progress), for H. Bahlsens
Keksfabrik AG, Hanover, c. 1929.

5

Kurt Schwitters: *Merz 21. Erstes
Veilchenheft* (cover), 1931.

6

Kurt Schwitters: catalogue of the Karlsruhe
exhibition 'Dammerstock Housing Estate:
Die Gebrauchswohnung', 1929 (cover in
red cardboard). Balkenschrift and Futura
(inside).

7

Kurt Schwitters: Dammerstock housing
estate flyer, 1929. The repetition of the
word 'dammerstock' refers to the method
of building series of blocks in the construction of mass housing.

8

Kurt Schwitters: Dammerstock housing
estate leaflet, 1929.

druck: c. f. müller, karlsruhe i. b.

sie werden es sicher schon bemerkt haben, wenn sie im d-zug
sitzen und der kommt so richtig in fahrt, so ruft der immerzu:
**dammerstock, dammerstock, dammerstock, dammer-
stock.** er hat es mit seinem einfachen d-zug-verstand begriffen,
daß heute **der dammerstock die** siedlung ist, die sie un-
bedingt gesehen haben müssen. **dammerstock, dammerstock, dammerstock, dammerstock,** so rollt ein d-zug
nach dem andern in karlsruhe an. **dammerstock, dammerstock, dammerstock, dammerstock,** so fragen alle frem-
den, die in karlsruhe aussteigen; aber sie brauchen nicht zu
fragen, denn der weg zum **dammerstock** ist gut gekenn-
zeichnet. **dammerstock, dammerstock, dammerstock,
dammerstock,** so sagt noch nach 50 jahren der greis, wenn
er so recht in fahrt kommt, denn die **dammerstock-sied-
lung** ist ihm **das architektonische erlebnis** seiner jugend
gewesen.

DAMMERSTOCK
jüngste siedlung im zeilenbau

besuchen auch **sie** die ausstellung karlsruhe, **dammerstock-
siedlung, die gebrauchswohnung,** welche noch geöffnet
ist bis zum 27. oktober dieses jahres.   3. oktober 1929.

entwurf: k. schwitters, hannover.

7

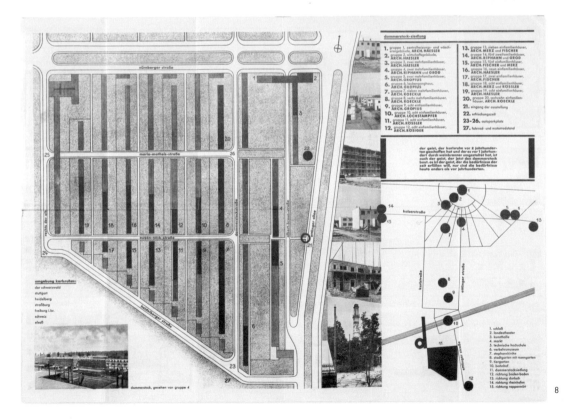

8

9

Kurt Schwitters: *KLEB* publication. *Kleb-Worte-Ziffern-Zeichen- Normierte Teilzeichnungen für Bauzeichnungen*, cat. 1, Berlin, year not specified (1931).

10

Kurt Schwitters: Bürgerschule, Hanover, timetable, 1930.

11

Kurt Schwitters: 'Zoological Garden of the Capital City Hanover', letterhead, 1932 (there were versions in Futura and Erbar-Grotesk).

12

P. 155 – Kurt Schwitters: *Städtische Bühnen Hannover, Spielzeit 1930/31*, advertising leaflet, 1930.

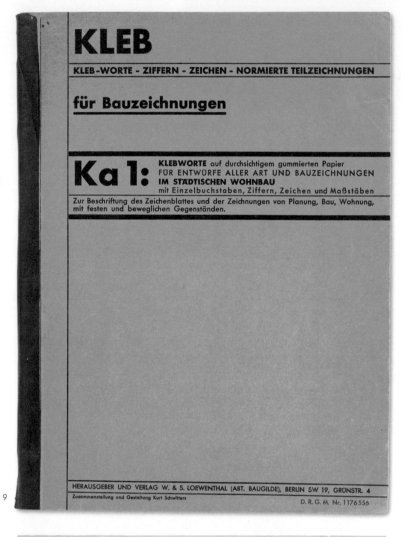

9

10

city of Hanover. In his home town, it was necessary to ensure that all official stationery was consistent with DIN standards.[25] This major commission, which was by no means an 'aesthetic affair',[26] involved 'informational records, announcements on paper or in poster form, letterheads and envelopes, postcards, newspaper advertisements (especially those for the municipal utilities, theatres, etc.), tickets, memorabilia, books, and similar print materials', for which a typeface was required.[27] Schwitters recalled in 1930 that 'among the Fraktur, Antiqua and Grotesk types that I presented in various weights to the urban planning authority', he selected 'the sans serif as the simplest and clearest type', and from the various sans serif types, he chose Renner's '"Futura" from the Bauer Type Foundry in Frankfurt a. M., and about a dozen printing houses that did not have this typeface purchased it.'[28] However, 'the use of "Futura" ... did not become standard' – the 'urban planning authority also approved other types for theatres, banks and facilities so that printers that did not own the Futura sans serif would also get work.'[29]

The majority of shops, however, acquired it immediately. As a result, between 1929 and 1934, hundreds of different 'informational' administrative publications were produced that were instantly presented at contemporary exhibitions as exemplars of design. They constitute a singular heritage – both for Schwitters, who was eventually forced to emigrate to Norway in 1937, and for Futura, which remained undiminished during the dark times that followed.[30]

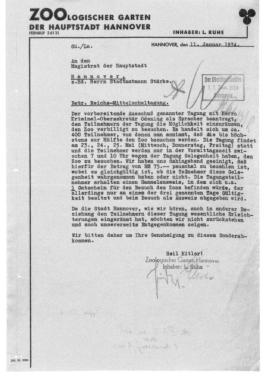

11

'Kurt Schwitters does not have the dryness of a preacher; with him, the mischievous spirit of the Dadaists always breaks through.'

PAUL RENNER
Der Künstler in der mechanisierten Welt
[The Artist in the Mechanized World],
1977.

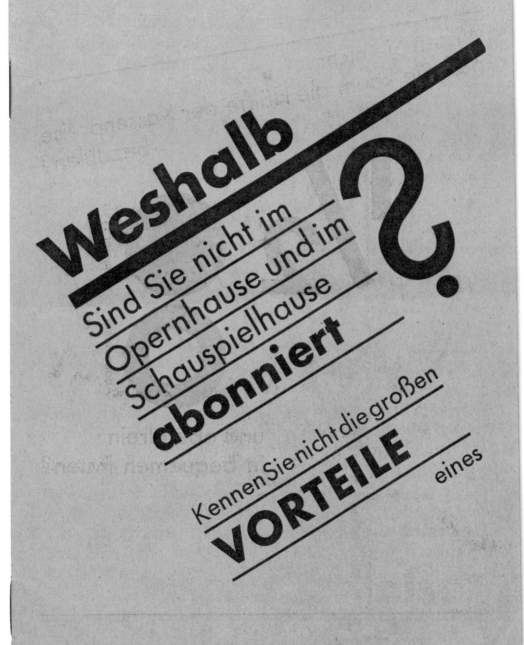

STÄDTISCHE BÜHNEN HANNOVER
SPIELZEIT 1930/31

Weshalb?

Sind Sie nicht im
Opernhause und im
Schauspielhause
abonniert

Kennen Sie nicht die großen
VORTEILE eines

12

STÄDTISCHE BÜHNEN
HANNOVER
Fernruf 20573 u. 21981

1. bis 7. Juni 1930

ABONNENTEN WERBEWOCHE

eine Auswahl der besten Werke des Spielplans

Zu Abonnementspreisen

Opernhaus			Schauspielhaus
Aida	Sonntag,	1. Juni	Kaiser von Amerika
Sly	Montag,	2. Juni	Tartüff
Meistersinger	Dienstag,	3. Juni	Andere Seite
Vier Grobiane	Mittwoch,	4. Juni	Affäre Dreyfus
Fidelio	Donnerstag, 5. Juni		Richard III
Zigeunerbaron	Freitag,	6. Juni	Menschen im Hotel
Schwanda	Sonnabend, 7. Juni		Napoleon greift ein
1,25 bis 6 Mk.	Preise		0,80 bis 4 Mk.

KARTENVERKAUF Vorverkauf für beide Theater drei Tage im voraus bei J. W. Söltzer, Seilwinderstraße 11 (Fernsprecher 21883), Sternheim & Emanuel, Gr. Packhofstraße 44 (Sammel-Nr. 50471), Henry Glißmann, Hildesheimer Straße 14 (Fernsprecher 82565), Verkehrs-Verein Hannover, Bahnhofstraße 8 (Fernsprecher 27010). NEBENSTELLEN: Paul Knauth, An der Lutherkirche 1, Lindener Reisebüro, Falkenstraße 6, Filiale Paul Most, Celler Straße 100 (Fernspr. 65721), Lorenz Salige, Nordmannstraße 1, Wilhelm Busch, Ricklinger Stadtweg. — An den Theaterkassen kein Vorverkauf. — Am Tage der Aufführungen: von 10-13½ Uhr, Sonntags 11-13½ Uhr, für beide Theater an den Kassen des Opernhauses; abends an den Theaterkassen (im Opernhaus 1 Stunde vor Beginn, im Schauspielhaus von 17½ Uhr an). **Bestellungen werden jederzeit entgegengenommen.**

Typographie: Kurt Schwitters, Hannover. Druck: C. L. Schröder, Hannover.

PROPAGANDA FOR ARTISTICALLY DESIGNED ADVERTISING[31]

RING NEUE WERBEGESTALTER

'We are now a proper association with nine members. They are Vordemberge and myself, Trump, Burchartz, Michel, Baumeister, Tschichold, Dexel, Domela. We already have two magazines and five exhibitions. ... Would you like to join as a foreign member?' So reads a letter that Kurt Schwitters, as initiator of the ring neue werbegestalter (Circle of Contemporary Advertising Designers) sent to Piet Zwart in December 1927.[32] In 1928 the Dutch typographer accepted the invitation and became the first foreign member of the new association with international aspirations, which had been set up at Schmelzmühle, near Eppstein in Taunus – part of the estate of the married artists Ella Bergmann-Michel and Robert Michel.FIG.15 P.159 From the very beginning, the association had set itself the goal of expanding both geographically and in terms of numbers, and by means of targeted invitations like the one above, it developed into a European network. (Symptomatic of the period, all members were men.) These progressive architects and artists, who dedicated themselves to applied art and worked as commercial graphic designers in order to have an influence on the design of the everyday culture of their time, added to their numbers by recruiting skilled typographers Jan Tschichold and Georg Trump. Trump taught at the Kunstgewerbeschule Bielefeld, and then in 1929 switched to a position as a teacher at the Münchner Meisterschule für Deutschlands Buchdrucker (Munich Trade School for Germany's Book Printers), where Tschichold worked. In the early days of the Ring, Tschichold worked on his essential guide for practitioners, which was published in 1928 with the title *Die Neue Typographie – ein Handbuch für zeitgemäss Schaffende* (The New Typography – a Handbook for Contemporary Creators) in Berlin by Verlag des Bildungsverbandes der Deutschen Buchdrucker.

Each member was supposed to follow his own visual strategy and demonstrate, through pioneering works, the equal merits of the genres, but especially the artistic merits of typography. Thus, this association of like-minded artists deliberately operated without a defined programme.[33] Information was circulated among its members via newsletters written by Schwitters, covering topics such as meetings, publications, exhibitions and lectures, for which an archive of slides containing the materials of the members was organized.FIG.14 P.159

13
Kurt Schwitters: 'Städtische Bühnen Hannover', poster, 1930.

The association's members, some of whom were friends, deliberately followed the concept and organizing model laid out by architects of the New Architecture, who in 1926 had formed an association called Der Ring. The image of a complete, geometrical, self-contained form with no beginning and no end was part of their agenda, which, with a typographical connotation, could also symbolize the ideal of the New Advertising Designers. Unsurprisingly, there were personal overlaps: Ernst May, who as head of Frankfurt's urban planning authority was a member of the Berlin Ring, was put forward by Michel as an honorary member of the ring neue werbegestalter, but he refused, 'saying that he preferred to sympathize with us and our views from a distance'.[34] His sympathy for the concerns of Schwitter's Ring had already been expressed in the magazine *Das Neue Frankfurt*, FIG.7 PP.68–69. which, under the leadership of Michel and Hans Leistikow, was intended to function as the publication medium of the Ring and to publish 'reports, circulars and news'.[35] Although the architect Adolf Meyer, who was also involved in the architects' association, was accepted as a full member, there was an absence of consensus among the representatives of the Bauhaus. In response to the invitation 'of the head of the advertising department of the Bauhaus to become a member, so long as Hannes Meier [sic] is director', and 'to support each other as separate organizations', according to Schwitters, 'the committee only laughed'.[36] Since the Ring feared that

its 'aims would be seen as influenced by the Bauhaus'[37] and lumped together with 'Bauhaus Typography', a decision was made not to cooperate with the school and 'not to enter into any obligations vis-a-vis the Bauhaus'.[38] The Ring instead recruited private members among skilled typographers.

'Who knows Erbar?' came the question from Schwitters to his colleagues in 1928.[39] This was Jakob Erbar, whom Schwitters nominated for election to the group. Erbar had been working at the Cologne Werkschulen as a teacher of type since 1926 and was the author of Erbar-Grotesk, released in 1926 by the Frankfurt-based type foundry Ludwig & Mayer. This was one of the earliest sans serif types of its time and was referred to constantly as a model for Renner-Grotesk, particularly as a result of the different letter variants. Kabel, which was released in 1927, several months after Futura light; Elegant-Grotesk, which was released in 1928 and similar to Futura in style; and Gill Sans from the same year (1928/29) were among the favourite types of the organization's designers.

In an attempt to expand the reach of the Ring, and since a high point in terms of exhibition activities had already been reached, with presentations in Stuttgart, Basel, Munich, Copenhagen, Aarau, Stockholm, Essen and Amsterdam, the collective attempted to collaborate with the Bauer Type Foundry in 1931.[40] Schwitters outlined the plan, in which Futura played a major role as a key marketing tool:

'In response to Dexel's question as to what should be done to accelerate the new surge in the Ring's activities, I followed a suggestion by Paul Schuitema, which I revised according to my own thoughts, and offered a booklet or book to the Bauer Type Foundry, which would be designed by members of the Ring free of charge. Do not complain because firstly, 100 marks will flow into the Ring's fund, which will save you your annual contribution, and secondly, the Bauer Type Foundry must pay if it wants to buy any design for itself; but thirdly, it is to be a book with which the Ring will present itself to a broad public. It would therefore be good if every member could commit to one or more pages. The book will somehow on the envelops – please forgive me, that was the typewriter's fault! I of course

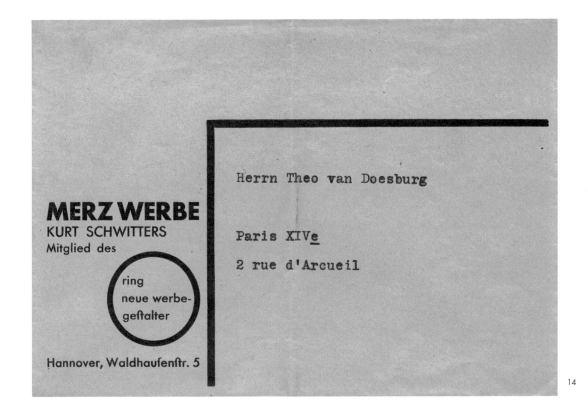

14

14
Kurt Schwitters: envelope with the emblem of the Ring, 1928 or later.

15
Friedrich Vordemberge-Gildewart: advertising sticker, after 1927.

PROPAGANDA FOR ARTISTICALLY DESIGNED ADVERTISING

16

16

Max Burchartz: Folkwang Schools Essen, prospectus, promoted in *Gefesselter Blick* (The Captive Gaze), 1930.

17

Max Burchartz: second German Dance Conference, invitation card with envelope, published in *Gefesselter Blick*, 1930. Combination of lead type and a stereotypical photograph as an example of 'mechanized graphics'.

18

Kurt Schwitters (ascribed): *Sonderschau Neue Typographie*, prospectus for a Ring exhibition in Magdeburg, August 1929.

17

meant 'envelope', be clearly marked to indicate that it is the first publication of the Ring. Who is willing to design the text and content of the cover so that it can serve as a model for a series of ring-bound books? Then there will be an introduction describing the aims of the Ring and the nature of the work of the individual members, if they have contributed to the book. Each person should promptly send me a general Ring text and briefly describe his special art. Then pages will follow praising Futura. The text for these pages will be supplied by Bauer. Every page will be designed by a different member of the Ring. The printing and deliveries will also be done by Bauer, and each employee will receive 100 copies. ... Once the book is available, one could contact other companies, thereby creating a series of publications. It may even be possible to receive a fee ...'[41]

THE CAPTIVE GAZE

This attempt, with the help of Futura and the Bauer Type Foundry, to imitate the successful concept of the brothers Heinz and Bodo Rasch – who, in 1930, had published 25 monographs of important contemporary advertising designers through the Stuttgart-based academic publishing house Dr Zaugg & Co. – failed. Therefore, *Der Gefesselte Blick* (The Captive Gaze),[42] which brings together the material of the Ring exhibition that the Rasch brothers had organized at the Graphische Klub in Stuttgart,[43] with the official participation of the Swiss trade association, constitutes the legacy in print of the Ring.[44]

Even its contemporaries recognized the 'cultural and historical value' of the publication, and its very practical use.[45] Jan Tschichold wrote to the two editors, 'I find the book excellently accomplished in every respect. There is an almost comprehensive overview of the most important attempts at the creation of a new typographic design'.[46] Friedrich Vordemberge-Gildewart, in his acknowledgement letter, prophesied: 'Your book is a wonderful weapon in my field of work in Hanover.'[47]

The international reception of the anthology designed by the Stuttgart brothers, with its eye-catching transparent cover, was a result of the fact that 'among the outstanding examples of suggestive

19
Friedrich Vordemberge-Gildewart:
tube design for Peligom glue, 1929.

advertising ... almost exclusively everyday examples from real practice were exhibited'.[48] To the reviewers, 'they were more insightful than all the examples of idle graphic artists and schools because the client was also behind them.'[49] They demonstrated in their composition, functionality, colour, photography and type the understanding that commerce and industry possess of these trends, which, by the way, will not be stopped.'[50] The goal formulated with regard to Ring's exhibition projects FIG.18 P.161 was clearly expressed: 'To document through a carefully compiled selection that, all over Germany, artists are concerned with the problem of advertising design, and that today there is an artistically high level of advertising. ... It is therefore propaganda for artistically designed advertisements.'[51]

During the global economic crisis of the time, 'every single one of the most prominent typographers marches by in alphabetical order' in *Gefesselten Blick*, but shortly afterwards, the political opponents of the avant-garde 'closed their ranks' too.[52] The existence of the Ring came to an end in 1931, although Bodo Rasch organized another exhibition in 1932 with the participation of Ring members, and he added a type-design section to the *Stuttgarter Werbeschau*, comprising works by Josef Albers, Herbert Bayer, Jan Tschichold and others, where Futura was, of course, also present.

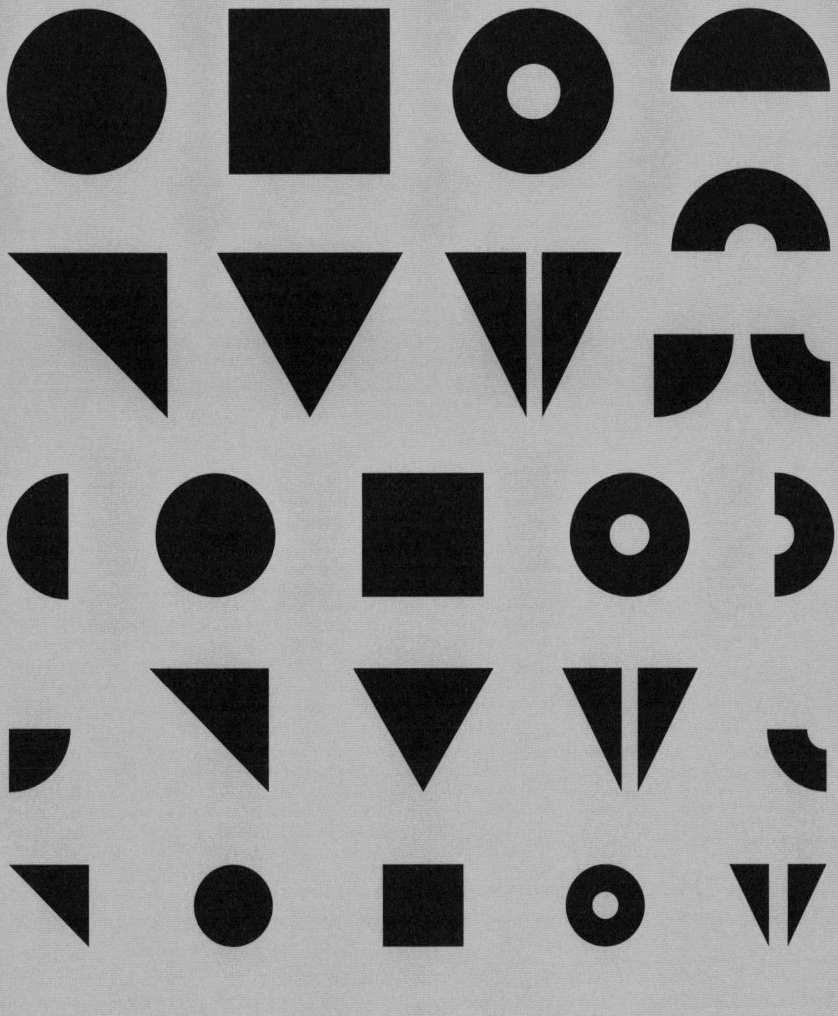

Futura Schmuck.

1

Cited in Kurt Schwitters: *Das literarische Werk*, ed. Friedhelm Lach, 5 volumes, Munich 2005 (first edition, Cologne 1973), vol. 2 (Prose 1918–1930), p. 28. The German name of the city is 'Hannover'.

2

Kurt Schwitters: 'Der Rhythmus im Kunstwerk'. In: *Hannoversches Tageblatt*, 17 October 1926, 4th supplement. Cited in: Schwitters: *Das literarische Werk*, vol. 5 (Manifestos and Critical Prose), p. 246. Friedrich Haarmann, a mass murderer who was born in 1879 and arrested in 1924, and Peter Behrens, the architect of the office building of Continental-Werke (1912), can be seen in this personal context as representing the polar nature of urban life before World War I in this personal context. This atmosphere is also vividly described in Theodor Lessing: 'Haarmann. Die Geschichte eines Werwolfs', Berlin 1925. In: *Aussenseiter der Gesellschaft. Die Verbrechen der Gegenwart*, ed. Rudolf Leonhard, vol. 6, pp. 9–17.

3

Schwitters: 'Der Rhythmus im Kunstwerk', p. 246. He justified this as follows: 'While it is true that over time Hanover went into decline when the art went astray, it has completely caught up. ... In contrast to the so-called art cities, our advantage is that we are not tied to an outdated tradition, and so instead, we have an exemplary artistic culture in Hanover. The Kestnergesellschaft showed us more or less everything that is being done today, and our museum is the only one in Germany that has a room for abstract paintings. It is therefore not surprising that there are no fewer than four abstract painters living in Hanover: Vordemberge, Ritschke, Buchheister and myself. And I think that a city like Hanover has given me the most MERZ-like inspiration' (ibid). Cf. Michael Erlhoff: 'Der Versuch, Revon auf die Füsse zu stellen'. In: *Kurt Schwitters Almanach 1984*, ed. Michael Erlhoff and Sabine Guckel, Hanover 1984, pp. 17–34.

4

Cf. El Lissitzky: 'Topographie der Typographie'. In: *Merz*, no. 4, (July) 1923.

5

Cf. *Merz*, no. 11, (November) 1924 ('Typoreklame Pelikan-Nummer').

6

Kurt Schwitters (1930). In: Schwitters: *Das literarische Werk*, vol. 5, p. 336.

7

Kurt Schwitters: *Werbe-Gestaltung: Die neue Gestaltung in der Typographie*, Hanover, year not specified (1930), 16 pages. In: Schwitters: *Das literarische Werk*, vol. 5, p. 227. Cf. fig. 1, p. 148.

8

Kurt Schwitters: 'Ich und meine Ziele' (1931). In: Schwitters: *Das literarische Werk*, vol. 5, p. 346.

9

Friedhelm Lach: Foreword. In: Schwitters: *Das literarische Werk*, vol. 1 (Lyric), p. 10.

10

Schwitters: 'Der Rhythmus im Kunstwerk', p. 246.

11

Letter from Kurt Schwitters to Helma Schwitters, Bad Ems, 14 August 1927, cited in Kurt Schwitters: *Wir spielen, bis uns der Tod abholt. Letters over five decades. Selected and with a commentary by Ernst Nündel*, Frankfurt am Main and Berlin 1986, p. 127.

12

In a letter to Walter Borgius on 2 July 1927, Schwitters wrote: 'It must be called optophonetic because the phonetic language must be indicated by an equivalent optical script. A new alphabet therefore needs to be created because the old, customary one is insufficient. There are no characters for ng, sch, ch; there are no specific symbols for the palatal r and the trilled r, for ch in 'noch' and ch in 'mich', for j in 'jeder' and j in 'jamais', for soft th and hard th (in English), for hard s and soft s.' Cited in: ibid, p. 120.

13

F(ritz) H(elmuth) Ehmcke: *Schrift. Ihre Gestaltung & Entwicklung in neuerer Zeit*, Hanover 1925, p. 66, fig. p. 67.

14

Thus, the prototype letterforms for a, g, m, n, ä, & and the oldstyle figures of Futura were offered as special characters, but in 1928 they were abandoned, along with the characteristic r. Regarding Systemschrift, cf. Kurt Schwitters: 'Anregungen zur Erlangung einer Systemschrift'. In: *i 10*, vol. I, no. 8/9 (August/September) 1927, pp. 312–16. Printed in Schwitters: *Das literarische Werk*, vol. 5, pp. 274–78.

15

Kurt Schwitters: 'Thesen über Typographie. These I'. In: *Merz*, no. 11, Hanover 1924, p. 91 ('Typoreklame Pelikan-Nummer'). Printed in Schwitters: *Das literarische Werk*, vol. 5, p. 192. Paul Renner's *Typographie als Kunst* was published in Munich in 1922.

16

Kurt Schwitters: 'Thesen über Typographie. These X'. In: *Merz*, no. 11, Hanover 1924, p. 91.

17

Kurt Schwitters: 'Gestaltende Typographie'. In *Der Sturm*, vol. XIX, no. 6, (September) 1928, pp. 265–69. Printed in Schwitters: *Das literarische Werk*, vol. 5, pp. 311–15.

18

Schwitters: *Werbe-Gestaltung*, p. 227. Here wrongly dated 1925. Cf. figs. 1–3, p. 148 et seq.

19

Ibid.

20

Cf. Schwitters: 'Ich und meine Ziele'.

21

There are numerous references by Schwitters to the New Architecture. His critiques and other writings demonstrate a preference for purposeful, 'constructive architecture', in line with his preferences for the development of typography. As early as 1925, his publishing house, Aposs, had released *Grosstadtbauten* (Big-City Buildings) by Ludwig Hilberseimer, the first and only publication in a planned series called *New Architecture*. Schwitters also designed *Die billige, gute Wohnung* (The Cheap, Good Apartment), a collection of floor plans published by the National Research Society for Economic Construction and Housing. In this regard, cf. Brigitte Franzen: 'Die Grossstadt – ein gewaltiges Merzkunstwerk? Versuch über Kurt Schwitters und die Architektur'. In *Neues Bauen der 20er Jahre: Gropius, Haesler, Schwitters and the Dammerstock Housing Estate in Karlsruhe*, 1929, (exhibition catalogue, Baden State Museum et al.), Karlsruhe 1997, pp. 123–38.

22

Cf. WZ 153, in *Typographie kann unter Umständen Kunst sein: Kurt Schwitters. Typographie und Werbegestaltung*, ed. Volker Rattemeyer and Dietrich Helms, with the collaboration of Konrad Matschke, (exhibition catalogue, Wiesbaden State Museum et al.), Wiesbaden 1990, p. 201.

23
Bauersche Giesserei (ed.): 'Drei Jahre Futura'. In *Renner Futura. Die Ergänzungs-Garnituren*, specimen, Frankfurt am Main, year not specified (1930), p. 2.

24
Ibid.

25
Serge Lemoine: 'Merz, Futura, DIN et cicéro'. In: *Kurt Schwitters*, (exhibition catalogue, Centre Georges Pompidou Paris, et al.), Paris 1994, pp. 186–93.

26
Preliminary remark on Kurt Schwitters: 'Über einheitliche Gestaltung von Drucksachen'. In: *Papierzeitung* (Berlin), vol. 55, no. 48, 1930, pp. 1436–40. Printed in Schwitters: *Das literarische Werk*, vol. 5, pp. 324–34.

27
Schwitters: 'Über einheitliche Gestaltung von Drucksachen', p. 324. Cf. Werner Heine: 'Der kurze Frühling der Moderne, oder – Futura ohne Zukunft. Kurt Schwitters' typographic works for the city administration of Hanover 1929–1934'. In *Typographie kann unter Umständen Kunst sein*, pp. 92–97.

28
Schwitters: 'Über einheitliche Gestaltung von Drucksachen', p. 325 et seq.

29
Ibid., p. 329. The imprints on the commercial prints indicate that the printing houses Gröhmann, Hahn, Osterwald, Schrader, Schöer and others worked with Futura.

30
In 1933 the city administration issued a 'Fraktur order' for new editions, but the printed forms set in Futura continued to be used for internal correspondence.

31
Cf. Kurt Schwitters: Mitteilung 17 and Abstimmung 20 (1928). Cited in *Typographie kann unter Umständen Kunst sein*, p. 114.

32
Kurt Schwitters, letter to Piet Zwart, 12 December 1927. Cited in: Kees Broos: 'Das kurze, aber heftige Leben des Rings "neue werbegestalter"'. In *Typographie kann unter Umständen Kunst sein*, p. 7.

33
Schwitters commented on the Ring in March 1930. Cf. Kurt Schwitters: *der ring neue werbegestalter*. In *Neue Werbe-grafik*, (exhibition catalogue, Gewerbemuseum Basel 1930), p. 4. Printed in Schwitters: *Das literarische Werk*, vol. 5, p. 337.

34
Kurt Schwitters: Mitteilung 20 (1928). Cited in *Typographie kann unter Umständen Kunst sein*, p. 118.

35
Kurt Schwitters: letter to Piet Zwart, 24 June 1928. Cited in: Broos: 'Das kurze, p. 8.

36
Kurt Schwitters: Mitteilung 19 (1928). Cited in *Typographie kann unter Umständen Kunst sein*, p. 115.

37
Ibid, p. 116.

38
Ibid.

39
Kurt Schwitters, letter to Piet Zwart, 24 October 1928. Mitteilung 22. Cited in *Typographie kann unter Umständen Kunst sein*, p. 120. 'Wer kennt Böhm, Frankfurt, Erbar, Köln, Lewi, Düsseldorf? Kommt von den Herren jemand für den Ring in Frage?'

40
Cf. the listing of the Ring's exhibitions in *Typographie kann unter Umständen Kunst sein*, p. 141.

41
Kurt Schwitters, letter to Piet Zwart, Mother's Day, 1931. In *Typographie kann unter Umständen Kunst sein*, p. 126.

42
Gefesselter Blick. 25 short monographs and contributions on modern advertising design, ed. and with an introduction by Heinz and Bodo Rasch, Stuttgart 1930. Cf. for context, Annette Ludwig: *Die Architekten Brüder Heinz und Bodo Rasch. Ein Beitrag zur Architekturgeschichte der zwanziger Jahre*, Tübingen/Berlin 2009.

43
The exhibition 'Gefesselter Blick. Internationale Ausstellung Moderner Typografie' (The Captive Gaze: International Exhibition of Modern Typography) was held 8–11 February 1930 at the Gustav-Siegle-Haus in Stuttgart. The Graphische Klub (Graphic Club) was founded in 1881 as the Gemeinschaft zur Förderung der Drucktechnik und Buchkultur (Society for the Promotion of Printing Techniques and Book Culture).

44
Cit. in the agreement between the Rasch brothers and the academic publishing house Verlag Dr Zaugg of 5 April 1929 (Bodo Rasch Estate). In their survey of potential contributors, which Schwitters supported through a circular distributed to the members of the Ring, the Rasch brothers had specified similar parameters. For example, as they write in a letter of 29 January 1930 to Hans Leistikow: 'in addition to your materials, we would like to kindly request you inform us briefly of your age and education. The book is structured in such a way that each of the artists represented therein has 2–4 pages for his examples and a proper title page bearing his name, and below that, his information in small type as well as his answer to the question: "what principles do you follow in the design of your types, or do you not follow any particular principles at all in this regard?" Given the diversity of the collected material, it will be important for the reader to comprehend quickly whether the artist is a painter, architect, printer or book maker, and which generation he belongs to' (Bodo Rasch Estate).

45
(Anonymous): Review of *Gefesselter Blick* (The Captive Gaze). In: *Zirkel* (Stuttgart), vol. 1, no. 1, 1 July 1933, p. 24.

46
Postcard from Jan Tschichold (Munich) to the Rasch brothers, 31 May 1930, unpublished (Bodo Rasch Estate).

47
Letter from Friedrich Vordemberge-Gildewart (Hanover) to the Rasch brothers, 4 December 1930, unpublished (Bodo Rasch Estate).

48
Review of *Gefesselter Blick* (The Captive Gaze). In: *Das Werk* (Zurich), vol. 19, no. 4, 1932, p. liii.

49
Ibid.

50
Ibid.

51

Kurt Schwitters: Mitteilung 17 and Abstimmung 20 (1928). Cited in *Typographie
kann unter Umständen Kunst sein*, p. 114.
He is referring here to a bid for an exhibition at the Galerie Nierendorf in Berlin.

52

Letter from the Rasch brothers to Willi
Baumeister (Frankfurt am Main), 17 January 1930 (Bodo Rasch estate).

BERLIN

At the end of the 1920s, Berlin had developed into a global city with a booming advertising industry. The most important media and publishing houses in Germany and the advertising agencies Mosse, Ullstein and Scherl were concentrated in Berlin's newspaper quarter, the area comprising Charlottenstrasse, Jerusalemerstrasse, Kochstrasse and Schützenstrasse. These companies sought to perfect the art of mass-media communication and employed external advertising agencies, consultants and experts, leading to the development of a strong, independent advertising industry, which in turn provided its customers with a professional presence across all forms of print media.[1] Berlin's increasingly important international role in advertising was also demonstrated at the International Advertising Conference of 1929, attended by advertising strategists and professionals from around the world to discuss the future of their industry.

Anyone who wanted a career as a commercial graphic designer went to Berlin: Lucian Bernhard and his colleague Fritz Rosen founded their own advertising design studio at the Ala-Haus (Allgemeine Anzeigen GmbH) on Potsdamer Strasse. After his departure from the Bauhaus, László Moholy-Nagy opened his own studio in Berlin, where he also employed former Bauhaus students.[2] Increasingly, branch offices of international – especially American – agencies also opened in Berlin, such as J. Walter Thompson at Unter den Linden, and Crawford's advertising agency in Potsdamer Strasse.[3] One important address for the design avant-garde was the German office of the New York agency Dorland, on Kurfürstendamm, where Herbert Bayer was artistic director, including for German Vogue.[4] In 1930 Bayer began to advance towards becoming an independent artistic director of dorland-studios, where

Kurt Kranz, Hannes Ferdinand Neuner, Xanti Schawinsky, Hin Bredendieck and even Moholy-Nagy worked, among others.[5] There, he skilfully combined typography, photography and graphics to create a new graphic language that demonstrated a fascination for alienation and illusion.[6]

PE

1

László Moholy-Nagy: advertisement for SS-Kleidung, 1931.

DEZEMBER 1928 DEZEMBE

GEBRAUCHSGRAPHIK
INTERNATIONAL ADVERTISING AR

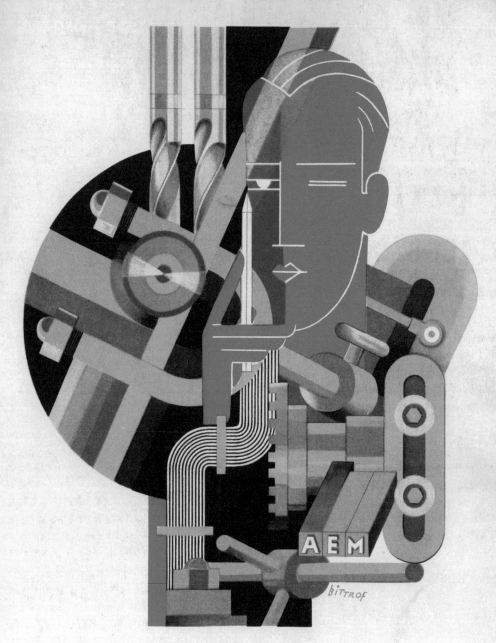

HERAUSGEBER PROF. H. K. FRENZEL, EDITC

PHÖNIX ILLUSTRATIONSDRUCK UND VERLAG GMBH., BERLIN SW 61, BELLE-ALLIANCE-PLATZ 7

ALLEINVERTRETER
FÜR DIE VEREINIGTEN STAATEN
VON NORDAMERIKA UND CANADA

THE BOOK SERVICE COMPANY
15 EAST 40TH STREET, NEW YORK CITY U.S.A.

SOLE REPRESENTATIVE
FOR THE UNITED STATES C
NORTH-AMERIKA AND CANAD

PETRA EISELE

FUTURA AND 'FORM UM 1930'

After the inflation of 1923, Germany experienced a major economic upturn. The increased production of industrial goods improved the finances of the population as a whole, which in turn led to higher sales of products.

For the design industry, this created a demand for new proposals for products that were suitable for industrial production. It also gave rise to a new industrial aesthetic based on standardization and typesetting that became widely employed. Beyond this, the higher rate of output, and the wider range of available goods, meant that products needed to be differentiated by means of advertising. Accordingly, many graphic designers were employed in the rapidly growing market for advertisements, posters and display windows.

In this context, the principles of the New Typography, which had been propagated aggressively by the Bauhaus and its avant-garde proponents, came together with the demands and requirements of reality. FIG.1 P.172

These principles were included in modified form in the curriculum of leading educational institutions open to modernism, such as the Frankfurter Kunstschule (School of Art), where Hans Leistikow and, after Paul Renner's departure, Willi Baumeister taught. Max

Burchartz taught in Essen, Johannes Molzahn in Magdeburg, and Georg Trump in Bielefeld, where, in 1929, he received an invitation to teach at Renner's Münchner Meisterschule für Deutschlands Buchdrucker (Munich Trade School for Germany's Book Printers), which was certainly the most important educational institution for the graphic arts in the 1920s. Its highly specialized graduates instigated a creative approach that was 'thought through, meticulous and flexibly applicable in daily work', and became widespread both in Germany and beyond.[7]

The principles of the New Typography were applied to the design of magazines, advertisements and large posters, and were thereby exposed to a big portion of the population in a professional, although extremely watered down, form. The combination of typography and photography that László Moholy-Nagy had called for in his programmatic text *Typo-Photo* of 1925 therefore grew to become an increasingly common element of day-to-day design and visual consumption. This new way of seeing, combined with the modern layout, modified by the technical and aesthetic requirements of traditionally trained experts, led to the development of a new 'modern' type of advertising design.

According to Gert Selle, it encountered a society whose technologically conscious elite increasingly cultivated a 'technoid daily culture' in which consumer desires focused on clean and smooth technological designs that had abandoned the social functionalism of the Bauhaus and the political goals of the

New Architecture.[8] Even the economic and political crises of the late 1920s and early 1930s did not prevent 'ever more beautiful yet functional products designed with highly professional skill' from being released on to the market.[9]

Selle describes the new, restrained 'Form um 1930' (literally 'design at the turn of the decade around 1930', a term introduced by the design historian Gert Selle) as cool, elegant and austere: 'These new technoid forms compete with the opulence of the world of consumer goods supersede them in trendy consumer circles that feel an attachment to a modern identity.'[10] The most popular objects among this elite class of technology enthusiasts were cars, aeroplanes and technical gadgets, while the most sought-after, high-end household goods were made of glass, porcelain or the latest plastics. With their detached elegance and immaculate surfaces, these anonymous mass-market products offered no means of expression for the individual at all.[11]

In graphic design and typography, 'Form um 1930' was expressed in the form of a cool elegance, and it was in this context that Futura progressed to the prototype stage in 1930. With its sleek lines, Futura light evoked a particular elegance in its reduction to the basic geometric shapes derived from classical Antiqua, it was both abstract and traditional. The way in which Futura was marketed at the time supports the notion that this typeface was very well suited as a typographic tool for 'Form um 1930'. While advocates of the New Typography were still strongly attached to the combination of black and red, a cool colour palette dominated around 1930. Accordingly, blue and silver were used for the campaign 'Drei Jahre Futura' (Three Years of Futura) in 1930. The second portfolio, *Futura – die sich die Welt eroberte* (Futura and How It Conquered the World), the new Futura specimen brochure and a brochure of pictures all combine a captivating silvery sheen with FUTURA in blue lettering. FIG.4,5 P.178 ET SEQ. In addition, the sample applications within are characterized by slim forms and elegant contours, as well as a discreet, muted colour scheme (often combinations of blue/brown/black/gold), giving the products an understated, distinguished air. The sample prints for Futura from about 1930 also display urban elegance in their choice of theme, featuring advertisements for machines and technical devices, as well as classic, elegant clothing that showcases a sophisticated big-city lifestyle spanning sportiness and refinement. FIG.6 P.181

2

P.174 — Technology provides the model for the clean, smooth techno-design look of 'Form um 1930': cover of the magazine *Gebrauchsgraphik*, December 1928. Illustration by Max Bittrof.

3

The car as the ultimate product of a new technology-loving class: 'Race and Culture' are embedded in the cool, muted elegance of a de-individualized elite. Advertisement for the Opel company, 1928, from the collection Dr Christos N. Vittoratos, Frankfurt a.M.

3

SEVILLA **FUTURA**

FUTURA

FUTURA

FUTURA
FUTURA
FUTURA
FU
FU
FU

URA

BAUERSCHE GIESSEREI · FRANKFURT AM MAIN · BARCELONA · NEW YORK

1932

BAU
FRANK

FUTURA

FU

BL

FUTURA

DIE

SICH DIE WELT

EROBERTE

MAPPE

4

4

PP. 178–79. – Futura type specimens and
portfolios from 1927 to 1937.

5

Silver ring-bound Futura type specimen brochure, 1933, with three double
spreads presenting Futura Bold, Futura
Inline and Futura Display.

6

Advertisement for Lucile Paray, 1930.

IN PARIS IT'S
LUCILE PARAY

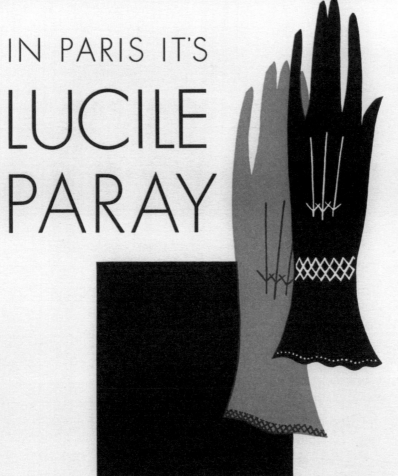

IN NEW YORK
WEAR RIGHT
Foremost in Gloves

WIMELBACHER & RICE · 1150 BROADWAY · NEW YORK CITY

FUTURA AS A
BEST-SELLING TYPEFACE

Futura was marketed both as a tool
for the New Typography, and as a tool
for contemporary, modern advertising,
with resounding success. Around 1930,
increasing numbers of magazines were
published in Futura. The magazine
Graphische Nachrichten began to be set
in Futura in 1930, [FIGS.7-11] while in August
1931 *Die Form* was published in Futura,
with the following explanation: 'This issue
is set in the Futura type, which is now
also available for use with typesetting
machines. ... It is a well-known fact that
it was designed by our colleague Paul
Renner. ... This type is now the most
well-known and beloved of the sans
serifs.'[12] From April 1932 the monthly
magazine *die neue stadt: internationale
monatsschrift für architektonische
planung und städtische kultur* (the new
city: international monthly magazine for
architectural planning and urban culture)
also was set in Futura.[13] Baumeister, who
was responsible for the design of the
magazine following the departure of
May and Leistikow in October 1930,
changed the entire layout by setting the
magazine title in right-justified, lower-
case Futura Bold.

COMBINED TYPES

Around 1930, the design avant-garde –
beginning to turn away from a New
Typography that they felt was increasingly
becoming a mere set of rules – called for
a more moderate use of sans serif type.
As early as 1928, Herbert Bayer had
condemned a superficial 'Bauhaus style',

7

8

7-9
Covers of the trade magazine *Graphische
Nachrichten*. April, December and
September 1930.

VERLAG GUTENBERG-BUND · BERLIN S 42 · LUISENUFER 1

GRAPHISCHE NACHRICHTEN

ACHZEITSCHRIFT GRAPHISCHER BERUFE

-6. OKT. 1930

10–11

Examples of the application of Futura in *Graphische Nachrichten*.

12

Advertisement for 'Die Futura: Eine Schrift erobert die Welt' (A Typeface Conquers the World), in *Gebrauchsgraphik*, 1930.

while Jan Tschichold had branded purely formal, conspicuous, user-orientated design elements, such as the circle, square and bar, 'sham constructivism' and 'formalism'.[14] In 1933 Moholy-Nagy wrote: 'Of course, the strict grotesque is insufficient for the varied range of work in today's advertising industry. The fear that all campaigns will look the same obliges typographers to consider other kinds of type.'[15] In fact, a new graphic and typographic style developed in modern advertising around 1930 that was inspired by the New Typography but was also emancipated from it. It demonstrated a confident approach to all graphic and typographic design methods that also fully exploited the new possibilities in manufacturing, such as two-colour printing.

Type combinations – a new typographic design technique – began to be used more frequently to highlight text and to emphasize headings and titles. Tschichold pointed out in 1935 that type combinations in 'advertising of all kinds' were becoming 'increasingly important' for creating 'an individual appearance'.[16] For example, Joost Schmidt combined a sans serif type and a delicate English handwriting in his folding map for the city of Dessau, while Futura was combined ever more frequently with Antiqua types over the course of the 1930s.

Futura can therefore be rightfully described as the typeface of its time. Its triumph in the 1930s was partly thanks to a flourishing international advertising industry whose technology-loving target audience favoured the 'Form um 1930'. The lighter weights of Futura in particular, with their echoes of the avant-garde and classicism, fulfilled the new demand for a sophisticated and refined aesthetic.

13

13
Herbert Bayer: promotional advertisement for the agency Dorland, featured in *Gebrauchsgraphik*, 1929.

14

15

14

László Moholy-Nagy (design): invitation to the 'exhibition of the architect b.d.a. walter gropius', 1930.

15

László Moholy-Nagy (design): *Ausstellung Walter Gropius: Zeichnungen, Fotos, Modelle* (exhibition catalogue, featuring drawings, photographs, models), 1930.

16

Futura Black in an early application for a guidebook by Heinz Johannes on New Architecture in Berlin, 1931.

17

Futura Black, used by the Berlin-based *Deutscher Kamera-Almanach*, 1932.

18

László Moholy-Nagy (cover design): *Foto-Qualität: Zeitschrift für Ware und Werbung*, 1931.

(UB) The magazine was actually called *Qualität*. Its editor, Carl Ernst Hinkefuss, often used it to publicize and support the Bauhaus, and his advertising company benefited from its reputation. The name of this issue – *Foto-QUALITÄT* (Photo Quality) – signifies the quality of both Moholy-Nagy's photogram and the publication itself. The title appears to have been stencilled, but in fact, Futura Black supplied the forms for the handmade supplementary type; immediately after Futura Black's release, people were enthusiastically tracing its forms.

16

17

SCHRIFTLEITUNG UND
KUNSTLERISCHELEITUNG:
CARL ERNST HINKEFUSZ
BERLIN

HERAUSGEGEBEN VON C. DÜNNHAUPT · GMBH · DESSAU

foto-QUALITÄT

ZEITSCHRIFT FÜR WARE UND WERBUNG

IX.
1·2

19

19

László Moholy-Nagy (cover design):
Erwin Piscator: *Das politische Theater.*
Berlin: Adalbert Schultz, 1929.

(UB) An immense crowd of people swells
from the back of the cover to the front,
waiting to enter the spherical visionary
structure. This consists of elements of
revolutionary stage technique, which was
known to be compatible with the most
modern media. The latest graphic elements are therefore also used for the title
of this scene. The white cut-out geometric
letterforms look like light projected onto
a red canvas. The darkened line of characters was created by rasterizing these
handcrafted, simplified letters, reminiscent
of Futura Black, and printing them with
the red plate. With the muted white as
an overtone, image and type become
inextricably linked.

According to the advertisement (in
Die neue Bücherschau, vol. 7, no. 8,
August 1929), the book was intended
to be published with the 'first 11,000
copies' issued at the end of August 1929,
in time for the reopening of the theatre in
Nollendorfplatz.

20

Type specimen for Futura Black, c. 1929.

21

Futura Black, English specimen brochure,
The Bauer Type Foundry Inc., New York
City, 1929.

20

21

22

22

(UB) László Moholy-Nagy (cover design): *Walter Gropius: bauhausbauten dessau* (*Bauhausbuch* no. 12). Munich: A. Langen, 1930.

In this work, Moholy-Nagy suggests using typography, paper and print to create an original plan drawing, which is featured as a protective sleeve around the architect's book. Naturally, the title is not set in Futura Black. It is drawn, which can be seen, for example, in the different openings in the **b**. It is therefore a double game of mimicry: firstly, a typeface mimics the character of the manual stencil, and then a typeface is imitated manually, and all for the sake of flat geometry, which at that time still held an important association. Artistic production was supposed to be economical, functioning as part of the production process, the end point of which was the labelling of a prepared and packaged box – rationally legible and applied with a stencil.

23

László Moholy-Nagy (cover design): László Moholy-Nagy, *The New Vision: Fundamentals of Design, Painting, Sculpture, Architecture*, New York: W. W. Norton & Company Inc., 1938.

23

Futura Black.

1

Print was the most important advertising medium at the time. Radio and film accounted for an insignificant share of advertising, with film constituting only about 1 per cent of all advertisements.

2

However, it is not clear what jobs they were working on. Cf. Ute Brüning: 'Praxis nach dem Bauhaus'. In: *Das A & O des Bauhauses. Bauhauswerbung: Schriftbilder, Drucksachen, Ausstellungsdesign*. Catalogue edited for the Bauhaus Archive by Ute Brüning, Leipzig, 1995, p. 269.

3

Cf. advertisements of J. Walter Thompson: Umfassender Werbedienst in 4 Erdteilen in the magazine *Gebrauchsgraphik*, July 1927.

4

Herbert Bayer: *Die Berliner Jahre – Werbegrafik 1928–1938*, ed. for the Bauhaus Archive by Patrick Rössler, Berlin 2013, pp. 32–33.

5

Alexander Schug: 'Herbert Bayer – ein Konzeptkünstler in der Werbung der Zwischenkriegszeit'. In: *Ahoi Herbert! Bayer und die Moderne*, published by Lentos Kunstmuseum Linz, Weitra 2009, p. 177.

6

Bayer's role as a commercial graphic designer for the Nazi party is problematic. For example, he designed the exhibition 'Wunder des Lebens zur deutschen Rassenhygiene' (The Miracle of Life for German Racial Hygiene) in 1935, and was the exhibition manager of the 'Deutschland Ausstellung' (Germany Exhibition) for the National Socialists in 1936, both in Berlin. Cf. *Inszenierung der Macht. Ästhetische Faszination im Faschismus*, ed. Klaus Behnken and Frank Wagner, cat. of the NGBK, Berlin 1987, p. 286 et seq.

7

Robin Kinross: 'Das Bauhaus im Kontext der Neuen Typographie'. In: *Das A & O des Bauhauses*, p. 12.

8

Heiner Boehncke: 'Design im Nationalsozialismus'. In: *Hitlers Künstler. Die Kultur im Dienst des Nationalsozialismus*, ed. Hans Sarkowicz, Frankfurt am Main/Leipzig 2004, p. 282; Gert Selle: *Geschichte des Design in Deutschland*. Updated and expanded, new ed., Frankfurt am Main 2007, pp. 182–84.

9

Selle: *Geschichte des Design in Deutschland*, p. 184. Selle, in turn, refers in his text to the following: Klaus-Jürgen Sembach: *Stil um 1930/Style 1930*, Tübingen 1971.

10

Selle: *Geschichte des Design in Deutschland*, p. 182.

11

Ibid, pp. 183–85.

12

Die Form: Zeitschrift für gestaltende Arbeit (Berlin), vol. 6, 1931, no. 8, p. 320.

13

die neue stadt was the successor of the magazine *Das Neue Frankfurt*.

14

Herbert Bayer: 'typografie und werbsachengestaltung'. In: *bauhaus. zeitschrift für gestaltung* (Dessau), vol. 2, 1928, p. 10; Jan Tschichold: *Die neue Typografie. Ein Handbuch für zeitgemäss Schaffende*, Berlin 1928, p. 85.

15

László Moholy-Nagy: (Reply to) 'Im Kampf um neue Gestaltungsfragen'. In: *Typografische Mitteilungen*. Magazine of the Educational Association of German Book Printers (Berlin), vol. 30, January 1933, p. 3.

16

Jan Tschichold: 'Schriftmischungen'. In: *Typographische Monatsblätter* (Bern), vol. 3, 1935, no. 2, p. 32.

MUNICH

THE AVANT-GARDE AND NATIONAL SOCIALISM

In the 1920s, Munich was not a modern city that could be compared with Berlin or Frankfurt. Indeed, it was the very antithesis of the fast-paced world city of Berlin.

'Munich is Hitler's city, the German leader of the fascists, the city of the swastika, this symbol of popular defiance and an ethnic aristocratism, whose conduct is nothing less than aristocratic', wrote Thomas Mann in 1923, describing the city on the River Isar.[1] In fact, Hitler's political career began in Munich. It was there that he formed the NSDAP and that the party acquired its official organ, the *Völkischer Beobachter* (People's Observer). In the early 1920s the formerly liberal Munich middle class had become increasingly re-ceptive to anti-democratic, Social Darwinist, reactionary sentiments, so in November 1923 Hitler felt strong enough to carry out a coup attempt, which was later idealized as the 'March to the Feldherrnhalle'.[2]

However, political battles were still playing out in Munich. Paul Renner openly expressed sympathy with the intellectual liberals and anti-fascists, on occasions such as his speech at the large demonstration 'Battle for Munich as a Cultural Centre' in the Munich Tonhalle in November 1926, initiated by Heinrich and Thomas Mann. In 1930 an article by Renner appeared in the magazine *Gebrauchsgraphik*, in which the director of the Meisterschule für Deutschlands Buchdrucker (Trade School of Germany's Printers) and creator of Futura described the New Typography as firmly established but not entirely opposed to a 'political idiocy, growing more violent and malicious every day', which 'may eventually sweep the whole of Western culture to the ground with its muddy sleeve'.[3] Renner expressed himself even more clearly in his publication *Kulturbolschewismus?* (Cultural

Bolshevism?), in which he criticized the pseudo-biological racial doctrine of the National Socialists and mentioned the names of numerous artists and designers who had been accused of being Jewish (although it was public knowledge that this was not the case), in order to discredit them and their works.[4] Renner was particularly opposed to Paul Schultze-Naumburg, who fought uncompromisingly against artistic modernism. Renner ascribed not only racist propaganda to him, but also brutal, bloody attacks in public lectures against those who challenged his arguments.[5]

On 31 January 1933 the Nazi section of the municipal council expressed its delight that 'a citizen of Munich had advanced to the position of Chancellor for the first time in the history of the German Reich since 1870'.[6] National Socialist art and cultural policy soon spread, via a 'uniformly designed' art and press, un-hindered throughout the 'Hauptstadt der Bewegung' (capital city of the movement).

PE

1

Meisterschule für Deutschlands Buchdrucker, Munich, brochure.

Meisterschule für Deutschlands Buchdrucker

München

CHRISTOPHER BURKE

MUNICH AS A CENTRE FOR TYPOGRAPHY 1926–1933

In a typically irreverent speech given in 1928 at the Werkbund conference in Munich, Kurt Schwitters stated: 'Incidentally, it is difficult to imagine that somebody from Munich could feel comfortable in another city; for a start, they would never in their life be able to get used to illuminated signs.'

Munich was still so conservative at this time that illuminated signs were prohibited in the city. Unlike Frankfurt or Berlin, the Bavarian capital remained largely untouched by architectural modernism. The designer of Futura, Paul Renner, sought to change that situation and spoke passionately about modernization at an event entitled 'Kampf um München als Kulturzentrum' (Struggle for Munich as a Cultural Centre), which was held on 29 November 1926 in Munich's Tonhalle (concert hall). Among the other speakers, in front of a packed audience, were Thomas Mann and Heinrich Mann. Renner's speech called for Munich to be brought into the new era. He lamented the fact that Munich, known as a 'city of art', was lagging behind the new movement in design. He blamed this on Munich's proximity to the southern home of humanism and on its still largely rural Bavarian location: 'Here is the real cultural problem of Bavaria. The European culture of today is not a rural one, but an urban one.' The New Architecture, as a return to basics from the stagnant classical tradition, embodied for Renner 'a new feeling for unity of content and form' in which 'our time has found its creative virtue'.

Munich had not traditionally been a centre for the printing trade to the same extent as Leipzig, for example. There were no major type foundries based exclusively in Munich. But, in early 1927 the Meisterschule für Deutschlands Buchdrucker, Schule der Stadt München und des Deutschen Buchdrucker-Vereins (Master School for Germany's Printers, School of the City of Munich and the German Printers' Association) was established there. Renner led the campaign to establish this national school in Munich and he was its founding director.

Renner had been director of Munich's Graphische Berufsschule (Graphic Design School) since Easter 1926, a position he took after spending a year teaching typography at the Frankfurter Kunstschule (Frankfurt School of Art). Renner heard that funds had been made available by the Deutscher Buchdrucker-Verein to set up a school for the training of prospective printing-house managers.

2
Meisterschule für Deutschlands Buchdrucker, Munich, brochure.

München *und* **Südbayern**

Herausgegeben vom Verkehrsverband München und Südbayern

3

Probably created by Meisterschule students under Jan Tschichold's guidance: Munich and Southern Bavaria, brochure, ed. Verkehrsverband München und Südbayern (Transport Association of Munich and Southern Bavaria), c. 1930.

4

Overview of Professional Schools in the City of Munich, after the academic year 1925/26.

5

German Trade School of Fashion, brochure – possibly by Meisterschule students under Jan Tschichold's guidance, c. 1930.

6

Graphische Berufsschule der Stadt München/Tagesfachschule für Buchbinder (Graphic Design School of the City of Munich/College for Book Binders), brochure, supplements in *Graphische Nachrichten*, typeset and printed by Meisterschule students, c. 1930.

Printing organizations in Leipzig and Berlin were bidding to be host to the school, and Renner saw a chance to secure its establishment in Munich. In collaboration with the Verein Münchner Buchdruckerei Besitzer (Union of Munich Printing-House Proprietors), he negotiated with the Deutscher Buchdrucker-Verein. The advantages of the Munich bid were local government support of 50,000 marks, and the donation of free premises in the building already occupied by the Graphische Berufsschule.

The two Munich schools were distinct from each other: the Berufsschule trained apprentices for the trade, and the new Meisterschule offered an all-round theoretical and practical education for those who would go on to run printing establishments. However, the staff and their approach to teaching seem to have served both schools alike. Workshop teaching was combined with lectures and demonstrations, and instruction at the Meisterschule encompassed typesetting, all reprographic and printing techniques, business theory, bookkeeping, legal theory, printing-house organization and colour theory. The school also ran a varied course of lectures by visiting speakers: among them was Walter Gropius, who gave a lecture on 'Neues Bauen' (New Architecture) in 1931.

Renner was a suitable figurehead for the Meisterschule: he had become a noted typographer owing to his work with the Munich publisher Georg Müller between 1907 and 1917, and then a cautious advocate of the New Typography. During the years of

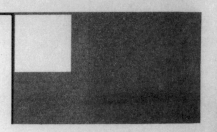

LEHRKÖRPER

MÄNNLICHE ABTEILUNG MIT 9 DIREKTORATEN		WEIBLICHE ABTEILUNG MIT 3 DIREKTORATEN	
Oberstudiendirektoren	9	Oberstudiendirektoren	—
Schuldirektoren	31	Schuldirektoren	3
Lehrkräfte im Hauptamt	183	Lehrkräfte im Hauptamt	112
Insgesamt	223	Insgesamt	115
Nebenamtliche Fachlehrkräfte	201	Nebenamtliche Fachlehrkräfte	45
Summe der Lehrkräfte	424	Summe der Lehrkräfte	160
Summe der hauptamtlichen Lehrkräfte			338
der nebenamtlichen Lehrkräfte			246
Insgesamt:			584

KOSTEN IM RECHNUNGSJAHR 1926

MÄNNLICHE ABTEILUNG		WEIBLICHE ABTEILUNG	
Ausgaben Mk.	2 688 824	Ausgaben Mk.	1 111 945
Hievon trägt:		Hievon trägt:	
die Stadt	2 248 140	die Stadt	858 010
der Kreis	400 684	der Kreis	233 935
der Staat	40 000	der Staat	20 000
GESAMTAUFWAND:			3 800 769 MK.
Hievon trägt:		die Stadt	3 106 150
		der Kreis	634 619
		der Staat	60 000

ÜBERSICHT
ÜBER DIE

BERUFSSCHULEN

DER STADT MÜNCHEN

NACH DEM SCHULJAHR 1925/26

Deutsche Meisterschule für Mode

Höhere Fachschule der Stadt München und der einschlägigen Reichsverbände:

Reichsverband der Innungen für das Damenschneidereigewerbe, Berlin

Reichsverband des deutschen Schneidergewerbes, Elberfeld

Reichsverband für Wäscheschneiderei und angeschlossene Gewerbe, Hamburg

München 2 M, Oberer Anger 17, Telefon 91606

GRAPHISCHE BERUFSSCHULE DER STADT MÜNCHEN

Leitung: Oberstudiendirektor Paul Renner

Tagesfachschule für Buchbinder

Professor Georg Trump

Gewerbehauptlehrer Gustav Keilig

Sommersemester von Ende April bis Mitte Juli. Wintersemester von Anfang Oktober bis Ende März. Schulgeld monatlich 9.— bzw. 10.50 RM. Der Eintritt kann jederzeit erfolgen.

Auskunft durch das Sekretariat der Graphischen Berufsschule, Pranckhstraße 2, Ruf 57268.

establishing the Munich schools he was simultaneously engaged with the lengthy design and production process of Futura, and wrote several essays about the necessity of finding 'the typeface of our time'. He recognized Jan Tschichold – author of the manifesto 'elementare typographie' (1925) – as a critical theorist of New Typography, and contacted him initially to suggest that Tschichold take over the position Renner had left vacant in Frankfurt. The two men evidently discovered some common ground (not least the fact that they had both been accused of being Bolshevists in a printing trade magazine), and Renner invited Tschichold to teach in Munich instead.

Tschichold began teaching at the Graphische Berufsschule in June 1926, and also became a principal tutor for Schriftschreiben (formal writing/typographic sketching) and type composition at the Meisterschule. Both Renner and Tschichold believed that tactile engagement with creating letters through the self-contained activity of handcraft was still the most effective means of learning about the qualities of letterforms. This contrasted with the more Constructivist approach to letter design at the Bauhaus. The manual skills taught at the Munich schools were embodied in the two instructional books that Tschichold wrote while employed there – *Schriftschreiben für Setzer* (Calligraphy for Compositors, 1931) and *Typografische Entwurfstechnik* (How to Draw Layouts, 1932). These demonstrate exercises featuring a range of

script styles, from frakturs to sans serifs. While the printed work produced at the Munich Meisterschule tended towards a relaxed asymmetry, increasingly typeset in Futura, traditional styles and typefaces were not excluded, and this helped to create a 'Munich style', which Philipp Luidl described as 'an undogmatic tendency, marked by reason and aesthetic feeling'.[7]

7

8

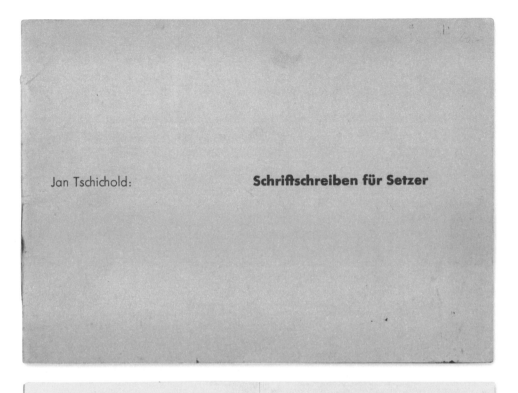

7

Works from the Munich Meisterschule
für Deutschlands Buchdrucker, supplement in *Graphische Nachrichten*, set
and printed by students, c. 1930.

8

Works from the Meisterschule, supplement for *Archiv für Buchgewerbe und
Gebrauchsgraphik*, set and printed by
students, 1931.

9

Jan Tschichold: *Schriftschreiben für Setzer*
(Lettering for Compositors), Frankfurt:
Klimsch, 1931; cover and double spread.

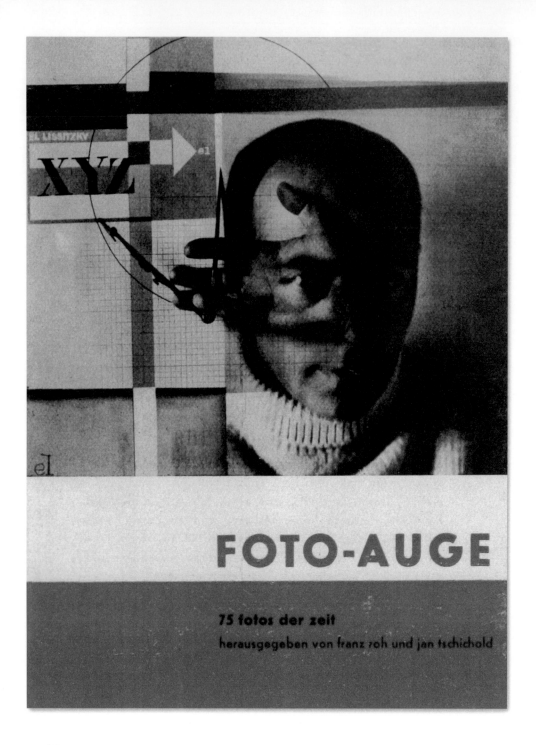

10

Advertising leaflet for *Foto-Auge: 75 Fotos der Zeit*, collected by Franz Roh and Jan Tschichold, Stuttgart: F. Wedekind, 1929. Photomontage: El Lissitzky.

JAN TSCHICHOLD AND FUTURA

Jan Tschichold's widow, Edith, commented late in her life that her husband had advised Renner about the form of Futura. The two men may well have discussed the matter of 'the typeface of our time', which preoccupied both of them, but there is no firm evidence that Tschichold contributed to the design of Futura. The personal relationship between Renner and Tschichold seems not to have been very close: they were from different generations – Renner was rooted in the nineteenth century; Tschichold was born in the twentieth. (Yet, although Renner's modernism did not burn as brightly as Tschichold's, it lasted longer.)

Tschichold's book *Die neue Typographie* (1928) was the most important document of its subject and, designed by the author, it was fully typeset in sans serif. The first three weights of Futura had been released in early 1928, but it is likely that the printer of *Die neue Typographie*, the publishing house Buchdruckerwerkstätte in Berlin, had not acquired it before the book was typeset. Instead, it was composed in Aurora, a sans serif of the common, nineteenth-century style. Such typefaces provided the aura of objectivity (*Sachlichkeit*) required by the New Typography, yet Tschichold was unwilling to admit that their visual qualities were entirely acceptable.

He claimed to have used such a sans serif for composing the text of *Die neue Typographie* in order to demonstrate how legible it could be, but simultaneously offered a veiled apology for the typeface itself, explaining that his particular choice was limited by what the printer had available. Indeed, as he pointed out, it was not usual in the 1920s for printers to hold sufficient quantities of sans serif type to compose a whole book. Mechanical typesetting had not yet become that common in Germany.

In his book, Tschichold stated that the 'so-called "Grotesque" or block-letter' was the only typeface 'in spiritual accordance with our time', and continued: 'There is no doubt that the sans serif types available today do not yet fulfil the requirements of an entirely satisfactory typeface. The specific characteristics of this type have scarcely been worked out yet: the small letters especially are still too dependent on the humanist minuscule.'[8]

Tschichold preferred the 'old anonymous sans serifs' to the new designs, such as Erbar and Kabel, which were too individualistic; but he conceded that Futura made 'a significant step in the right direction'. Tschichold continued to favour the grotesque style of sans serif in his practical work, although he did begin to use Futura in publicity and books that he designed for the publisher Der Bücherkreis in the early 1930s. Futura was the text typeface in his book *Schriftschreiben für Setzer*, and he also featured it as the sans serif example in *Typografische Entwurfstechnik*, although he simply called it a 'grotesque'. (Incidentally, Renner rejected the term 'grotesque' as a description of his Futura typeface.) Futura did, however, meet one of Tschichold's stated requirements for an ideal sans serif – the eradication of calligraphic features from the small letters. It was really the typeface that came closest to the ideal described by Tschichold and other modernist typographers; and perhaps the immediate success of Futura prevented Tschichold from trying to have a sans serif design of his own produced by a German type foundry before 1933.

Tschichold stated in *Die neue Typographie* that no single person could design the requisite typeface; instead it would be the work of a group, among whom he thought 'there must also no doubt be an engineer'.[9] Nevertheless, between 1926 and 1929 he designed a sans serif typeface that could be interpreted as a suggestion for his ideal letterform. It obviously bears some similarity to Futura, and to Bauhaus alphabets, because he was trying to reduce letters to an elemental form in a similar way. Indeed, Tschichold cut out an advertisement page for Futura from a magazine and used it as a basis for visualizing three weights of his own typeface. It is understandable that he would not want to offer his sans serif as direct competition to Futura in the German type market, in which Renner's typeface was proving a great success; instead, he sent it to the French foundry of Deberny & Peignot. He cannot have been pleased when they answered that they had just agreed to market Futura in France, which they did under a different name – Europe. So they returned his drawings to him.

After this refusal, Tschichold reworked this design into a presentation of his ideas for orthographic reform. This was a single alphabet (a mixture of capital and minuscule letterforms) rendered as a geometric sans serif, in an elegant light weight. It was published in 1930 with the title 'Noch eine neue Schrift' (Yet another new script).

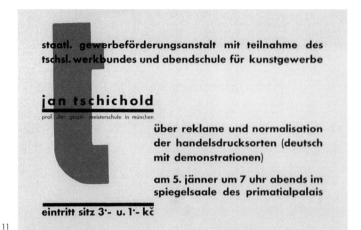

11

11

Window display card announcing a lecture by Jan Tschichold on advertising and the standardization of commercial printing, letterpress, 1931.

12

Jan Tschichold: advertisement for Futura, revised by Tschichold, 1929 (and detail).

13

Jan Tschichold (design): O. Mänchen-Helfen, *Drittel der Menschheit: Ein Ostasienbuch.* Berlin: Der Bücherkreis, 1932.

14

Jan Tschichold (design): Erich Grisar, *Mit Kamera und Schreibmaschine durch Europa: Bilder und Berichte.* Berlin: Der Bücherkreis, 1932.

12

13

14

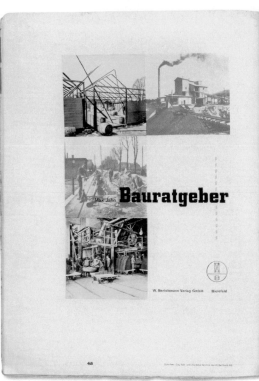

City halbfett

H. BERTHOLD AG Berlin SW 61 Mehringdamm 43

Nach Entwürfen von Prof. Georg Trump, München, geboren am 10.7.1896
in Brettheim. 1926 Professor in Bielefeld und München,
1931 Direktor in Berlin. 1934 bis 1953 Direktor der Meisterschule
für Deutschlands Buchdrucker in München, seit 1953 freiberuflich tätig
als Schriftkünstler, Maler und Graphiker.

Geschnitten in 8 10 12 14 16 20 24 28 36 und 48 p

WEITERE GARNITUREN

mager
fett

Erstguß im Jahre 1930
Signatur: Normal
Zifferndicke: Bildweite

Ziffernhöhe:
H123H

KLASSIFIKATION

Drucktypenverzeichnis

abcdefghijklmnopqrstuvwxyz chck ß

ABCDEFGHIJKLMNOPQRSTUVWXYZ

1234567890 & .,:;'-/])!?§*†„"»«äöü ÄÖÜ

Akzente

áàâéèêëíìîïóòôúùûç

æœ ÉÈÊË Ç ÆŒ

Übersetzer ab 24 p

╱ ╲ ╱╲ ..

Punkturen ab 12p nur

.,:;'-/)!?»«

Verwendung der Schriften nur gemäß den Lieferbedingungen
der Schriftgießerei. Nachbildung verboten.
Schriftmuster-Kartelkarte nach DIN 16 517.

Bth. 69

GEORG TRUMP

Examples of work done at Munich's Graphische Berufsschule were shown at a major international printing exhibition held in Cologne in 1928, known as 'Pressa'. A group from the Munich schools that most probably included both Renner and Tschichold visited 'Pressa', where examples of typography done at the Kunstgewerbeschule in Bielefeld were also on display. A successful graphic design workshop had been built up at that school under the direction of Georg Trump, and Renner, who was impressed by its work, invited him to teach at the Meisterschule. Renner's action was partly prompted by an expectation that Tschichold would not remain in employment there much longer. He also felt that Trump was one of the few young candidates with real practical experience in composition and printing.

Trump began teaching at the Meisterschule in the second half of 1929. He was a remarkably fine practitioner of the New Typography, in addition to being a prolific and innovative typeface designer. His slab serif typeface City (1930) has, like Futura, proved to be an enduring legacy of German New Typography. However, Trump did not initially stay long in Munich, leaving in 1931 to teach at the Berlin Kunstgewerbe- und Handwerkerschule, although he would return in 1934 – one year after Renner and Tschichold were dismissed by the National Socialists – as director of the Meisterschule.

15
Work by Georg Trump in *Archiv für Buchgewerbe und Gebrauchsgraphik*, vol. 68, no. 9, 1931.

16
Georg Trump: City Medium, typeface index card, H. Berthold AG, 1930.

'In the same way that every window of a building has an almost human physiognomy, so every typographic character has a face; it shows a personality, an attitude. Everything that can be said about the character of a human being also applies to the character of a typeface. A typeface is noble or ordinary, it is proud or anxious, it is clear or confused, decisive or indecisive.'

PAUL RENNER, 1929.

ISABEL NAEGELE

FUTURA ON THE ROAD TO SUCCESS

Little is known about the authorship of Futura Schmuck, released in 1927, FIG.18 P.215 apart from the fact that Renner wanted to distance himself from the contents of the font and its geometric ornaments. Renner had opposed 'schematization in typography' several times in his publications, and specifically formalism in 'elementare typografie'.[10] It can only be assumed that Futura Schmuck (meaning Ornament) was the Bauer Type Foundry's nod to the contemporary market for advertisements in the style of the New Typography, which used geometric forms, particularly circles, as distinctive structural elements. Numerous patterns could be designed using these geometric segments and basic shapes. The significance of this ornamental trend is reinforced by the release of two other typefaces at that time – Blickfang Schmuck, by Schriftguss AG in Dresden, and Elementare Schmuckformen, by its competitor D. Stempel in Frankfurt.

Renner's design for Futura Black, a stencil type, followed in 1929. FIG.21 P.189 In comparison with Josef Albers' Schablonenschrift, FIG.44 P.119 which was based on a limited number of basic geometric shapes, Renner's design, which was used in type combinations for posters and books, was the more legible overall, and so the more practical design. Unlike Albers' conceptual approach, Renner's design reflects the work of an experienced type designer: a 'stroke-and-ball' r makes a new appearance in the lower-case letters. Incidentally, this r can also be found in the character set of Plak, a poster type by Renner that was released in about 1928 by Stempel. It was offered in wood, and later in synthetic resin, too, in large sizes of 72 to 624 point in bold, bold condensed and bold compressed weights. It is interesting to note that it was intended to supplement the type designed with the cooperation of Wilhelm Pischner – Neuzeit-Grotesk – which was considered Futura's competitor.

THREE YEARS OF FUTURA

In his text 'Drei Jahre Futura' (Three Years of Futura, 1930/31), Renner describes the development of the type family that was now expanded with light oblique, medium oblique and demibold weights: 'through the typesetter's work with Futura, it was found that an oblique type was required. Typesetting for advertisements requires certain parts of the text to be clearly distinguishable from others. In addition to the differentiation resulting from the varying degrees of brightness in the type, differentiation is also achieved by a variety of slants. Typographic practice has also dictated that in addition to Futura Bold for the display type, a bold condensed should be provided.'[11]

Futura Book followed in 1933, a set somewhere between the light and medium weights that was recommended for use in book typography. Renner proved with the design of his book *Mechanisierte Grafik* (Mechanized Graphics) of 1931 that both Futura Medium and the lower-case 'stroke-and-ball' **r** could also be used for highly legible running text. The jury of the Buchkunst Foundation considered this book to be one of the 50 most beautiful books of the year. However, in practice, Futura Book filled a gap between the very delicate Futura Light in small sizes and Futura Medium.[12] An interesting but unfortunately undated proof in book oblique with English text, probably from the 1930s, shows experiments with the lower-case **r** and lower-case **t**, both with a downstroke.<u>FIG.42 P.451</u> The text indicates that this was a sample for the American advertising market. It is striking how these interventions make the type look more closed, and the characters less differentiated.

Futura Inline, released in 1931, and the cursive sets are largely based on Renner's ideas and sketches, but were eventually finalized in detail by Heinrich Jost's staff. Despite difficult years for Renner, living in exile, additional sets followed between 1937 and 1950, expanding the successful and comprehensive Futura family: Futura Medium Condensed (1937), Futura Bold Oblique (1938), Futura Book Oblique (1939) and Futura Light Condensed (1950). As members of the Futura family, these sets eventually also made a substantial contribution to the financial status of Renner and his descendants.

17

17
Paul Renner, *Mechanisierte Grafik*, Berlin 1931.

18
Futura Schmuck type specimen, c. 1929/30.

19
The 13 sets: Futura type specimen with reduced pages and paper of different colours, after 1938.

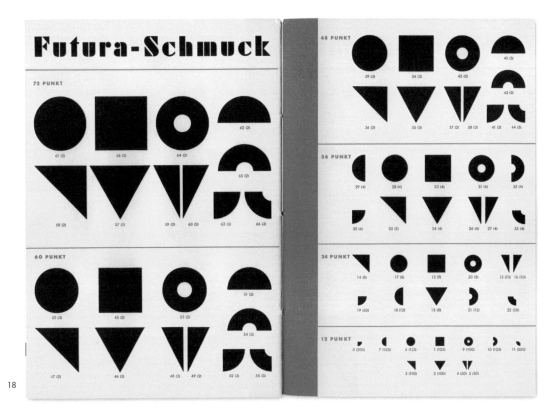

Wass

SWISSAIR

Das Land

des ewigen

Kasperlegeschichten von Hans Barth

ZIPP

FRIDOLIN

DAS
BASTEL
WUNDER

1 Holländer

2 Dreirad

3 Roller

NEW AND RECENT TYPEFACES

In 1937 Berthold released Renner's Ballade, a black letter type, which, as a response to the times, attempted to reconcile the features of Schwabacher with Antiqua by means of curved, wide forms. In 1939 Stempel followed Renner-Antiqua with the release of a very sleek, upright Antiqua in two weights, which were used in newspapers such as the *Süddeutsche Zeitung*, and in other publications, until the end of World War II.[13]

Research by Burke on staggered payments from Stempel to Renner between 1939 and 1942 indicates that another four type designs were in development but never completed, to Renner's disappointment.[14]

However, another comprehensive type project did manage to see the light of day, even if with a delay: Renner-Grotesk and Steile Futura. Unlike Futura, Renner-Grotesk, according to Renner, was intended to be a 'true' grotesque. After long, unsatisfactory test runs in about 1936 at Stempel, Renner gave the design to the Bauer Type Foundry, where it was finally released in 1951, after many changes and additional developments for commercial reasons, as part of the Futura superfamily of the 1950s.[15] The type specimens of the Bauer Type Foundry from September 1938 contain the first proofs in 48 point.[FIG.44 P.455] This so-called Steile Futura is slim, upright and based, unlike Futura, on a construction principle of the rectangle. In addition, it bears clear elements of handwriting in its upstrokes and downstrokes, like small 'stumps' – the cursive **r**, for instance, has a downstroke – the forms of which must have been in tune with the tastes of the 1950s. In any case, formal similarities with Futura Schlagzeile can be observed from 1933 in right-angled shapes. And a sheet of paper from 14 February 1931 bears designs for a Futura Unziale,[FIG.23 P.219] which also contains similarities to some letters from the later Futura Schlagzeile. Further developments to the predecessors of Futura Schlagzeile over several years and additional obstacles are not improbable. In this respect, the name 'Steile Futura' is somewhat misleading and can be explained only as an attempt on the part of the Bauer Type Foundry to latch on to the great success of the Futura brand.

20

Applications of Futura: portfolio of commercial jobs from c. 1953/54.

31.5.39

Bauersche Gießerei, Frankfurt a.M.

Lieber Herr Jost, ich schicke Ihnen beiliegend die Zeichnung für die magere Kursiv der Steilen Futura '(Orthogonal,
wird der Name im Ausland sein müssen!)

Einige Zeichen sind doppelt gezeichnet, die bessere Form hat
auf beiliegender Photographie ein kleines Kreuz.

Bei den Ziffern ist die 5 hier wohl etwas zu schwach

Bei den Großbuchstaben müßten folgende in den angegebenen
Teilen wolh einen Hauch stärker werden:

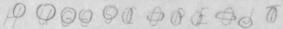

Dagegen sind die von links unten nach rechts oben führenden
Striche wieder zu schwer in den Zeichen:

X Y W Z

Bei R dürften die beiden Qzuerstriche leichter sein.

                              Mit besten Grüßen in der
                    Zuversicht, daß es Ihnen und Ihren erfahrena
                    Mitarbeitern gelingen wird, etwaige andere
                    Mängel noch auszugleic hen

                                        Ihr ergebener

                                        P. Renner

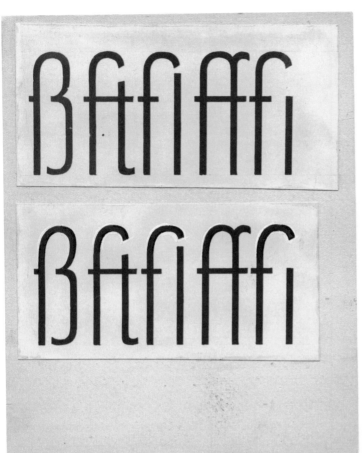

21

Letter from Paul Renner to Heinrich Jost on 31 May 1939 regarding Steile Futura Light Cursive, with detailed corrections.

22

Drawings of designs for the ligatures **ß**, **ft**, **fl**, **ff** and **fi** of Steile Futura Light. Corrections were made using opaque white.

23

Renner's design for Futura Unziale, 14 February 1931. Corrections were made using opaque white.

22

23

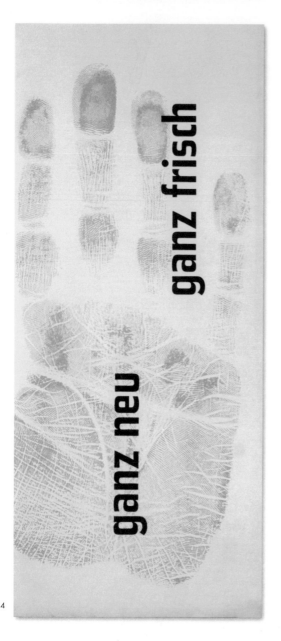

24

24

Ganz neu ganz frisch (Totally New and Fresh), Bauer Type Foundry advertising leaflet for Steile Futura, c. 1953.

25

Es geht wieder aufwärts (On the Way Back Up), Bauer Type Foundry advertising leaflet, after 1945.

26

Type specimen for Futura Display. Leaflet printed on coloured paper.

27

PP.222–23 – portfolio of commercial print jobs using Steile Futura Bold from c. 1953/54.

28

PP.224–25 – portfolios and type specimens from c. 1950/53.

► Nr. 105006   6 Cicero

PRUNK Hochzeit 1

► Nr. 105008   8 Cicero

MODE Ware 2

► Nr. 105010   10 Cicero

CHEF Arzt 3

► Nr. 105012   12 Cicero

Südpol 4

► Nr. 105016   16 Cicero

Funk 5

FIGURENVERZEICHNIS

ABCDEFGHIJKLM
OPQRSTUVWXY
ÄÖÜÇ

abcdefghijklmno

qrstuvwxyzäöüch

!?('&

890

CAFÉ SCHWARZ

Jede Nachzeichnung zum
die im Widerspruch zu
eht.

Verlagsanstalt Alexander Koch GmbH. Stuttgart · 60. Jahrgang 1952

27

Bauersche Giesserei Frankfurt am Main   Futura

STEILE
FUTURA
KURSIV

halbfett

1953

FUTURA

1950

A fett

CHRISTOPHER BURKE

CRISIS, 1933 – THE POLITICIZATION OF FUTURA

Futura has now become an icon of neutrality, often used in publicity by political parties of all persuasions. But at the beginning of the Third Reich it was explicitly politicized by the National Socialists in order to punish its designer, Paul Renner, for his criticism of Nazi cultural policy.

More than any other city, Munich served as a base for the gradual acquisition of power by the National Socialists during the 1920s, and in November 1928 Adolf Hitler received a rapturous reception for a speech he gave at Munich University. In 1930 the Nazi Party (NSDAP) remodelled Barlow Palace in central Munich for its national headquarters; this came to be known as the Braunes Haus (Brown House). In the previous year, the first public event of the Kampfbund für Deutsche Kultur (Fighting League for German Culture) had been held in Munich. This organization (formed by Alfred Rosenberg, editor of the National Socialist newspaper *Völkischer Beobachter*) officially adopted the racist views on 'art and race' propagated by the conservative architect Paul Schultze-Naumburg. He embarked on a lecture tour of German cities to expound his theories, and his talk in Munich was so well-received that he gave a second, which

Renner attended. Schultze-Naumburg showed slides of Asian art and modern, avant-garde Western art, describing their distorted representation of human figures as products of perverted minds. The young Munich painter Wolf Panizza interrupted with the question, 'But where is the good modern art?', and was consequently beaten up and seriously injured by Nazi thugs. Renner was outraged by this incident, and gave an account of it in a short book he wrote in criticism of Nazi cultural policy, *Kulturbolschewismus?*, published in 1932. He sent the manuscript to two German publishers, both of whom rejected it, so he submitted it to his friend Eugen Rentsch in Zurich. The anti-Nazi polemic of Renner's essay was clearly too dangerous for German publishers to handle at that time.

The expression 'cultural Bolshevism', which Renner questioned (literally with a question mark) in the title of his book, had become a reproach directed against the New Architecture by the *Völkischer Beobachter* by about 1930. In his book, Renner attempted to counter the anti-Semitic and anti-Communist rhetoric of the Nazis with an appeal to reason, but there is no doubt that the publication marked him as an enemy of the NSDAP. Indeed, Renner sensed the trouble his book was attracting and withdrew it from circulation.

Hitler was appointed Chancellor at the end of January 1933, as part of a compromise prompted by the reigning political chaos. The majority of Germans shared the suspicion of the short-sighted power-brokers who had levered him into power, that he would not last long. Yet

Paul Renner

Kultur-
bolschewismus?

Eugen Rentsch Verlag

29
Pamphlet against National Socialist
cultural policy: Paul Renner's *Kultur-
bolschewismus?*, Erlenbach-Zurich/
Munich/Leipzig: Eugen Rentsch
Verlag, 1932. Title set in Futura Display.

Renner harboured graver sentiments. In a contribution to a survey on the 'state of graphic design' for the magazine *Gebrauchsgraphik*, published in that same month, he commented: 'Political idiocy, growing more violent and malicious every day, may eventually sweep the whole of Western culture to the ground with its muddy sleeve.' Renner's comment was duly noted, and later used as evidence against him.

The success of the National Socialists in the election of March 1933 allowed them to seize power in Germany. They wasted no time in implementing a programme of arresting dissidents, and Renner must have been fully aware of its effects. Indeed, his colleague Jan Tschichold was arrested in the middle of March, a few weeks before Renner's own arrest. Tschichold received notice of his dismissal from the Meisterschule after only the first few days of his internment. As director of the Meisterschule, Renner complained on Tschichold's behalf, but Tschichold remained in prison for four weeks.

In March 1933 Renner supervised the design of the German exhibit at the fifth Milan Triennale. For this international exhibition, the German display was entrusted to the Werkbund, which decided to restrict its contribution to the output of the German graphic design trade. Renner took charge of selecting the material and designing the display; the architect Walther Schmidt also contributed to the final layout of the German stand. Renner's particular contribution was a slideshow illustrating the historical progression of style in letterforms. He used four projectors, and each series of slides in the 60 stages of the sequence featured an image of script alongside illustrations of other arts from the same period.

While Renner was busy designing the Milan exhibit, he was being increasingly harassed by the authorities. Both his home and his office at the Meisterschule were searched on 25 March 1933. A caretaker let the 'political police' into Renner's office, and they seized photographic slides featuring examples of photomontage that the authorities described afterwards as 'Russian propaganda against Germany'.

On 31 March 1933 Renner was visited at the Meisterschule by Johannes Sievers, a long-time Werkbund supporter from the Foreign Office, and Eberhard Hanfstaengl, the director of the National Gallery in Berlin. They were sent to verify that the material chosen by Renner for the Milan exhibition was suitable in terms of foreign policy. Several objects were found to be unfit for display, and Hanfstaengl complained specifically that there was an imbalance in favour of roman type over gothic. (Gothic script was becoming a key feature of the Nazi propaganda machine at this time.) Renner was not happy with this interference, and his obstinacy was noted.

Renner was taken into custody at 23:30 on 4 April 1933, and released the next day, on the condition that he report to the police every other day. His almost immediate release was thanks to a fortuitous, indirect family connection to Rudolf Hess, Hitler's deputy. Nevertheless, on

31

30
P.229 – entrance to the German exhibit at
the 5th Milan Triennale in 1933. Renner's
slide projections are in the background.

31
View of the German exhibit at the 5th
Milan Triennale. The exhibition space
was designed by Munich's government
architect, Walther Schmidt.

11 April Renner was temporarily relieved of his post at the Meisterschule, and his case was examined under the statutes of the Gesetz zur Wiederherstellung des Berufsbeamtentums (Professional Civil Service Restoration Act), which was instituted by the Nazis on 7 April (three days after Renner's release).

In attempting to dismiss Renner, the Nazi authorities sought to establish firm links between creative work and political ideology. Although Renner had often expressed the view that art and life should be united in creative work, he cannot have envisaged the facile injection of politics into culture carried out by the Nazis. There was no evidence that he was affiliated with the Communist Party, and so the Nazi examiners admitted that he could be convicted only if his 'artistic activity' could be established as 'Communistic'. The Nazis then had to face the consequences of their own loose employment of political terminology: the officials realized that they could not adequately judge Renner's design activity 'because it is not clearly established what is to be understood as Communistic art in the field of graphic design'. They solved this problem by suggesting a stylistic link between his typeface Futura and the forms of the New Architecture, which was commonly held to have Russian associations. Renner's renunciation of the traditional forms of gothic type in Futura was deemed anti-German.

Renner was permanently dismissed from his position at the Meisterschule on 16 February 1934 by the Bavarian Reichsstatthalter (Reich lieutenant) Franz von Epp, not on grounds of Communist activity, but on grounds simply of 'national untrustworthiness'.

Renner's status as a modernist branded him subversive. By supporting the New Architecture and New Typography, he associated himself with the avant-garde. These new design styles were the products of an elite, and were consequently antipathetic to the populist notions of traditional village life promoted by the Nazis, who propagated strong myths about German identity, intended to stir the hearts of the majority. The Nazi accusations of Communist influence in artistic activity were a convenient propaganda exercise designed to remove potential dissidents.

Futura, attuned to the new taste for unornamented form, was labelled anti-German by the authorities. In 1928 the graphic design magazine *Gebrauchsgraphik* (printed in German and English) had adopted Futura as its typeface for text, followed by the Werkbund journal, *Die Form*, in August 1931. The scope of these periodicals was truly international, dealing with design from all over Europe and America. Futura emerged as a principal component of typographic modernism: by differentiating itself from roman and gothic with its simplified forms, the typeface carried an aura of international neutrality. Although Tschichold and the Bauhaus typographers were the most vocal proponents of a sans serif constituting a rejection of 'national' styles in letterforms, Renner also proposed his Futura as a universal letterform. It was easy for the Nazis to construct a logical short circuit connecting it to the international Communist effort. Yet, as Robert Bringhurst has observed: 'Except by incidental association, there are no Marxist (or Christian or Muslim or Jewish) scripts, any more than there is a Marxist or Christian arithmetic or, in music, a communist C-sharp.'[16]

Futura, which had already become a successful typeface by 1933, did not disappear from use in Germany altogether, and it was not outlawed by the Nazi regime. Indeed, official documents of the Third Reich were sometimes composed in Futura, most probably because of its availability and suitability. There was a cultural tendency towards the modern within the Nazi Party, led by Joseph Goebbels (and approved by Hitler to some extent), and it was this tendency, allied to political expediency, that triumphed over the *völkisch* (folk) element in 1941 with the secret decree banning gothic script in favour of roman as the 'normal script'.

Ironically, after his arrest and release, Renner received the Grand Diploma of Honour for his work on the German exhibit at the Milan Triennale, which finally opened on 10 May 1933. The judges were especially impressed with the slideshow presentation. Futura was shown in a specially typeset quotation from Mussolini: 'We dare not plunder the inheritance of our fathers, we must create new art.' This exhibition seems to have been decisive in spreading the popularity of Futura around Europe, and in Italy a sans serif inscriptional letter, very close to Futura in form, was developed for public lettering on buildings of the Fascist regime. The allusion to classical Roman majuscules in Futura capitals accorded neatly with the undoubted intention of the Italian Fascists to evoke imagery from the Imperial Roman past.

32

In the background is Paul Renner's honorary degree certificate for his contribution to the German exhibit at the Milan Triennale of 1933. In front is the accompanying letter of 9 September 1935 from the Minister for the People's Enlightenment and Propaganda. It bears a handwritten note by Renner on the subject of the denunciation, 1935.

Der Reichsminifter
für Volksaufklärung und Propaganda

Geſchäftszeichen: **I 1212/6.9.**
(In der Antwort anzugeben)

Berlin W8, den 9.September 1935.
Wilhelmplatz 8—9
Fernsprecher: A 1 Jäger 0014

An

Herrn Paul Renner
Leiter der Meisterschule für Deutschlands
Buchdrucker

in

M ü n c h e n

*Ob nicht nach der
Bekanntgabe dieser
Ordensverleihung eine
Denunziation erfolgt
ist? Denn warum hat
gerade 1935 das Propagan-
daministerium meine
Bücher auf die Liste der
schädlichen Bücher gesetzt?*

In der Anlage übersende ich Jhnen

das Diplom über das Jhnen von S.M. dem König

von Jtalien verliehene

Offizierskreuz

des Ordens der Jtalienischen Krone.

Jm Auftrag

gez. Dr.Greiner

Beglaubigt

Kanzleiangeſtellter.

234 MUNICH

'Whoever forbids art to perceive the shadowy side, the other side of life, which is not always beautiful and dignified, has understood just as little of the meaning of life as of the essence of art itself.'

33
Portrait of Paul Renner, probably 1946.

PAUL RENNER
Kulturbolschewismus?, 1932.

FUTURA AND THE NSDAP

Fanatical Nazis assailed Futura, designed by a critic of the regime, as an ideological abomination. Yet not all Nazis were as dogmatic. A schism existed between modern and anti-modern camps, the latter led by the chief party ideologue, Alfred Rosenberg, who enforced *Gleichschaltung* (or Nazification of all things German). Among the bêtes noires of the pro-moderns were the ideologically approved typefaces – Fraktur and Schwabacher – as well as other so-called kitsch aspects of art and culture. Italian Fascism, after all, was defined by modern art. But the pro-modernist faction was doomed, once Hitler had decreed that modernism was degenerate in all its representations.

Banning non-Germanic (indeed Jewish or Bolshevik) typefaces was one of Rosenberg's propaganda themes, at least from 1933 to 1935. It was made manifest in an aggressive campaign, promoted using stickers with slogans advocating 'Schöne Deutsche Schrift' (Beautiful German script). A Nazi journal devoted to lettering and type, *Die zeitgemäße Schrift* (Contemporary Lettering), sponsored annual German lettering competitions and taught students that blackletter faces – spiky Fraktur, Schwabacher, Textura and Rotunda – were intertwined with German *völkist* tradition.

However, pragmatism ultimately trumped dogma when, after 1938, high-ranking Nazis realized that party-approved blackletter typefaces challenged legibility, especially in occupied countries. The Nazi party secretary, Martin Bormann, decreed that Antiqua (Roman) would become the official script (*Normalschrifterlass*), replacing Schwabacher 'Jewish letters' for all official signs and publications. This opened the door to further sans serifs as well.

Futura appeared in a volume of *Lehrgang Typographisches Skizzerieren und Drucksachenentwerfen* (Typographic Sketching and Print Design), the official typesetting handbook of the DAF (the Nazi Labour Front), where it was actually prominently credited to its designer, Paul Renner, who was labelled a 'cultural Bolshevik'. Hitler's long-time personal photographer, Heinrich Hoffmann, also issued merchandise catalogues (*Nationalsozialistischer Bilder Sortimentskatalog* – National Socialist Picture Publishers' Full-Range Catalogue) filled with Nazi picture postcards, wall hangings, portfolios, card decks and loose-leaf folios of the Führer's watercolour paintings, with cover titles typeset in upper- and lower-case Futura Bold.

34

35

34

Sans serif types such as Futura and black letter types were not objected to in Georg Schautz's *Lehrgang Typographisches Skizzieren und Drucksachenentwerfen* (Typographic Sketching and Print Design), edited by the national organizational head of the NSDAP. Commissioned and edited by the Office for Professional Education and Management of the Deutsche Arbeitsfront (German Labour Front). Berlin: Lehrmittelzentral der Deutsche Arbeitsfront, 1939.

35

Hitler's personal photographer, Heinrich Hoffmann, produced his own product catalogues – which included watercolours by the Führer for sale – set in Futura Bold. The catalogues included art prints, photo enlargements, postcards, watercolours, books and sculptures. Munich/Berlin et al.: Verlag nationalsozialistischer Bilder, c. 1940.

FESTTAGE DER NATION

Von HEINER KURZBEIN

Wenn man vor 1933 zehn Männer beauftragt hätte, die zehn Fotografien zusammenzustellen, die im Laufe der vergangenen 5 Jahre auf das deutsche Volk den stärksten Eindruck gemacht haben, so hätte man 100 verschiedene Bilder vorgelegt bekommen. Würde man die gleiche Aufgabe im Jahre 1938 stellen, so zeigte sich wohl, daß die zehn Männer zu den gleichen Ergebnissen kämen. Denn sie alle stellten fest, daß die stärksten Bildeindrücke ausgegangen sind von den neuen Festtagen der Nation.

30. Januar:
TAG DER MACHTÜBERNAHME

5. Sonntag vor Ostern:
HELDENGEDENKTAG

(14)

Die grundlegende Wandlung, die sich seit dem 30. Januar 1933 in Deutschland vollzogen hat, findet einen sichtbaren Ausdruck in den neuen Feiertagen des deutschen Volkes. Sie traten neben die altüberkommenen Feste, sind jedoch von einem gänzlich anderen Sinn und einer anderen inneren Berechtigung erfüllt und getragen. Wenn die alten Festtage – Ostern, Pfingsten, Weihnacht – mehr oder weniger aus dem Jahreslauf und im Kreise der deutschen Familien ihre Bedeutung und Festlichkeit erhielten, sind die neuen Festtage aus

20. April:
GEBURTSTAG DES FÜHRERS

1. Mai:
NATIONALER FEIERTAG
DES DEUTSCHEN VOLKES

(15)

36

OSTLAND

MONATSSCHRIFT
DES REICHSKOMMISSARS
FÜR DAS OSTLAND

PORTAL DER GROSSEN GILDE IN REVAL
FARBAUFNAHME VON HANS SCHUMACHER, KÖLN

APRIL 1944 NR. 10 JAHRGANG 2 RIGA

37

AUSSTELLUNG

DIE STRASSE

MÜNCHEN 1934

Hoheitszeichen in Holz, modelliert von HANS PANZER, München. Geschnitzt in Holz von Münchener und Berchtesgadener Schnitzern

Insignia in wood modelled by HANS PANZER, Munich carved in wood by carvers from Munich and Berchtesgaden
Photo: Jaeger & Goergen, München

Eingangshalle
Architektur   Architecture
Prof. THEO LECHNER

Entrance Hall
Photo: Regierungsbaumeister Walter Müller-Grah, München

54

38

36

'Festtage der Nation' (The Nation's Festivals) – Renner's Futura, used for Nazi propaganda in the magazine *die neue linie*, which at one time was celebrated as a manifestation of modernism; 1938.

37

Futura used for international communication: the title page of the magazine *Ostland*, published by the National Socialists in Riga, April 1944.

38

Report on the exhibition 'Die Strasse' (The Street) in the magazine *Gebrauchsgraphik*, 1934.

39–40

Title pages of the *Mitteilungsblattes der Reichsdeutschen in Rumänien* (Newsletter of Germans of the Reich in Romania), 1940 and 1944. The change made to this periodical, published in Bucharest, is an indication that black letter type was not considered legible outside Germany.

39

40

41

Hans Vitus Vierthaler: Poster for the
'Entartete Kunst' (Degenerate Art) exhibition, Munich Police Department, 1936.
The poster refers to a travelling exhibition
that began in 1933 in Dresden and paved
the way for the much more comprehensive exhibition of the same name at the
Haus der Kunst in 1937. It is interesting
to note how the techniques of the New
Typography, the 'Bolshevist enemy', are
referenced in the lettering, colour and
composition.

42

Invitation to a book-burning event in
Königsplatz, 1933.

43

P.243 – John Heartfield: 'The Meaning of
Hitler's Greeting: Small Man asks for Big
Donations. Motto: Millions stand behind
me!' Draft of title design A–1–2, 1932.

ENTARTETE KUNST

ausstellung von „kulturdokumenten"
des bolschewismus und jüdischer
zersetzungsarbeit. vom 4. III. bis 31. III. 1936

was wir in dieser interessanten
schau sehen, wurde einmal
ernst genommen!!!!

vierthaler

Ausstellung im Weißen Saal der Polizeidirektion, Neuhauserstraße, Eingang Augustinerstraße
Geöffnet: Werktags von 10 bis 21 Uhr, Sonntags 10 bis 18 Uhr
Eintritt: Für Einzelpersonen 20 Pfennig. Bei geschlossenen Führungen der Betriebe 10 Pfennig.
Anmeldung der Führungen im Gauamt der N.S.-Gem. „Kraft durch Freude" Abt. Propaganda

41

EINLADUNG

ZUM

VERBRENNUNGSAKT AM KÖNIGSPLATZ

AM MITTWOCH, DEN 10. MAI 1933, NACHTS 11³⁰ UHR.

Die Studentenschaften der Universität und der Technischen Hochschule München und der Kreis VII
(Bayern) der Deutschen Studentenschaft laden Sie zu der oben bezeichneten Kundgebung ein.

Mit dieser Karte haben Sie Zutritt auf dem abgesperrten Raum am
Königsplatz (vor der Staatlichen Kunstausstellung). Der abgesperrte
Raum muß um 11 Uhr nachts pünktlich betreten sein.

Nach 11 Uhr trifft d. Fackelzug d. gesamten Studentenschaft Münchens ein.

1. Die vereinigten Kapellen spielen Marschmusik
2. Beginn der Feier 11³⁰ Uhr mit dem Lied „Burschen heraus"
3. Rede des Ältesten der Deutschen Studentenschaft Kurt Ellersiek
4. Verbrennung volkszersetzender Bücher und Zeitschriften
5. Gemeinsamer Gesang der Lieder:
   „Der Gott, der Eisen wachsen ließ"
   „Deutschland Deutschland über alles"
   „Die Fahne hoch, die Reihen dicht geschlossen"

42

TYPOGRAPHY AND NATIONAL SOCIALISM

The visual representations of the Third Reich are both contradictory and consistent, and the phrase that can be used to describe both the era and the existence of National Socialism, in terms of design, is 'reactionary modernity': a modernity behind natural stone facades, a constant contradiction between a real and a predetermined goal, between form and content, between claim and implementation.[17] This can also be observed in its use of type. Just as architecture made use of historical references, with the construction of 'medieval castles' and neo-classical structures, alongside the highly functional industrial buildings in the style of the Bauhaus, typography used a mix of black letter fonts, Antiqua and sans serif types.

A distinction must, however, be made between the years leading up to 1933 and the 12 years of Nazi dominance. At first, the NSDAP made attempts to appear grounded and close to the people, which often gave rise to crude, 'wooden' designs using various kinds of Fraktur and Schwabacher types (which were also used by the other parties). However, examples of the use of sans serif types can also be found. With varying degrees of success, typesetters and graphic designers in the Third Reich played freely with the entire range of types. While

the poster for the 'Great German Art Exhibition', for example, was set in a gold, upper-case and centred Antiqua, lettering for a regional sports event might use black letter type. Similarly, the 'value' of the product often determined the care with which the type or types were chosen and applied.

Since it is not possible (and perhaps not even desirable) truly to monitor design against the use of ideologically suitable text – much of which also lacks professional competence – it is impossible to establish a consistent connection with the use of particular types. Design quality and choice of typeface were ultimately dependent on local officials and institutions – their demands, their abilities and their agenda, in addition to the technical possibilities. Naturally, though, an effort was generally made to appear 'German' and 'of the people', which is why black letter types played an important role until the 'type decree' of 1941.[18] The 'great achievements of German culture' were considered to be more appropriately represented by an Antiqua – or a sans serif, even if magazines such as *Betonstraßenbau* and *Die Straße* were considered representative of current technical standards and progress.

This was probably more of an emotional than a rational approach to type, which at that time was determined by the work in question:[19] If a winter relief poster was supposed to appeal strongly to the people, Antiqua capitals were simply not appropriate, since they were considered to be somewhat elitist at that time. Black letter types were absent in almost all international media and applications. For example, no black letter type was used in the context of the 1936 Olympic Games in Berlin. The same applied to recruitment posters in the Netherlands and Denmark. The different target audiences among the German reading public also played an important role in the choice of type. For example, the difference in terms of typographic style and design between the *Völkischer Beobachter* and the weekly periodical *Das Reich* was similar to that between *Bild* and *Die Zeit* today.

To grasp design (among other things) in the Third Reich, it is worth examining the magazine *Gebrauchsgraphik*, which was undoubtedly the most important vehicle of the industry at that time. One thing immediately catches the eye: it uses Futura[20] – despite the destiny of its author. In fact, Paul Renner's famous typeface (and other sans serif types) began to appear more frequently, demonstrating their modernity and power in instances where they were used to replace an older type as part of a design revision. That Futura's potential was tested in type combinations for the Waffen-SS is a bitter irony. Its 'self-evident, noble figure, free from any influence of fashionable form, and whose crystal-clear purity is always pleasant and fresh to the eye,' could, as the examples show, also be used for negative purposes.[21]

Futura was promoted from Frankfurt by the Bauer Type Foundry in almost every issue of *Gebrauchsgraphik*, often with advertisements covering an entire page, although interestingly – and certainly not coincidentally – without naming its author (the foundry did not otherwise hesitate to exploit famous names). There is one exception: the comprehensive announcement of Renner's 65th birthday, which at first glance does not appear to be an advertisement, and which presents in a preceding editorial piece what are presumably the most conservative works of his output.[22] Even those who rejected 'Bolshevik design', Constructivism and contemporary modernism could not escape Renner (who was driven from his professional post as quickly as possible in 1933) or his Futura. This remains just as true today, as Renner's most famous type, acting in his stead, continues to outlive all people and all things.

Motto:
**MILLIONEN
STEHEN
HINTER MIR!**

Kleiner Mann bittet um große Gaben

Futura Medium oblique lower-case l

Futura Medium lower-case l and upper-case i
The lower-case l on the left overshoots the
upper-case i

1

Thomas Mann, cit. in *Die zwanziger Jahre in München* (Schriften des Münchner Stadtmuseums 8), commissioned by the Munich City Museum and ed. Christoph Stölzl, Munich 1979, p. xiv.

2

Günter Hockerts: 'Warum München? Wie Bayerns Metropole die "Hauptstadt der Bewegung" wurde'. In: *München und der Nationalsozialismus*. Catalogue of the Munich Documentation Centre for the History of National Socialism, ed. Winfried Nerdinger, Munich 2015, p. 387.

3

Paul Renner: date not specified (examination of the current status of graphic design). In: *Gebrauchsgraphik* (Berlin), vol. 10, January 1933, no. 1, p. 34.

4

Cf. Paul Renner: *Kulturbolschewismus?* Photomechanical reprint of the first edition of 1932 from Eugen Rentsch Verlag, Erlenbach-Zurich, Munich and Leipzig, ed. and with commentary by Roland Reuss and Peter Staengle. Frankfurt am Main/Basel: Stromfeld 2003, pp. 10–19.

5

Ibid, p. 9.

6

Cited by Klaus Schumann: 'Kommunalpolitik in München zwischen 1918 und 1933'. In: *Die zwanziger Jahre in München*, p. 15.

7

Philipp Luidl: 'München – Mekka der schwarzen Kunst'. In: *Die zwanziger Jahre in München*, p. 195.

8

Jan Tschichold: *Die Neue Typographie: ein Handbuch für zeitgemäss Schaffende*, Berlin 1928, p. 75.

9

Ibid, p. 76.

10

Paul Renner: *Mechanisierte Grafik: Schrift, Typo, Foto, Film, Farbe*, Berlin 1931, p. 71; and 'Gegen den Schematismus in der Typografie'. In: *Klimschs Jahrbuch* (Frankfurt am Main), 1933, p. 25.

11

Paul Renner: 'Drei Jahre Futura'. In: *Type specimen Futura: die Ergänzungsgarnituren*. Frankfurt am Main 1930/31.

12

The present book also uses the book weight for its running text, in addition to Futura Light.

13

Christopher Burke: *Paul Renner: The Art of Typography*, London 1998, p. 163.

14

Ibid. The list of payments on acount of over 500 Reichsmarks includes additional cuts of Renner-Antiqua, a Carus-Antiqua and Hapag.

15

The war and Renner's health problems, including a stroke in 1948, were partly the cause of the delay.

16

Robert Bringhurst: *The Solid Form of Language: An Essay on Writing and Meaning*, Kentville, Nova Scotia, 2004, p. 25.

17

Cf. Peter Reichel: *Der schöne Schein des Dritten Reiches – Faszination und Gewalt des Faschismus*. 3rd ed., Munich/Vienna 1991, p. 101 et seq.

18

This decree forbade the use of black letter scripts – they were referred to as 'Jewish letters' and were to be replaced by 'normal German lettering' (Antiqua). The background, however, was different, with a view to the 'final victory' and an advance into the east. While the intention was to switch to a type that would be legible anywhere, the progression of the war meant that this initiative, as well as others, quickly became obsolete.

19

Cf. Andreas Koop: *Die Macht der Schrift. Eine angewandte Designforschung*, Sulgen/Zurich 2012, pp. 240–41.

20

From 1930 and until long after World War II; superseded only in 1962 by Helvetica.

21

Advertisement in *Gebrauchsgraphik*, no. 9, 1933 (unpag. front part).

22

Book 5, 1943. PP. 9–16 in a paginated editorial section and clearly a 'regular' article; it is followed by a 12-page insert (in the same format but on different paper) with three articles by Renner that generally date back before 1933. The 'Beilage' (supplements) were ordered by the Mergenthaler Setzmaschinen-Fabrik GmbH in Berlin and set in Linotype-Renner-Antiqua.

VIENNA

After World War I and the collapse
of the Austro-Hungarian Empire, administration of the once brilliant capital city of
the Habsburg dual monarchy transferred
to the Social Democratic Party, leading
to the nickname 'Red Vienna'. The city's
housing shortages were addressed with a
series of affordable-housing projects. These
involved the construction of cheap, simply
equipped dwellings whose residents would
share communal facilities such as laundries,
baths, kindergartens and playgrounds.
The best-known residential complex was
the Karl-Marx-Hof, built between 1926
and 1930, which also made a political
statement with its red facade. In addition
to the usual shared services, social and
medical facilities, business premises, meeting rooms and a library were provided.

Worker emancipation and a neutral
exchange of information were the focus of

educational reforms, as was the case at the Gesellschafts- und Wirtschaftsmuseum (Museum of Society and Economy) in Vienna, founded in 1925. Its director, Otto Neurath, had set himself the task of enabling labourers to hold informed opinions. For the museum, he developed large viewing panels that displayed social information using standardized graphic symbols and specially chosen colours: each symbol indicated a certain quantity, and was repeated as required to indicate a total quantity. Replacing words, letters and numbers with symbols was an attempt to test a new form of communication – one that would convey information simply and quickly, without language barriers and, if possible, free from cultural connotations.

PE

CHRISTOPHER BURKE

OTTO NEURATH AND THE VIENNA METHOD OF PICTORIAL STATISTICS (ISOTYPE)

Otto Neurath was a polymath whose life's work encompassed political economy, sociology, philosophy, urbanism and visual communication. He was the leading figure in the work that is now most commonly termed 'Isotype' – an acronym for International System of Typographic Picture Education. Isotype was initially known as the Vienna Method of Pictorial Statistics (Wiener Methode der Bildstatistik), having been developed at the Gesellschafts- und Wirtschaftsmuseum (Museum of Society and Economy) in Vienna, which opened in 1925 under Neurath's direction. The museum's work in visual education formed part of the cultural programme of the socialist municipality of Vienna during the First Austrian Republic. Workers' education was the starting point for the museum, but the Vienna Method had an inherent potential for wider application and an international scope. The name Isotype was adopted in about 1935, after Neurath and his closest collaborators were forced to flee Vienna, initially re-establishing themselves in the Netherlands.

Isotype was a method for assembling, configuring and disseminating information and statistics through pictorial means. Neurath described it as a 'language-like technique', characterized by consistency in the use of graphic elements. The basic elements are pictograms – simplified pictures of people or things, designed to function as repeatable units – but a verbal element was almost always essential to Isotype charts for contextualization and explanation. In the early years of the Vienna Method, both pictures and lettering were drawn by hand. The principal objective of the method was educational, and its creators did not set out to practise graphic design per se, yet both Neurath and his principal collaborator (and later wife), Marie Reidemeister, possessed acute visual sensitivity, and were not satisfied until the visual qualities of Isotype had acquired a graphic modularity and powerful simplicity.

Part of this process of maturation was the employment of Futura, typeset in-house at the Vienna museum, for all verbal content on charts. Neurath likened the simplicity of Futura to the clarity he required of pictograms (which he begins by referring to here as 'signs'): 'The individual signs should be easily understood, quickly recognized and strongly differentiated from each other. This can sometimes be achieved by signs drawn in a complicated way, as shown with the Fraktur script, the individual letters of which are occasionally more characteristic than those of roman. But in the interest of teaching it is advisable to use both signs and letterforms that are easy to reproduce, like sans serif types (Renner's Futura, etc.), the legibility of which in accompanying text could possibly be disputed. Optically, they also best suit the quantity-pictures in the Vienna Method, which is why they are used for the inscriptions on them.'[1]

1

Use of Futura in *Gesellschaft und Wirtschaft* (Society and Economy), a portfolio of pictorial statistics by the Gesellschafts- und Wirtschaftsmuseum in Vienna, consisting of individually printed multicoloured sheets that communicate complex information with the aid of a standardized visual language: cover page, 1930.

GESELLSCHAFT
und WIRTSCHAFT

 farbige Tafeln
Bildstatistisches Elementarwerk
des Gesellschafts- und Wirtschaftsmuseums in Wien

PRODUKTIONSFORMEN
GESELLSCHAFTSORDNUNGEN
KULTURSTUFEN
LEBENSHALTUNGEN

1 Verlag des Bibliographischen Instituts AG. in Leipzig

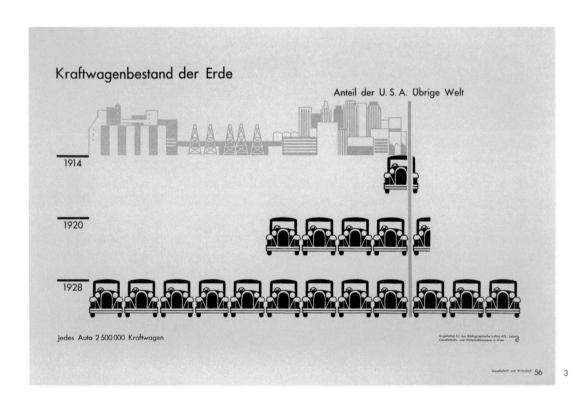

Herrn Professor R e n n e r
Direktor der Fachschule für
Typographie M ü n c h e n

Internationales Archiv für bildhafte Pädagogik
Ausstellungsinstitut   Orbis - Produktion

Wien XIV. Ullmannstrasse 44
Telefon: R 35-4-68 Telegramm: Mundaneum Wien

| Ihr Zeichen Votre référence Your reference | Ihre Nachricht vom Votre lettre du Your letter of | Unser Zeichen Notre référence N/Jä Our reference | Datum Date 5.8.1931. |

Lieber Herr Professor !

Das Deutsche Museum, Baubüro für das Studiengebäude
sendet uns folgendes Schreiben :

Auf der Deutschen Bauausstellung in Berlin haben wir
den vorbildlichen österreichischen Pavillon mit den von Ihnen
ausgeführten statistischen Darstellungen besichtigt.

Wir sind gerade mit der Beschriftung der Bibliotheks-
räume des Deutschen Museums beschäftigt und wären Ihnen sehr
dankbar, wenn Sie uns Muster in verschiedenen Größen von der
Schrift zukommen ließen, die Sie bei dem in Berlin gezeigten
Ausstellungsmaterial verwendet haben.

Aus Wien will man Münchner Schrift ! Wir haben mit-
folgende Antwort geschrieben :

Sehr geehrte Herrn !

Es freut uns sehr, dass Sie unsere Schriftwahl so
günstig beurteilen. Wir verwenden nur gesetzte Schrift. Es ist
die Type Futura Ihres nächsten Nachbarn Professor Renner, München, mit dem Sie sich vielleicht am besten unmittelbar in Ver-
bindung setzen.

Wir benützen die Gelegenheit gerne Ihnen einiges von
uns und über uns zu übersenden, vielleicht ergibt sich einmal

4

2-3

'Mächte der Erde'/'Kraftwagenbestand der
Erde' (Labour Force/Number of Cars on
Earth), *Gesellschaft und Wirtschaft*, 1930.

4

Letter from Otto Neurath to Paul Renner,
5 August 1931.

CHRISTOPHER BURKE

GERD ARNTZ

As Neurath had suggested, Renner's attempt to reduce roman letters to their geometrical foundations was akin to the efforts made in Vienna to design simplified pictograms depicting people, animals and objects – especially after Gerd Arntz was appointed chief artist at the museum. Arntz, a German artist specializing in woodcut prints, was the third key member of the museum team. He went to work there in September 1928, around the time that Futura began to be used in Isotype work. The museum acquired the typeface soon after its release, but it seems that Arntz was not directly responsible for this; he recalled that the Futura metal type had been delivered to the museum by the time of his arrival, but that the fonts had not yet been unpacked.[2]

Arntz was aware of the New Typography (his work was featured in Jan Tschichold's book on the subject), and he later claimed to have followed its principles in combining pictures with text. Indeed, from this point onwards, Isotype charts generally exhibit a relaxed asymmetrical layout, with type ranged left, as the statistical pictograms often were.

Arntz's great skill in pictogram design was his ability to produce modular picture units that could be repeated in sequence along a line – like characters of a picture script – without making them excessively rationalized or geometric. For example, his pictograms for different kinds of people are recognizable human silhouettes. The apparent simplicity of the images belies the great subtlety of his drawings. In this sense Arntz's pictograms are analogous to Futura, for which Renner and his colleagues at Bauer also moderated pure geometry with subtle compensations so that the typeface would appear geometric to the observer.

The Isotype pictograms for 'man' and 'woman' are marked by a lesser degree of schematization than their successors used on public signs, such as the ubiquitous DOT pictograms found on most toilet doors. Ellen Lupton suggested that the DOT male pictogram could be called 'Helvetica man', likening it to Swiss typography. By extension, perhaps, the generic Isotype pictogram for 'Man' could be labelled 'Futura man'.

5
'Mann' (Man), page from *Isotype Bilder Wörterbuch* (Isotype Picture Dictionary), a collection of pictogram templates.

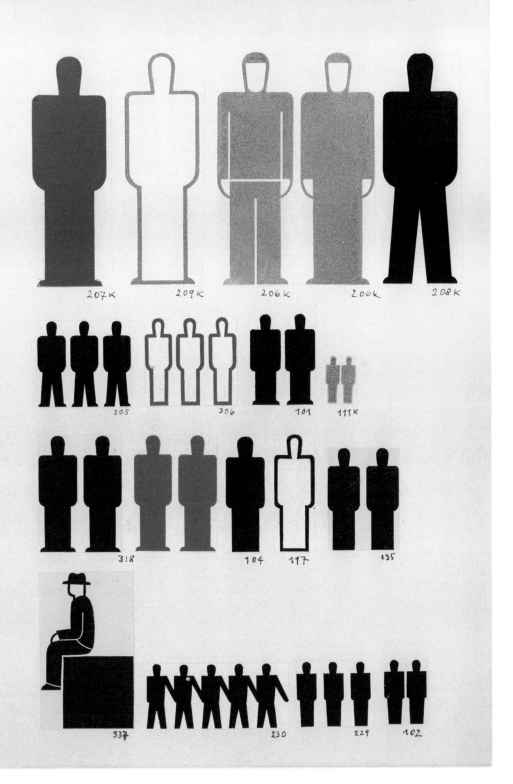

207 K 209 K 206 K 206 K 208 K

305 306 101 111 k

318 104 117 135

337 230 229 102

GERD ARNTZ

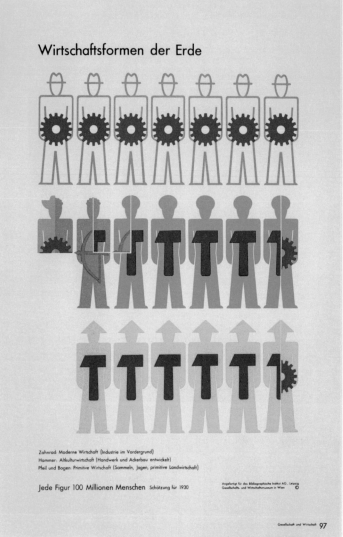

6

'Wirtschaftsformen der Erde' (Economic forms of the Earth), from the portfolio *Gesellschaft und Wirtschaft* (Society and Economy), 1930.

7

'Gesellschaftsgliederung in Wien' (Demographics of Vienna), from *Gesellschaft und Wirtschaft*, 1930.

8

P.260 – 'Arbeitslose' (Unemployed), from *Gesellschaft und Wirtschaft*, 1930.

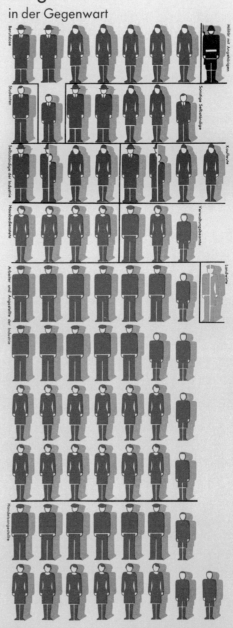

Gesellschaftsgliederung in Wien

um 1700   in der Gegenwart

Jede Figur 2500 Menschen   Jede Figur mit Grau 25 000 Menschen

Angefertigt für das Bibliographische Institut AG., Leipzig
Gesellschafts- und Wirtschaftsmuseum in Wien

7

259 GERD ARNTZ

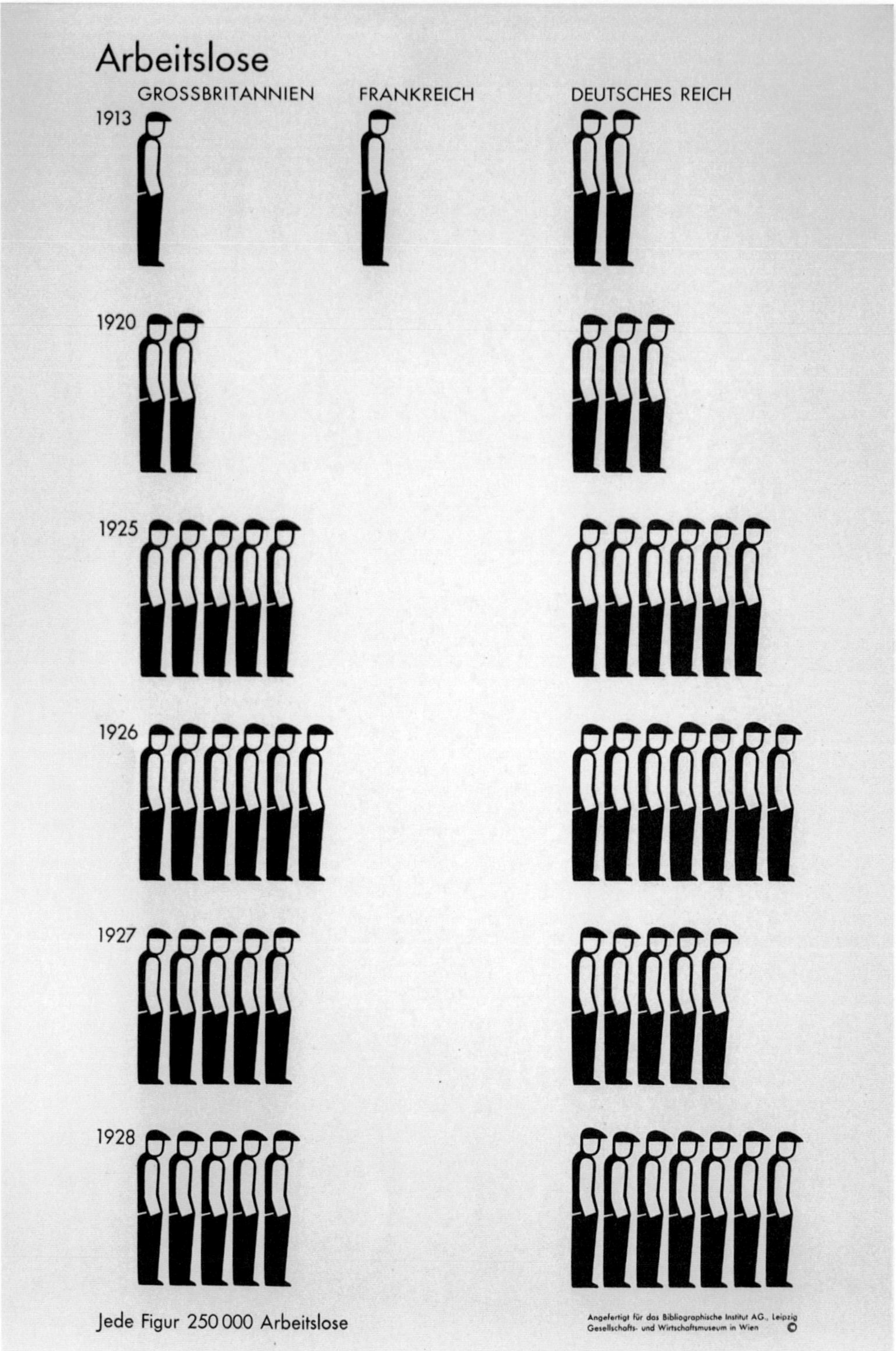

Arbeitslose

GROSSBRITANNIEN   FRANKREICH   DEUTSCHES REICH

1913

1920

1925

1926

1927

1928

Jede Figur 250 000 Arbeitslose

Angefertigt für das Bibliographische Institut AG., Leipzig
Gesellschafts- und Wirtschaftsmuseum in Wien ©

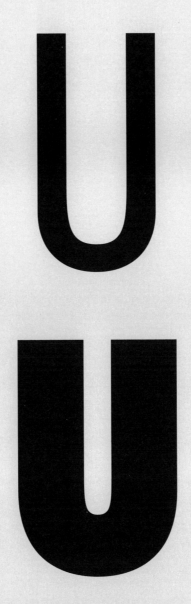

1

Otto Neurath: 'Bildstatistik nach Wiener Methode in der Schule' (1933). In: *Otto Neurath. Gesammelte Bildpädagogische Schriften*, ed. Rudolf Haller and Robin Kinross. Vienna 1991, pp. 282–83.

2

Robin Kinross: 'The Graphic Formation of Isotype'. In: Christopher Burke, Eric Kindel, Sue Walker: *Isotype: Design and Contexts, 1925–1971*. London 2013, p. 134.

PRAGUE

The use of Futura in what became the Republic of Czechoslovakia after World War I was not only closely linked to the avant-garde movement in that country, but also heavily influenced by the use of sans serifs in twentieth-century Czech typography. Futura's story demonstrates how a typeface can reflect the spirit of its times, not only through its appearance, but also in the political and social circumstances of its use.

In the early 1920s those working in Czech avant-garde artistic circles were eager for a modern type that could express the qualities of the machine age. In particular, young Czech architects sought an appropriate typeface for their publications, which had almost always been printed in a bold sans serif from the nineteenth century.[1] During the 1920s, avant-garde books, magazines and posters were forced to improvise when it came to typefaces, often depending on the meagre offerings of the Czech printing houses, which in turn relied on imports from the German foundries. Some artists and writers chose to construct sans serif headlines themselves – the prominent avant-garde writer and artist Karel Teige, for example, adapted Bayer's Universal for his own use.

In the second half of the 1920s professionals in the printing industry – printers, typesetters and others, who belonged to the well-organized Typografia labour union – published an influential monthly magazine (*Typografia*), in which Constructivism and the use of sans serifs were widely discussed in the didactic texts of Jan Tschichold, Teige and others. Their rational arguments gained much support among young printers and typesetters, who felt that the geometric simplicity, economy and scientific (psychotechnic) properties of sans serifs reflected the zeitgeist. Sans serifs had become part of a new universal style, sought since the art nouveau period.

This new generation of typesetters, printers and typographers embraced sans serifs with enthusiasm. But there was resistance among the older members of the industry, who rejected the notion that the typeface of the new era should be impersonal, de-nationalized, international, universal. Some in the printing industry felt that, following the creation of the Republic of Czechoslovakia in 1918, it was time to develop a national typography based on Slavic roots. The older generation's mistrust was also fuelled by the political context of sans serifs, linked as they were to a leftist/socialist vision of social transformation, including the abolition of social classes and private property. The most prominent Czech foundry (Česká slévárna písem v Praze) eventually released two different sans serifs, Patrona and Bold Empiriana.

Their character was more decorative than Constructivist, and they were used widely in advertising and commercial printing.

When Gill Sans was released in 1928, its use was widespread in Czechoslovakia, appearing not only in prints by avant-garde designers, but also in large works created by typesetters working in printing houses. During the 1930s, sans serifs dominated in all kinds of headline – in the advertising industry, and for book and magazine covers. Gill Sans and other sans serifs, whether Czech or imported from Germany (Kabel, by Rudolf Koch, was particularly popular), were recognized as a basic element of a new visual style.

IK

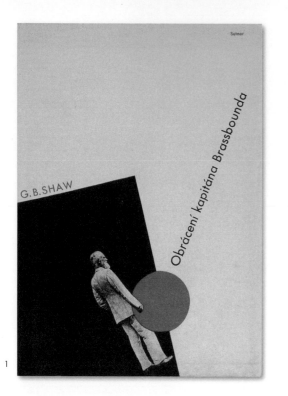

IVA KNOBLOCH

SEARCHING FOR THE TYPEFACE OF OUR TIME

Futura, released in the 1930s, was used mostly by Czech designers and architects who were part of the wider European modernist community, whose work bore close relation to that being produced in Germany at the time. This typeface was seen as a ray of light coming from the great German lighthouses of Constructivism and functionalism. In comparison with Gill Sans, Futura, with its simplified, more geometric shapes (**a**, **t**, **g**), was considered better suited to being read at speed – that key component of all things modern – and the expanding adoption of Futura over the coming years would constitute a kind of manifesto in itself. For a deeper understanding of this, it is worth focusing on a few key designers and their particular use of the typeface: Ladislav Sutnar, František Muzika, Zdeněk Rossmann and František Kalivoda.

At the time of Futura's release, Sutnar was one of the country's leading modernist designers, and a key modernizing force in design and printed communication. He was the art director of DP (Družstevní práce), one of Prague's main publishing companies, and its modern design studio, Krásná jizba (Beautiful Chamber); he was also soon to become the director of Prague's state college of graphic arts. Sutnar's work embraced several disciplines – graphic design, textiles, toys,

and product and exhibition design – and his writing, organizing and networking activities introduced a Bauhaus-inspired influence on both the operations of the Czech Werkbund (Svaz československého díla) and the contemporary Czech lifestyle in general. At the end of the 1920s, Sutnar constructed his own sans serif, based on a geometric grid, for the creation of two logos: his famous 'dp' (for the publishing house of that name), and 'baba' (created for the Baba functionalist housing estate built by the Czech Werkbund, inspired by a similar estate in Stuttgart).

It seems that Sutnar used Futura for the first time for the poster of an exhibition of Czech applied art in Stockholm in 1931. According to him, he designed it in haste in the Stockholm printing house itself, having

just arrived there by train from Prague – circumstances that could explain the apparent subconscious influence on it of a poster by Jan Tschichold.[2] This direct Tschicholdian inspiration would occur a few more times in Sutnar's poster design work. In the 1930s appropriation of Tschichold's works was not seen as a violation of copyright, but as a contribution to the expansion of this new

6

7

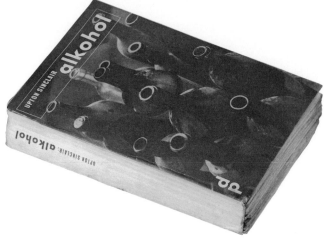

8

1–4

P.270 – Ladislav Sutnar: book covers for George Bernard Shaw, 1930–33.

1

Obrácení kapitána Brassbounda.
Prague: Družstevní práce, 1932.

2

Člověk nikdy neví.
Prague: Družstevní práce, 1931.

3

Trakař jablek.
Prague: Družstevní práce, 1932.

4

Drobnosti: Výstřižky z novin, Prohlédnutí Blanco Posneta.
Prague: Družstevní práce, 1933.

5

P.271 – Ladislav Sutnar: poster for an exhibition of Czech applied art in Stockholm, 1931.

6

Ladislav Sutnar: book cover for Upton Sinclair's *Pout lásky*, 1930 and 1932. Logo design 'dp'.

7

Ladislav Sutnar: book cover for Upton Sinclair's *Utajované zlo* (Classified Evil). Prague: Družstevní práce, 1931.

8

Ladislav Sutnar: book design for Upton Sinclair's *Alkohol. Román.* (The Wet Parade. A novel). Prague: Družstevní práce, 1933.

9–10

Ladislav Sutnar: book design and chapter separation pages for Tilschová-Úlehlová's *Jak a čím se živit* (How and What to Eat). Prague: Družstevní práce, 1935.

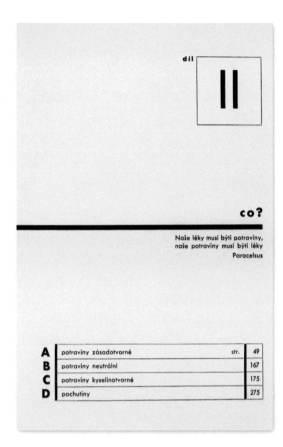

díl **II**

co?

Naše léky musí býti potraviny,
naše potraviny musí býti léky
Paracelsus

A	potraviny zásadotvorné	str.	49
B	potraviny neutrální		167
C	potraviny kyselinotvorné		175
D	pochutiny		275

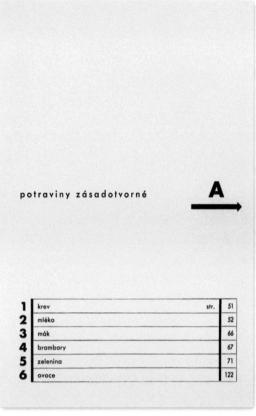

potraviny zásadotvorné **A** →

1	krev	str.	51
2	mléko		52
3	mák		66
4	brambory		67
5	zelenina		71
6	ovoce		122

9

10

visual language. On this poster, Sutnar used Futura in lower case; the words in Swedish stress Futura's characteristic **t** and round **o**, and its geometric organization in space. The colour scheme, which demonstrates Futura Bold in positive and in negative on an orange background, contributes to the eye-catching effect and the purpose of Futura: speedy legibility.

For book design, Sutnar preferred Gill Sans, but his use of Futura in this field was still highly distinctive. In the early 1930s he used it for a series of books by George Bernard Shaw. The title line intersects with the 'G. B. Shaw' and the photography in odd and unexpected positions, with the photography remaining the centre of attention – which was why Sutnar chose not to use Futura in bold. In other book series, such as for a number of titles by Upton Sinclair, Sutnar used Futura in bold and lower case in the frame. Typography and photography are used here to create one communication unit – a 'typofoto'.

Sutnar's sophisticated approach to the Futura typeface is demonstrated well by a healthy-eating guide from 1935, *Jak a čím se živit* (How and What to Eat) by Tilschová-Úlehlová. That same year, Sutnar answered a survey about cover design: for him, a book's cover was the same as a facade for an architect, reflecting the principles of a house's ground plan. In the same way, a cover should reflect the structure of its book. Designing a book is a structural project in which all the meaningful elements are coordinated and integrated in a visual flow. In the healthy-eating guide, Futura is used for the title on the cover and on the chapter separation pages, where the structure of each chapter is signalled. In this particular book, Futura serves as a mean's of transmitting key information, and was selected for its precision and clarity. Futura thus becomes an important means of organizing information and defining its structure, thereby communicating the most relevant content.

Zdeněk Rossmann was one of the most radical of the leftist Czech avant-gardists, a frequenter of the Bauhaus, from where he was eventually dismissed because of his communist activism.[3] He presented himself as an architect, but he understood his true mission to be the transformation of society, using his talents in the fields of stage, exhibition and graphic design. As a 22-year-old student he used a sans serif in lower case for the complete design of the *almanach fronta* (1927). The use of a sans serif was in itself a manifesto of socialist international universalism: austere, ascetic and highly 'scientific'.

After returning from the Bauhaus, Rossmann became a teacher of advertising and typography at the Škola umeleckych remesiel (School of Craft), a highly progressive educational institution in Bratislava – today the capital of Slovakia – not far from Vienna. The management and teachers were young and, thanks to the programme designed by the modernist thinker and pedagogue Josef Vydra, the college was known as the 'little Bauhaus', or 'School of the New Vision'. Rossmann's dynamic contribution to the college was fundamental, and today he is recognized as the key player in the modernization of Slovak interwar graphic design. In the 1930s Rossmann entered into a close correspondence with Tschichold, who became his mentor regarding methods of teaching.

Rossmann introduced Tschichold's rules concerning teaching practices into the Czech pedagogy of typography. Tschichold's *Typografische Entwurfstechnik* inspired Rossmann to produce his own book of *Entwerfen, Druck/Design* (Print Designs), a collection published in 1936. In it Rossmann writes, in text set in Futura, that typographic construction should be technically perfect, pure, clear and precise, and should lessen fatigue: 'The aim of the typography is to inform through type in the fastest and most economical way.'[4]

This premise explains how Futura, exclusively in lower case, came to be Rossmann's most favoured type during the 1930s. He used it for the School of Craft's visual identity and all of its printed communications, as well as for his own business

11

12

11
Zdeněk Rossmann: *Písmo a fotografie v reklamě* (Type and Photography in Advertising). Bratislava: Index Olomouc, 1938.

12
Jan Tschichold: *Thesis, Antithesis, Synthesis*: exhibition catalogue for the Lucerne Art Museum, 1935.

card. It also appeared on his poster design for the first exhibition on wood construction in the building industry, 'Výstava byvania v dreve', in 1932. Futura was also present in his educational exhibition design, and in the experimental children's book *Kapka vody* (Drop of Water; 1935), in which the text is followed by photomontages, rebuses, icons and typographic symbols. This book might well be categorized among the illustrated works that provoked a new perceptual sensitivity at the time, inspired by the visual vernacular of modern metropolitan culture.

13

Another pedagogic memento by Rossmann appears in his book *Písmo a fotografie v reklamě* (Type and Photography in Advertising; 1938): Futura, he argues, ranks first among the sans serifs that may be employed for advertising. According to psychological tests, typefaces constructed on a basis of lines and circles are the most legible. Furthermore, Futura's long-stemmed **d**, **k**, **l** and **f** mean that while reading, the upper parts of these letters stand out more clearly. Advertising aims to inform rationally, and so Rossmann, in his recommendation of the use of Futura, also stressed its lack of sentimentality, in addition to its technicality and economy. The text is followed by a

very important pictorial section, in which he presents different disciplines of advertising, including exhibition design. In the examples given of other European avant-garde modernist typographers, we predominantly see Futura. The exhibition catalogue by Tschichold for the Kunstmuseum Luzern in Lucerne, in particular, reveals Futura to be an extraordinarily well-balanced type. Futura was, for Zdeněk Rossmann, a truly modern type, and he used it as a manifesto of modernization – a progressive utopia of being and becoming modern.

The architect František Kalivoda is not widely known. He was an active member of the Brno avant-garde, working across various media, with a specific focus on experimental cinema as the leader of the film and photography section of the Czech Left Front, a 1930s leftist organization of artists and architects. He used Futura for his ambitious magazine projects *Ekran* and *Telehor*, published as an international platform for an international audience. Neither project was ever fully achieved – only their first issues appeared – but both publications rank among the most interesting European avant-garde magazines covering experimental film and photography. Kalivoda was not only their publisher and editor, but also their graphic designer.

The stated purpose of *Ekran*, issued in 1934, was to support new cinema against the threat of the film industry, while that of *Telehor*, a 'magazine for visual culture', was to develop the interrelationship of art, photography, film and light experiments. Its sole issue appeared in 1936 and focused exclusively on the work of László Moholy-Nagy, with an introduction by

Siegfried Giedion. Kalivoda used Futura in lower case throughout both publications, for titles and body text. Phrases were divided by blank space, an effect that is optically very disturbing and was criticized even at the time. But typography was not itself of primary interest to Kalivoda, and his opinion was shared by Moholy-Nagy. Typography's function was redefined: not legibility nor speed nor economy, but a means to 'free vision'. Through his promotional leaflets for *Ekran*, Kalivoda challenged people to develop a new sensitivity to multimedia in terms of how they communicated and interacted with each other. His language, rich in pathos, recalls the words of Le Corbusier in *Vers une architecture nouvelle*, but it also tackles the new obstacle of the cynical forces of capitalism

15

14

13
Zdeněk Rossmann/J. V. Pleva: experimental children's book *Kapka vody* (Drop of Water). Bratislava: Index Olomouc, 1935.

14
Ekran no. 1, magazine on the art of cinema, 1934. Editor and designer: František Kalivoda.

15
Special issue of the Czech magazine in four languages *Telehor 1-2*, by and about László Moholy-Nagy, 1936. Editor and designer: František Kalivoda; title design based on the work of Moholy-Nagy.

inhibiting freedom and the progression of spirituality and visual culture.[5]

Futura seemed to be the typeface best suited to this mission. Its geometric design, simplicity, lightness and rhythmic qualities through blank space suggested a similarity between typesetting and the techniques of film editing. Typography itself was not in question, but rather the intermediality of light, photography, film, art and, finally, type.[6]

František Muzika, a painter and graphic designer, belonged to Prague's avant-garde circles. His activities centred on literature and stage design, and, as the art director of the publishing house Aventinum, he tried to harmonize modern fine art and literature. His concept of book design was based on new typographic principles, but his personal inclination in 1920s and 1930s was towards classic harmony. He used Futura in titles as a painter, and carefully composed its pure and geometric shapes not only as an optical, but also as a plastic element. He was seduced by the pure circle of the **O**, which he used with playfulness – as a sign, circle or abstract element flying in a photographic landscape. In his Futura-based book covers from the late 1930s we can already see his deep typographical sensitivity and the seeds of his later interest in the plastic beauty of the typeface.

16

František Muzika: cover for Karel Čapek, *Hordubal*. Prague: Fr. Borovy, 1935.

FUTURA'S TIME COMES TO AN END

The political situation in 1930s Germany provoked a wave of nationalism in Czechoslovakia. Slavic decor was again promoted in the fashion and textile industry, for example. And in typography, the movement against imported German typefaces in the professional community grew stronger, with many voices calling for home-grown Czech typefaces, and expressing enthusiasm for the typographic innovations coming from the Soviet Union.[7]

In 1939 an issue of *Typografia* magazine was devoted to sans serif types[8]. The large-scale use of sans serifs was seen as the era's biggest revolution in typography, but its domination was declared over by many writers. The cherished quality of speedy legibility held by Futura and other sans serifs was now sharply criticized as an illusion, specifically in blocks of text. Professionals advocated the return of roman types, particularly in book typesetting, and the use of sans serifs was recommended only in combination with other typefaces.

THE POSTWAR RECEPTION

Discussion of the rules for the New Typography and the status of sans serif types continued in the Czech professional community after World War II. Tschichold's conversion to classicism was seen by some as a kind of intersection, criticized by leftist designers, but acclaimed by most professionals, who directed sharp criticism at the interwar years' cult of the sans serif and its overuse.[9]

It was the interwar avant-gardist Muzika who was the first to make an intensive study of historical typefaces, and whose own designs followed Tschichold's classicism. Muzika held an influential position in the world of post-war typography as head of the type studio at the Academy of Art, Design and Architecture in Prague, the most important design school in Czechoslovakia. He imparted to his students his passion for type and its history, and created a precedent of historical sensitivity in the study of typefaces that lives on today. In 1958 he published a monumental two-volume publication, *Krásné písmo v historii latinky* (Beautiful Type in the History of Latin Script), which was translated into German as *Die schöne Schrift* in 1965. This historical overview, with its rich and perfectly printed pictorial material, still ranks among the most important works written on typography to this day.

Krásné písmo v historii latinky was published at a time when ideological demagogy and indoctrination remained strong. The hostility of official political culture to interwar avant-garde works, interpreted as bourgeois formalism, still prevailed, so Muzika looked carefully for arguments explaining the historical contributions of Constructivism and functionalism. His reasoning was based on the fact that the most progressive ideas after World War I had come from the Soviet Union. This strategic introduction (to satisfy the censors) allowed him to analyse the Futura typeface carefully. He appreciated it more than Gill Sans and other sans serifs of the period for its balance, namely in the letters **M**, **a** and **g**, but he stressed also the disharmony of the **u**. Muzika's monumental publication finishes with a polemic on Renner's idea that sans serifs respond to the zeitgeist of the modern era. Muzika did not see Futura as the right choice for typesetting books.

This opinion was not shared by Oldřich Hlavsa, another influential

Czech typographer whose three volumes, *Typographia 1-3*, published in the 1970s and 1980s, resonated not only in Czechoslovakia but also in the West, and became a standard reference work for the use of modern type. Hlavsa saw the typeface as a medium for optical experimentation and preferred less monoline, more idiosyncratic types. He appreciated Futura as one of the modern neutral types: good for the typesetting of books, much like Helvetica or Univers, which he himself preferred.

An epilogue: a recently published book about Rossmann[10] – one of the pioneers of the use of Futura in the 1930s – is set in Zirkel, which resembles Futura, having also been constructed on a geometric basis, although it contains optical improvements that contribute to better legibility. The legacy of Futura is still very much alive.

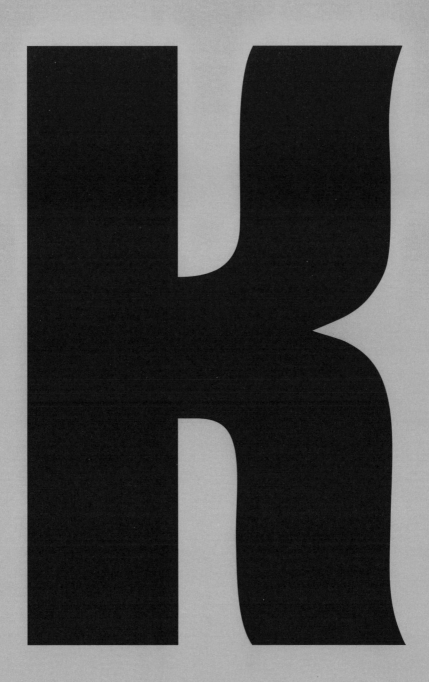

K, Futura Display.

1

Cf. the magazine *Život*, one of the editors
of which was the architect Jaromír Krejcar.

2

Iva Knobloch (ed.): *Mental Vitamins:
Sutnar in Texts*. Catalogue of the Prague
Museum of Decorative Arts. Prague 2010,
p. 180.

3

Cf. Susanne Anna (ed.): *Das Bauhaus
im Osten: Slowakische und tschechische
Avantgarde 1928–1939*. Catalogue of
the Bauhaus Dessau Foundation et al.
Ostfildern-Ruit 1997.

4

Zdeněk Rossmann: *Typography Designs*.
Prague 1936, page not specified.

5

Zuzana Marhoulová: 'František Kalivoda
as Film Critic and Editor'. In: *Studia minora
Faculatatis Philosophicae Universitatis
Brunensis* (Brno), no. 2, 2005, p. 138.

6

Cf. the texts of František Kalivoda in the
advertising brochure for the magazine
Ekran in 1934: *We are looking for new
ways, we are working for freedom of your
eyes.*

7

Cf. the magazines *Dorost Knihtiskařský*
and *Typografia*, vols. 1935 and 1936.

8

Cf. *Typografia* (Prague), 1939, no. 11.

9

Jindra Vichnar: 'Au Revoir the New
Typography'. In: *Typografia* (Prague),
XLIX, 1946, no. 4, p. 138.

10

Marta Sylvestrová and Toman Jindřich
(eds): *Zdeněk Rossmann. Horizonty modernismu* (Horizons of Modernism: Zdeněk
Rossmann, 1905–1984). Brno 2015.

PARIS

Evolving out of pre-war painting styles – particularly Cubism, Fauvism and Futurism – art deco developed after World War I into France's dominant commercial style during the 1920s and 1930s.

Art deco is an abbreviation of the French term 'arts décoratifs', a label that can be traced back to the international applied arts exhibition, the Exposition Internationale des Arts Décoratifs et Industriels Modernes, held in Paris in 1925. At this exhibition, a clear tendency could be observed in three-dimensional applications of design – in architecture, interior design, furniture and stage design – towards stereometric shapes and decoration based on geometric elements. Expensive pieces were usually individually designed and handcrafted from extremely high-quality materials for a new urban class wanting to showcase its exquisite taste and luxurious lifestyle.

In the graphic arts, particularly poster art, abstract representations dominated, with flat, geometrically constructed forms modulated by soft colour sequences, creating cascading motifs that formed a decorative effect.

One particularly prominent figure was Adolphe Jean-Marie Mouron, an immigrant from Ukraine who went by the pseudonym A. M. Cassandre. His graphic use of luxurious motifs such as cars, locomotives and ocean liners demonstrated sophisticated understatement, which he combined with the imposing power of modern machines – often supplemented with his own sans serif types set in capitals, which evoked exactitude and precision as well as dynamism.

Typography played an important role in the design of art deco posters because type was seen as an essential component of the graphics. Often, bizarre and barely legible alphabets were specifically developed. However, use was also made of extensive type families that exploited the interaction between wide and narrow, constructed and gestural, light and dark.

The French version of Futura was known as Europe, and it was given a special character: a lower-case **a**. ^{CF. P.315} This was reminiscent of a reduced Carolingian lower-case letter, or a streamlined car, the entire curvy contour of which cannot be perceived at once owing to its great speed. Through this distinctive special form, Europe acquired a 'French' look without losing its geometric character, which was well suited to the art deco style. As Paul Renner himself pointed out, Futura (or Europe) looked modern, even when used for regular text – a claim that was also made by the French foundry Deberny & Peignot.

PE

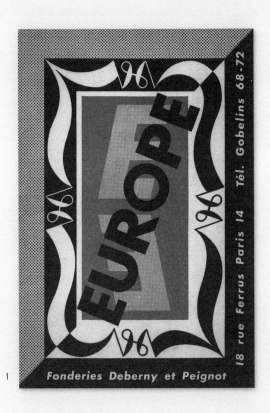

1
Deberny & Peignot, advertisement, 1937.

2–4
P. 290 et seq. — Maximilien Vox:
'Europe et le Studio', *Divertissements
typographiques*, no. 4, 1931.

EUROPE
ET LE
STUDIO

NUMÉRO 4 DES DIVERTISSEMENTS TYPOGRAPHIQUES

PUBLIÉS SOUS LA DIRECTION DE MAXIMILIEN VOX

PAR DEBERNY PEIGNOT

PRINTEMPS 1931

MICHEL WLASSIKOFF

THE BEGINNINGS OF FUTURA IN FRANCE

The French magazine for print and the graphic arts, *Arts et métiers graphiques*, published a contribution by Bertrand Guégan in its sixth issue (July 1928) entitled 'Le Futura', which presented the first three type series: Light, Medium and Bold. Guégan commented on Paul Renner in his introduction to the second type sample of Futura released by the Bauer Type Foundry, highlighting the typographer's 'ambitious undertaking' to provide 'us with Futura, the "typeface of our time". Our art industry and our architecture, says Mr Renner essentially, indicates the victory of the simple line; and that the lines of modern type are characterized by sobriety. Drawing inspiration from handwriting would be the wrong path, as would borrowing elements from earlier types.'

Guégan ascribed elegance and finesse to the design of the letters. At the same time, he complained of an exaggerated severity and eventually concluded that French readers would quickly tire of Futura, predicting that the use of this type would be limited to 'fun catalogues, pretty brochures and posters'.

Although this comment is restrained, the *Arts et métiers graphiques* advertisement in itself for Futura was remarkable and unprecedented. The magazine had been created in 1927 by the type foundry Deberny & Peignot and was primarily intended to publicize the typefaces sold by that foundry. If Futura appeared on its pages, this was owing to the old connections between the two type companies, Bauer and Deberny & Peignot, as well as the friendly relationship between the German magazine *Gebrauchsgraphik*, which switched to Futura very early on, and *Arts et métiers graphiques*.

In 1928 Draeger Frères, one of the most famous printing and publishing houses in France, began using Futura, which it had purchased directly from Bauer. Known for its high-quality prints and creative workshop, which primarily designed expensive catalogues for major car brands, Draeger ensured, through this presentation of Futura to an educated audience, that many printing houses followed suit. Draeger had previously worked almost exclusively with Deberny & Peignot; that the leading French type foundry still did not offer a modern type almost certainly contributed to this switch.

At Deberny & Peignot, Maximilien Vox had only recently (1927) started working as a typography advisor. He was also responsible for the foundry's trade journal, *Divertissements typographiques*. Vox was concerned by the lack of a type that took the new requirements of the public into account. In July 1929, in the magazine *Art et Décoration*, he expressed his opinion regarding the future of typography in France, deploring the lack of type foundries offering contemporary typefaces. At

ABCDEFGHIJ
KLMNOPQR
STUVWXYZ

abcdefghijklm
nopqrstuvwxyz

ABCDEFGHIJ
KLMNOPQR
STUVWXYZ

abcd
efgh
ijkl
mno
pqrs
tuvw
xyz

ABCDEFGHIJ
KLMNOPQR
STUVWXYZ

abcd
efgh
ijkl
mno
pqrs
tuvw
xyz

the end of 1929, shortly after this article was published, a dispute broke out in the boardroom of the type foundry regarding the actions needed to acquire a modern typeface. Vox encouraged the Bauer Type Foundry to sell Futura. Given the increasingly widespread use of Futura, as demonstrated by its purchase by Draeger, Vox offered his resignation to the foundry's board of directors without reservation, 'if Deberny & Peignot do not firmly accept my proposal to take action immediately to buy the typeface.'[1]

THE BIRTH OF EUROPE

The decision to buy Futura can be traced back to Charles Peignot himself, who supported Vox during the crisis meeting of his company and travelled to Frankfurt as soon as possible to strike a deal with Bauer. The rights were acquired according to a 'franchising' procedure: Deberny & Peignot distributed Futura under the name Europe, a renaming that has been ascribed to Charles Peignot. However, distribution was restricted to France and its colonies, as well as Egypt, Syria, Turkey, Greece and French-speaking Switzerland.[2]

The release of Europe was announced in the spring of 1930 in issue no. 3 of *Divertissements typographiques*, as follows: 'We are releasing a type that will be a great success: EUROPE, an Antiqua in three sets, the finest, most precise and "most usable" of all modern sans serif type-faces.' At the same time, *Arts et métiers graphiques* started using the type for its titling. In March 1930 the latter magazine published a special issue dedicated to photography, the cover page of which displayed the word in white three-dimensionally on a black background and in Futura/Europe capitals. In the preface to the issue, the title of the article by Waldemar George, 'Photographie vision du monde' (Photography Vision of the World), is shown in three different sets. Next come eight pages on the work of Maurice Tabard and the Studio Deberny & Peignot, which had recently been opened under the leadership of Peignot and specialized in the design of advertising prints. Through the work of this studio, Europe became known as an excellent typeface for use in combination with photography.

In March 1931 Deberny & Peignot published issue no. 4 of *Divertissements typographiques* with the title 'Europe et le Studio' (Europe and the Studio) and the subtitle 'Europe – 3 graisses – complément indispensable de la photographie publicitaire' (Europe – in three weights – an indispensable complement to advertising photography), followed by several sample applications of the typeface in works by Studio Deberny & Peignot as well as in whimsical designs by Vox. The accompanying text reads: 'Europe is the typeface of our time. ... It is an Antiqua: but a sufficiently versatile, flexible Antiqua for densely set texts: "editorial" articles, catalogues containing important text, circulars, etc.' The type was apparently 'designed to be the perfect companion for photographs'. The Europe/Futura typeface performed a particular role for Peignot and Vox: it was wonderfully suited to headings and was advisable for short texts, but was not intended for books or long texts. Peignot and Vox held the view that with the new developments in France, a typeface would arise that could represent the 'type of our time' and be used in all aspects of typography, from large sizes of type to running text in books. Europe was supposed to be the link between the developments of modernism from the 1920s and a more explicit type that needed to come about as quickly as possible. This explains why Deberny & Peignot did not include Futura Book, which was published by Bauer in 1932, in the repertoire of Europe.

THE SUCCESS AND
RISE OF EUROPE

The Europe typeface enjoyed great success from the very beginning. Charles Peignot compared it with the success of the Cochin type family, published in 1912. Deberny & Peignot supplemented the initial three weights with one light and one medium weight, followed by a bold italic. By contrast, the foundry's narrow Europe was an in-house design, with no counterpart at Bauer, that was clearly distant from Futura in its structure. This kind of type, a classic French Antiqua, was later supplemented by a bold condensed variant, and in 1938 a type in a light weight was released on to the market under the name Mont Blanc.

Europe was 'cast' by Deberny & Peignot, as indicated in the type sample brochures. This means that the printers

were provided with three series, beginning with the templates set by Bauer. Lastly, punches were produced for all the typefaces and sizes, particularly Europe Condensed, which was a proprietary design. A poster type that Bauer did not have was also produced in wooden letters. This variant contains a surprising design for the **a** that was later ascribed to Cassandre, although his authorship was never proven. Eventually, Deberny & Peignot introduced designs and punches for non-Latin series: the Greek characters of Europe in light, medium and bold in 1932, and Europe for Vietnamese, also in three weights.

In the meantime, Cassandre developed Acier, a semi-light headline type in two versions, which print black or grey, thus constituting an experiment between Bifur and Futura. It was released in 1932 by Deberny & Peignot. According to the specimen brochure, 'Acier is a typeface that will support all materials

currently available in Antiqua ... It can be used together with Europe and contribute to its great success.' With Film, Marcel Jacno presented Charles Peignot with an 'Antiqua for inscriptions'. Its publication was subsequently announced

6

DEBERNY ET PEIGNOT
UNE MODE QUI DURE
EUROPE
COMPLÉTÉ PAR
BANJO
ET
FILM
18 RUE FERRUS PARIS

4ᵉ CATÉGORIE

Corps 72
EURO PE

Corps 60
EURO PE

Corps 48
EURO PE

Corps 36
EURO PE

Corps 30
EU RO PE

Corps 24
EU RO PE

Corps 18
EU RO PE

Corps 16
EU RO PE

Corps 14
EU RO PE

Corps 12
EU RO PE

Corps 10
EU RO PE

NUMÉROS	CORPS	POUCES	POIDS
2441	10	30 A	1 k. 60
2442	12	25 A	1 k. 90
2443	14	20 A	1 k. 90
2444	16	15 A	2 k. 20
2445	18	15 A	2 k. 60
2446	24	6 A	1 k. 60
2447	30	6 A	2 k. 50
2448	36	6 A	3 k. 80
2449	48	5 A	5 k. 60
2450	60	3 A	4 k. 30
2451	72	3 A	5 k. 90
2452	10	30 A	1 k. 70
2453	12	25 A	2 k. 10
2454	14	20 A	2 k. 10
2455	16	15 A	2 k. 10
2456	18	15 A	2 k. 80
2457	24	6 A	1 k. 60
2458	30	6 A	2 k. 60
2459	36	6 A	3 k. 90
2460	48	5 A	4 k. 30
2461	60	3 A	4 k. 70
2462	72	3 A	6 k. 50
2463	10	30 A	1 k. 90
2464	12	25 A	2 k. 10
2465	14	20 A	2 k. 30
2466	16	15 A	2 k. 60
2467	18	15 A	3 k. 30
2468	24	6 A	2 k. 00
2469	30	6 A	3 k. 00
2470	36	6 A	4 k. 70
2471	48	5 A	7 k. 10
2472	60	3 A	5 k. 60
2473	72	3 A	7 k. 70

Les Initiales Europe existent en caractères très
de 6 cicéros à 40 cicéros.

Pendant longtemps les metteurs en pages des journaux crurent que le problème était pour eux de trouver chaque jour un caractère plus étroit qui leur permette un plus grand nombre de lettres sur la justification d'une colonne. Résultat catastrophique pour les yeux des lecteurs et la présentation du journal.

Maintenant les journaux qui veulent bien être mis en pages adoptent 2 ou 3 colonnes pour les titres importants d'où lisibilité, clarté et même élégance si l'on emploie les Initiales Europe qui ont d'ailleurs été créées pour répondre aux demandes incessantes qui nous étaient adressées par les directeurs et chefs de matériel des grands journaux.

DEBERNY ᵉᵗ PEIGNOT PARIS

4ᵉ CATÉGORIE

2555 - c. 60 - 4 A - F k. 40
BANJO

2554 - c. 48 - 6 A - 8 k. 76
BANJO

2553 - c. 36 - 8 A - 6 k. 00
BANJO

2552 - c. 30 - 8 A - 4 k. 80
BANJO

2551 - c. 24 - 8 A - 2 k. 60
BANJO

2550 - c. 18 - 20 A - 4 k. 20
BANJO

2549 - c. 16 - 30 A - 3 k. 70
BANJO

2548 - c. 12
BANJO

2547 - c. 10
BANJO

2546 - c. 8
BANJO

2545 - c. 6
BANJO

2541 - c. 6
BANJO
60 A - 2 k. 50

Après le long effort vers plus de sobriété, de rigueur et de pureté, après le succès universel de la formule du caractère Europe, il importe que la simplicité ne dégénère pas en pauvreté, la discipline en monotonie, la distinction en mélancolie. Voici donc, dans l'esprit des créations modernes, un caractère riant, d'une amusante fantaisie, et avec lequel on peut, littéralement, jouer : BANJO c'est le sourire de l'Europe.

CARACTÈRE A DEUX CHASSES

AA BB CC DD EE
FF GG HH I J
KK LL MM NN
OO PP QQ RR SS
TT UU VV W XX
YY ZZ Æ Œ Ç
Ç ( ) . , : ; ' - ‹ ‹ ! ?
1 2 3 4 5 6 7 8 9 0

Le policage indiqué comprend : une moitié de sortes larges et une moitié de sortes étroites.

Pour répondre à la demande d'un grand nombre de nos clients nous avons complété l'alphabet des sortes étroites qui doublent exactement les sortes larges. Il vous faut le caractère « Banjo » pour rivaliser avec la lettre dessinée.

DEBERNY ᵉᵗ PEIGNOT PARIS

CARACTÈRES

BOIS

DEBERNY ET PEIGNOT

in 1933: '[This] typeface has the ability to harmonize with the classical series, which it can serve as initials, as well as with the modern series, and particularly with Europe.'[3] Banjo, by Vox – who should have been a competitor with this typeface – was also referred to in relation to Europe: 'A brightly cheerful type full of delicious fantasy that you can literally play with: Banjo is the smile of Europe', wrote Vox in the preface to his typeface. In essence, Acier, Banjo and Film were not directly inspired by Europe. Acier and Film are only minimally similar to it at most, while Banjo was the product of Vox's earlier experiments with a typeface presenting a narrow and a wide version of every character. They all fulfilled the wish of Deberny & Peignot to expand the market for headline typefaces, which thrived in the 1930s. In type specimen books published after 1934, the company grouped the three kinds of type together as 'satellites' of Europe.

A SYMBOL OF MODERNITY

As the faithful mouthpiece of Deberny & Peignot, the magazine *Arts et métiers graphiques* disseminated Europe until the magazine was discontinued in 1939. Apart from a few exceptions, the typeface did not appear as running text, but in large point sizes it occupied a central position and was even used for the title from September 1933 to October 1934. Another magazine, *VU*, which was first published in 1928 by Lucien Vogel (a relative of Charles Peignot), was primarily dedicated to photography. Articles and dossiers left an unusually large amount of space for photo reportage as well as photomontages, accompanied by imposing headings and intermediate headings. While Europe was used frequently,

5

P.296 – catalogue of display types, Deberny & Peignot, c. 1935. Overview of Europe Medium, with the announcement of a new lower-case **a**.

6

P.297 – specimen brochure for Europe, which presents Acier, Banjo and Film as equally important typefaces, Deberny & Peignot, 1934, title page.

7

Specimen brochure for Europe, which presents Acier, Banjo and Film as equally important typefaces, Deberny & Peignot, 1934, double spread.

8

Album of wooden characters, Deberny & Peignot, c. 1935.

although not exclusively, it served as a model in this context.

The same applied to the use of Europe by leading French graphic artists in the 1930s, among them Jean Carlu in particular; Cassandre used it less frequently. Young creatives, members or friends of the Union des Artistes Modernes (UAM) used constructed sans serif types, particularly Europe: Francis Bernard, who used the typeface Acier for the running text, Jacques Nathan, Jean Picart-le-Doux and Marcel Jacno, who designed a noteworthy announcement in Europe for the Théâtre des Ambassadeurs.

SEARCHING FOR THE TYPEFACE OF OUR TIME

In 1934 Charles Peignot asked Cassandre to dedicate himself to the development of a true 'type of our time'; this seems to have been released on the occasion of the Paris World Exhibition in 1937, under the name Peignot. Although the concept was based on a clear and scientific rationale that was reminiscent of Futura, it was applied in the opposite way because Peignot wanted to remove the lower-case letters and print everything in Capitalis Monumentalis. The type became another economic failure, but it was widely used at the Paris exhibition. In addition to Peignot, which constituted the exhibition's typography section, constructed sans serif types were proudly displayed on facades, objects and prints in various country-specific and themed pavilions. The comments expressed in this regard were not always positive, as the reaction of a contemporary typographer

demonstrates: 'It was an excess of sans serifs and serifs drawn with a ruler or pair of compasses. ... It is not at all suitable for use in signs in Europe! One could find exceptions from among the otherwise uniform and international use of Antiqua, Futura, Europe and all their substitute forms from the last several years.'[4] The substitute forms he mentions refer to acquisitions that had been made by other major type companies in France: Fonderie Typographique Française (FTF) had Apollo (1934) and the type foundry Olive had Simplex (1937). However, the historian and lecturer at the École Supérieure Estienne Robert Bonfils published *La Gravure et le Livre* (Engraving and the Book) in 1938, a reference work set in Europe that has influenced generations of typographers by coining the term 'typographic genres'. For him, Europe/Futura was the epitome of the 'elegant genre'.[5]

9
Type specimen for Europe Medium, set by pupils of the École Municipale Estienne, as described by Paul Renner in a handwritten note on the reverse side.

Le gouvernement le plus confor-
me à la nature est celui dont la
disposition particulière se rapporte
mieux à la disposition du peuple
pour lequel il est établi. Les lois
doivent être tellement propres au
peuple pour lequel elles sont faites,
que c'est un très grand hasard si
celles d'une nation peuvent conve-
nir à une autre. Il faut qu'elles se
rapportent à la nature et au prin-
cipe du gouvernement qui est établi ou qu'on veut établir, soit qu'elles le forment comme font les lois
politiques, soit qu'elles le maintien-
nent comme font les lois civiles.
Elles doivent être relatives au phy-
sique du pays; au climat glacé,
brûlant ou tempéré; au genre de
vie des peuples, laboureurs, chas-

9

'The Europe typeface has captured its time; it is its perfect expression, in the same way as flat roofs and cubic buildings.'

ADRIAN FRUTIGER
'Les Linéales' (Monoline Types), 1960.

EUROPE AND UNIVERS –
EUROPE AND THE UNIVERSE

From 1952, Adrian Frutiger worked at Deberny & Peignot on the transition of the existing types to Lumitype, one of the first photosetting processes. After handling the classical types, 'an idea for an "Antiqua" design began to form. For Charles Peignot, it was clear that the best-selling type of the foundry, Futura – known as Europe in France – had to be included in the programme. I suggested another project to him because Europe was no longer current in my eyes.'[6] In actual fact, the sales figures of Europe were falling, which Frutiger commented on in his own words: 'The Europe typeface has captured its time; it is its perfect expression, in the same way as flat roofs and cubic buildings'.[7] Elsewhere, he wrote 'However, the modern concrete structures are not necessarily geometric; their forms are laden with tension and energy, just as a typeface should be.'[8]

The name of the new monoline type that was eventually selected is significant in every respect: 'We began with my working title "Monde", the world, because after "Europe" we wanted to look beyond the framework of Europe. ... And if we are going to think big, then we should think as far as the limits of what is thinkable: In the end, Charles Peignot chose "Univers".'[9] Frutiger preferred his typographic design to the one by Renner because it was compatible with all type systems: 'With Univers, text composed in different languages has a universally unified look – which is not the case with Futura.'[10]

As part of a discussion panel on the topic of monoline types during the Rencontres Internationales de Lure, where a jury of French and other European typographers attested in 1960 to the world domination of this type family, Gérard Blanchard seized the opportunity to inform Frutiger of his debt to Futura: 'You, Mr Frutiger, who designed Univers for the type foundry Deberny & Peignot, the intended successor to Europe – and I say successor deliberately, because you designed Univers on the basis of Europe – what do you think about Europe?'[11] Frutiger accepted the argument that Futura's time was behind it. Almost everyone who took part in these meetings in Lurs-en-Provence took a similar position: from Marcel Jacno to Albert Hollenstein, as well as Henri Steiner and Roger Excoffon. Europe was referred to as obsolete, and its use as old-fashioned. According to Jacno, as a result, Europe/Futura 'like all the direct or indirect results of the Bauhaus, satisfies reason but injures the elbows'.[12] Frutiger himself stated: 'The Germans still advocate Futura, but it is the wistfulness of people who were youths at the same time as Renner.'[13]

QUARTIERS DE NOBLESSE

The symbolic funeral of Futura in Lurs-en-Provence had, however, little to do with reality. In 1952 the great typographer Pierre Faucheux recalled, in a special issue of *Art d'aujourd'hui* dedicated to the relationship between graphic design and art, the emblematic nature of Futura, which he associated with modernity. Going against all the conventions of French typography, he subsequently made regular use of Futura for the running text of his designs for the publications of book clubs. In the 1960s he used it as a powerful title type for paperbacks for publishing houses such as Stock and Albin Michel. In order to reaffirm his law of the 'brutal contrasts of the body', which he applied to the cover pages and titles of the works, he used a reduced range of types: Plantin, Didot and Europe, which, with their very different bodies and cuts, could resist accusations of similarity. Faucheux thereby restored Europe/Futura to its rightful noble status.

10

11

10

Brochure of type specimens for Europe, Deberny & Peignot, 1950.

11

Advertisement for Europe Medium Condensed, Deberny & Peignot, c. 1935.

12

Marcel Jacno: brochure for the Théâtre des Ambassadeurs, Paris, 1934.

13

Advertisement for Louis Vuitton, 1931.

12

LOUIS VUITTON

INVITE A VISITER SON EXPOSITION DE MAROQUINERIE,
CRISTALLERIE, ARTICLES DE VOYAGE, INSPIRÉS D'ART
NÈGRE EN SON PAVILLON SIS A LA POINTE DE
MADAGASCAR A L'EXPOSITION COLONIALE.

PARIS
70 CHAMPS-ÉLYSÉES

NICE
I RUE PARADIS

CANNES
10 RUE DES BELGES

VICHY
RUE DU PARC

LONDON
149 NEW BOND St.

JEAN CARLU

Jean Carlu (1900–1997), together with Cassandre, Paul Colin and Charles Loupot, was one of the 'mousquetaires de l'affiche' (musketeers of the poster) who had a strong impact on French poster art during the interwar period. He was sympathetic to modernist artists and architects and was a co-founder in 1929 of the highly influential French artists' trade association Union des Artistes Modernes (UAM).[14] In the same year the Théâtre Pigalle, built by Charles Siclis, who was also a member of UAM, was opened in Paris, and Carlu designed the external signs and lights for it, as well as the courses and one brochure. This brochure, printed by Draeger, is a typographic manifesto: the running text in Futura is placed opposite full-page photographs by Maurice Tabard, showing the interior of the theatre. In its 13th issue (15 September 1929), the magazine *Arts et métiers graphiques* celebrated this 'splendid brochure printed in Futura with a silver coating', and printed further articles on the topic. As one of the first publications of Futura in France, it is an important example of modernist design.

Europe/Futura later became Carlu's favourite typeface. He used it on the title page of the first edition of *Publicité*, the annual special issue of *Arts et métiers graphiques*, as well as numerous studies, such as the design studies of the stand for the Paris electricity company CPDE at the Paris Household Goods Fair in 1934. With the onset of World War II, Carlu was forced to settle in the United States, where he worked for the US information service as well as the Container Corporation of America (CCA) and various publishing houses until the end of the war. While on the other side of the Atlantic, his advertising campaigns for the CCA contributed to the spread of Futura, and he also drafted an anti-Nazi poster in 1944 for the liberation of France from German occupation.

14
Jean Carlu: cover for *Publicité 34*, special issue of *Arts et métiers graphique*, 1934.

JEAN CARLU

NUMÉRO SPÉCIAL PRÉSEN

EUROPE
ET LE
STUDIO

**DEBERNY
PEIGNOT**

TANT A MESSIEURS LES

IMPRIMEURS

DIVERTISSEMENTS
TYPOGRAPHIQUES
PUBLIÉS SOUS LA DIRECTION DE MAXIMILIEN VOX
PRINTEMPS 1931

MAXIMILIEN VOX

Maximilien Vox (1894–1974) was an engraver, illustrator, publisher, journalist, critic and typography theorist. As the son of Pastor Wilfred Monod, one of the most important figures in Calvinism, he was baptised Samuel Monod. He converted to Catholicism and took the name Vox, with which he became famous. Vox's life and work were marked by a spiritual search and by his difficult relationship with the French Protestant tradition. He was recognized at a young age as one of the best typographers of his time, and in 1927 he was engaged by the type foundry Deberny & Peignot as a consultant. There, from 1928, he was entrusted in particular with *Divertissements typographiques*, a publication that focused on an appreciation of the foundry's heritage as well as the new developments taking place there. *Divertissements*, which was distributed free of charge to printing houses, contained original and amusing articles that, as Vox explained, 'for want of types, reinvent their usage'.[15] Vox was also heavily involved in the magazine *Arts et métiers graphiques*, which Deberny & Peignot had been publishing since 1927. It was not in this magazine, however, but in *Art et Décoration*, that Vox questioned the future of French typography in 1929. 'Will there be, as many claim, a "typeface of our time"?', he asked, quoting Paul Renner and the Bauer Type Foundry. Vox stressed that 'the type that will dominate all visible applications in the coming decade will not be Antiqua, but a further development of the Antiqua', 'a type with an almost perfect interplay of cuts, without serifs (until further consideration), with proportions of greater variety and liveliness than the former commonly used Antiqua fonts. There are already many versions of this type in Germany (Futura, Erbar, Kabel, Elegant, etc.) and one in England from the engraver and punchcutter Eric Gill (Gill Sans); in France, there are developments under way that are sure to be very successful. However, we will merely have to catch up; we refuse, vehemently and shrewdly, to be outpaced by the new times. France does not currently have a single specialized great designer of the calibre of a Koch, a Renner, Ehmke, Bernhard or other German typographic artists.'[16]

That Vox, who was otherwise a regular contributor to *Arts et métiers graphiques*, chose precisely this mouthpiece to make his opinion known is significant. In January 1929, Deberny & Peignot released Cassandre's Bifur, the design of which dated back to before the time of Vox's employment at the foundry, but it did not achieve the success expected of it. Vox did not take the commercial failure of Bifur too seriously. He wanted to distance himself from the politics with which Deberny & Peignot were reacting to the ever-growing demand for a 'modern' type, and made it very clear that another solution was needed. Vox saw the acquisition of Futura as an interim solution, since there was a lack of a modern type with a sufficiently broad application that could

FOUQUET'S

CHAMPS
ÉLYSÉES
PARIS

LE CHAPELIER DES GENS BIEN

GIBSON HATS
28, AVENUE DE L'OPÉRA, 28

fulfil, in particular, the recent resurgence in demand for advertising. What Vox liked about this option was the acquisition of Futura by the great printing house Draeger: 'The printing house Draeger Frères has recently made the purchase directly', he recorded in his notes at that time. 'If we want to assert ourselves in the market, we must not waste any time. I have made my position dependent upon it. Mr Girard and Mr Payet, in their surprise, tend to the view that there is nothing actually new about the type in question; that it is nothing more than our good old Roman Antiqua. Peignot, however, was clearly of the opposite opinion: he took control and made the decision himself.'[17]

In 1952 Vox published the type classification that bears his name and that was later taken over by Atypl, the Association Typographique Internationale (International Typographic Association). He replaced the old name 'Antiqua' with the term 'monoline Antiqua' and placed Europe/Futura at the top of the category of constructed types. The discussion panels on the topic of monoline types that took place during the Rencontres Internationales de Lure in 1960 brought together some of the leading typographers of all time, including Roger Excoffon and Adrian Frutiger. The yearbook *Caractère Noël*, which was later directed by Vox, published a long report on the topic.[18] Vox, who had fallen ill, was unable to participate in the discussions, but expressed himself in comment in his publication. He dedicates a chapter to Europe/Futura where he expresses vigorous criticism of this symbol of an elapsed modernity. Vox asks: 'Are we really doing something good now that we are giving our support to the Europe typeface? It does not hold the baseline very well, that is true; also, the original font is so poorly spaced that vertical letters – **i, l, t** – look spotty when set. One need only attempt to set "titille william". The lower-case **a** and **o** can scarcely be differentiated from one another. The error lies in judging Europe in plain bodytext. It is a noble typeface, like Garamont [sic], Baskerville, Didot, etc.'[19]

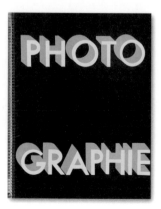

17

15–16
P.308 et seq. – Maximilien Vox: 'Europe et le Studio', *Divertissements typographiques*, no. 4, 1931.

17–19
'Photographie', special issue of *Arts et métiers graphiques*, no. 16, March 1930.

20
P.314 – Maximilien Vox: 'Europe et le Studio', *Divertissements typographiques*, no. 4, 1931.

SAY IT

WITH

MAYER
SIMON
& LŒBS
C°, INC°
312-313
WEST 41
N·Y·CITY

DOROTHY DUVAL
DUVAL DOROTHY
DOROTHY DUVAL
DUVAL DOROTHY
DOROTHY DUVAL
DUVAL DOROTHY
DOROTHY DUVAL

MODES

PARIS

3 R. DE

BERRY

ÉL. 17-11

Le cycle est désormais complet :
depuis un kilo de blancs jusqu'au matériel d'un catalogue complet, les
Fonderies Deberny Peignot mettent à
la disposition de l'imprimerie française

TOUT CE QU'IL FAUT

POUR

IMPRIMER

LETTRES ET

PHOTO

EUROPE
EUROPE
EUROPE

3

GRAISSES

COMPLÉMENT INDISPENSABLE DE LA PHOTO PUBLICITAIRE

FONDU PAR DEBERNY PEIGNOT

1

Maximilien Vox: 'Charles Peignot et son temps' (Charles Peignot and his Time). In: *Communication et Langages* (Paris) no. 14, June 1972, pp. 58–59.

2

In the entire literature relevant to Europe, whether in the publications of Deberny & Peignot or in *Arts et métiers graphiques*, not once are the origins of the typeface referred to. Neither the Bauer Type Foundry nor Paul Renner are named as the author of Futura/Europe. Everything indicates that the type foundry was anxious to conceal the origin of the typeface from a printing industry that was still strongly anti-German in sentiment, and to appropriate Futura/Europe as much as possible in order to create the impression that it was an explicitly French creation.

3

'Le Film, nouveau caractère de titre, gravé et fondu par Deberny & Peignot, d'après les dessins de Marcel Jacno' (The Film, a new type for large sizes, cut and cast by Deberny & Peignot according to designs by Marcel Jacno). In: *Arts et métiers graphiques* (Paris) no. 38, 15 November 1933.

4

Henri Colas: 'La lettre et l'enseigne à l'exposition'. In: *Le Courrier graphique* (Paris), December 1937.

5

Robert Bonfils: 'Psychologie du métier de typographe' (Psychology of the Typography Profession). In: *Ders.: La Gravure et le Livre*, Paris 1938, p. 183.

6

Adrian Frutiger: *Caractères: l'Oeuvre complète* (Typefaces: The Complete Works), ed. Heidrun Osterer and Philipp Stamm, Basel 2008, p. 88.

7

'Les Linéales' (Monoline Types), round table at the Rencontres Internationales de Lure. In: *Caractère* No. I, vol. 13, 1960.

8

Schweizer Graphische Mitteilungen (Zollikofer & St Gallen), February 1961, special issue Univers typeface, p. 10.

9

Frutiger: *Caractères*, p. 93.

10

Ibid, p. 100, caption 35.

11

'Les Linéales'.

12

Ibid.

13

Ibid.

14

Members of the artists' association UAM included A. M. Cassandre, Pierre Chareau, Paul Colin, Le Corbusier, René Herbst, Charles Loupot, Andre Lurçat, Robert Mallet-Stevens, Charles Peignot, Charlotte Perriand, Jean Prouvé and Maximilien Vox.

15

Dossier Vox, compiled by Fernand Baudin, 1975, p. 127.

16

Maximilien Vox: 'Typographie'. In: *Art et Décoration* (Paris), vol. LVI, July–December 1929, pp. 161–76.

17

Vox: 'Charles Peignot et son temps', pp. 58–59.

18

'Les Linéales'.

19

Ibid.

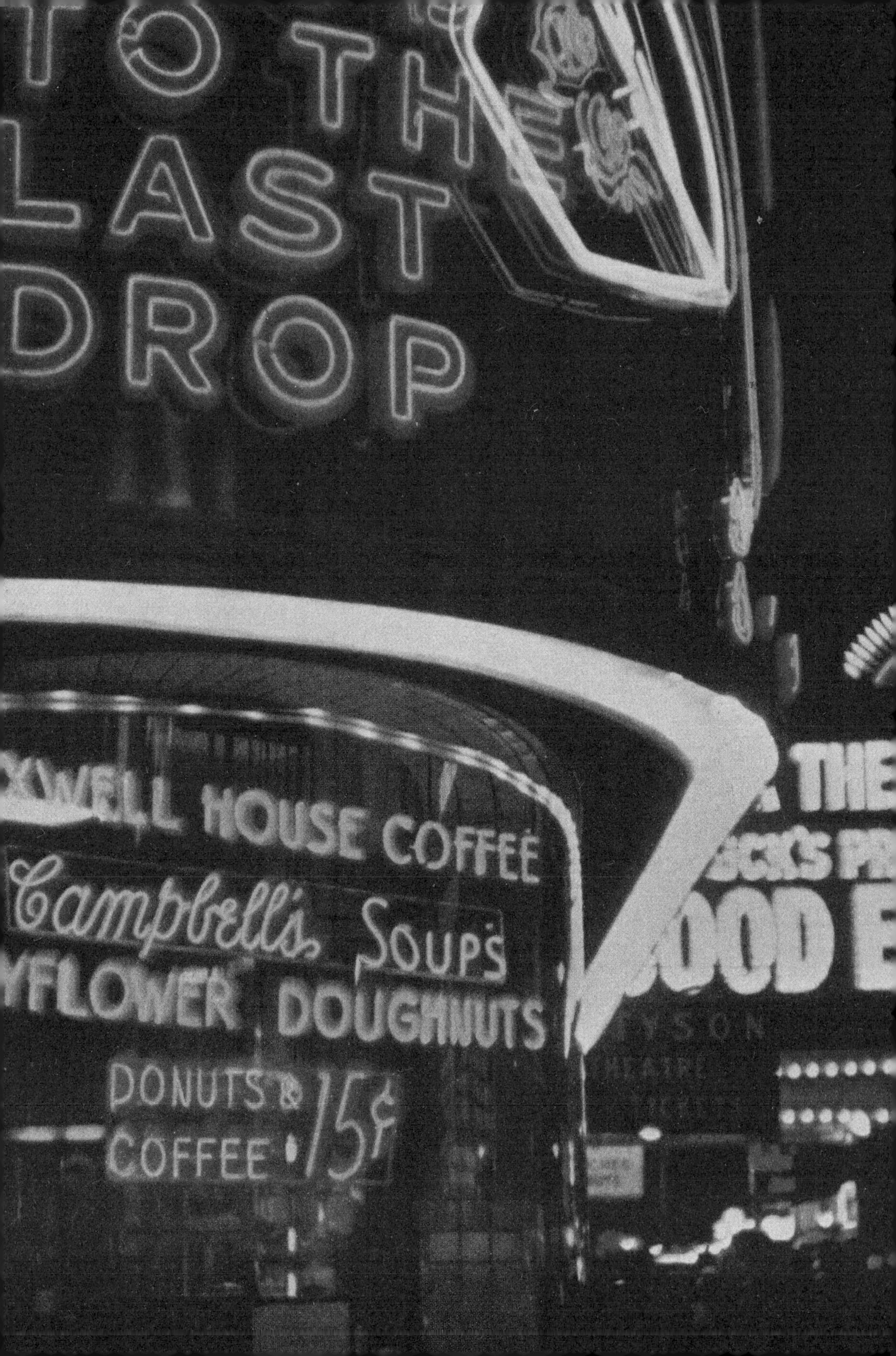

TO THE
LAST
DROP
XWELL HOUSE COFFEE
Campbell's Soups
YFLOWER DOUGHNUTS
DONUTS & COFFEE 15¢
THE

NEW
YORK

In the 1920s the graphic design profession in the US was becoming more formalized. By 1914, the year that the Institute of Graphic Arts was founded, commercial graphic design was already attracting a greater level of interest. Then, in 1920, the Art Director's Club was founded in New York, followed by the Society of Typographic Artists in Chicago in 1927.

New York's reputation as the new mecca of the advertising and graphic design scene led to a sharp rise in German businessmen establishing branches there, from the mid 1920s. By this time the famous German graphic artist and sculptor Lucian Bernhard had moved to New York and left the direction of his successful studio in Berlin to his colleague Fritz Rosen. In 1927 the Bauer Type Foundry opened an office in Manhattan, where Futura and many other types were enthusiastically received.[1]

In 1932 Paul Renner proudly wrote the following, in a moderate lower-case spelling: 'Today, when a modern type is desired, the printer chooses the sans serif without hesitation. This is not only the case in Germany and France; the Americans too now distinguish between "traditional types" and "modernistic types". According to the statistics of the magazine *The Inland Printer*, the most frequently used of these modern types is a sans serif from Germany: Futura.'[2]

At the end of the 1920s, the US experienced a boom in advertising and, correspondingly, magazines, which tended to use the modern picture and text compositions from Europe. In 1929 Mehemed Fehmy Agha, who had designed *die neue linie* in Germany and worked closely with Herbert Bayer at Dorland, received the commission to redesign *Vogue* and *Vanity Fair*, which he had set in Futura. By combining elements of art deco and Constructivist trends, which he had learned from Germany's New Typography, the magazines acquired a sophisticated and elegant look.

During the early years of the Depression, the prosperous graphic design scene came to a general standstill. But by the mid-1930s, the effects of Franklin D. Roosevelt's New Deal policy, which also supported artists and designers, were beginning to be felt. With the support of companies who were open to new ideas, American graphic designers such as Alexey Brodovich, Paul Rand, Lester Beall, Bradbury Thompson and Alvin Lustig carried out design experiments that, in turn, were decisive for the development of their respective styles.

With the rise of National Socialism in Germany and the public defamation of modern art, many intellectuals, architects and artists, as well as typographers and graphic designers, emigrated to the United States. Their first destination was New York, and particularly the cosmopolitan and creative scene of Manhattan. They brought with them the conviction that the sans serif should be seen as the type of the future. Many of them had already made use of Futura, or were at least familiar with its look, and they used the trusted German typeface in their new homeland – a tendency that was certainly also strengthened by Herbert Bayer's use of Futura in the catalogue design for the first major Bauhaus exhibition at New York's Museum of Modern Art in 1938.

PE

WOLFGANG HARTMANN

THE BAUER TYPE FOUNDRY IN NEW YORK

In 1927 Georg Hartmann decided to open a new office for the Bauer Type Foundry in New York. Previously, types had been delivered sporadically to North America, but the different type system there had caused difficulties: in the American point system, the letters were smaller in height and body, so they could not be combined with letters or spaces from the Didot system. Moreover, imports were subject to a very high customs tax, which prevented European types from being able to compete seriously with the domestic type foundries.

However, at the very same time as the branch office was established, advertising in America experienced a major boom. Agencies were requesting new types suitable for advertising, which the type foundries of that country could not deliver; Futura received an immediate and spectacular reception, and it was used enthusiastically for the design of advertisements. Bauer Bodoni, Beton, Bernhard and Corvinus also received a warm response. The type catalogues carefully printed by Bauer were collected by printers and used as a basis for their own applications.

In Frankfurt, types by American artists were acquired that enjoyed success both in America and Europe, such as Quick by Howard A. Trafton, and Flott by William S. Gillies.

The types were originally intended to be produced permanently in Germany, but this did not occur. In 1941 the US declared war, and products from Germany were no longer permitted for import. Hartmann therefore decided to transfer the production of the types with their Pica body size and height to Bauer's Spanish associate company, Fundición Tipográfica Neufville. In this way, the office in New York was able to continue its activity under a new name: Bauer Alphabets. It was crucial that the market for manual typesetting, which was very popular, would continue to be supplied.

Two men in particular were responsible for the great success of Bauer typefaces in the US. The first was Gustav Stresow, a young employee of Hartmann, who was sent to America in 1928. He led the company for two and a half years. His task was to visit the agencies and persuade them to use the types for the advertising of large companies, thereby motivating the printing houses to buy them. Fashion magazines were also seen as important clients because they were regarded as role models for good typography; many were inspired to imitate the types that they used.

The second man was Ludwig (Bill) Wolfgang Fröhlich, who took over the artistic direction of the Bauer office in 1935. Just one year earlier he had been studying at Goethe University in Frankfurt, before undergoing a brief period of training at the Bauer foundry there. Fröhlich had decided to emigrate to the United States on account of his Jewish background, and Hartmann helped him by offering him a position, and therefore an income, in the branch office there. Fröhlich was an extraordinary individual, who did much to increase the use of Bauer typefaces in the US. Just a few years after his arrival there, he founded his own advertising agency, Froehlich & Co., which specialized in the marketing of pharmaceutical products. Then, in 1954, he established International Marketing Services, which is now known as IMS Health. In 2014 it generated sales of $2.6 billion.

Fröhlich became exceptionally wealthy, and the owner of an elegantly furnished three-storey house with a large garden in the middle of Manhattan, surrounded by skyscrapers, and equipped with its own elevator for his invalid mother.

1
Offices of the Bauer Type Foundry Inc.,
235–247 East 45th Street, New York City,
c. 1927.

FUTURA
FUTURA
FUTURA
FUTURA
FUTURA
FUTURA
FUTURA
FUTURA
FUTURA
FUTURA
FUTURA
FUTURA
FUTURA
FUTURA
FUTURA
FUTURA

FUTURA
FUTURA
FUTURA
FUTURA
FUTURA
FUTURA
FUTURA
FUTURA
FUTURA
FUTURA
FUTURA
FUTURA
FUTURA
FUTURA

FUTURA BLACK

2

Intended for the American target audience: front and back cover of a specimen brochure for Futura Black, after 1930.

3–4

Sample applications for Concomo Pianos and Designers' Galleries; specimen brochure for Futura Black, after 1930.

5

Sample application and advertisement for the Bauer Type Foundry; specimen brochure for Futura Black, after 1930.

3

4

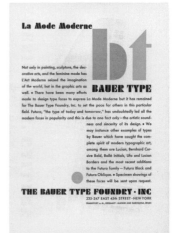

5

UTE BRÜNING

HERBERT BAYER: FUTURA IN THE MOMA CATALOGUE

In 1938 the *Katalog Bauhaus 1929–1928* was published in connection with the first exhibition of the Bauhaus in America at the Museum of Modern Art in New York. It transported pictures and ideas from the famous Weimar and Dessau schools into exile. The book, exhibition and a museum bulletin were designed by Herbert Bayer. His typographic concept united the three platforms, creating a contemporary Bauhaus identity that would not have come about without Futura. Why?

The transfer of content from the Old to the New World required many photographs, entailing an enormous amount of work to caption. A clear division into chapters using brief introductory texts was also necessary. In this way, types were just as important as pictures, although they were supposed to be regarded as subordinate. There was therefore demand for a type without individual characteristics, and which could be used in large as well as small quantities, in combination with images of any size, with any layout and with any content. Futura offered precisely these characteristics. While its geometric appearance can be considered from a certain angle as a subtext to Bauhaus design that makes use of basic shapes,

each sans serif requires a great deal of space, which can be generated with lighter strokes in light grey for Futura – a functional, graphic supplement for photo pages. As the former head of the printing house and advertising department, Bayer was particularly obliged to supply the Bauhaus contribution to the New Typography: this could only be an 'unadorned' type with a 'functional' design and layout. The book goes as far as featuring live demonstrations of the Bauhaus experiment with lower-case letters. It was one of the most important achievements of the former Bayer division, which had now been modernized into a 'typography workshop'.

With its changing layout from page to page, the book took on the nature of an album. This was all the more so since the usable area, which is positioned symmetrically in portrait, has corresponding centred page numbers on the right and left pages on the narrower external margin. With this arrangement, a series of varied two-page compositions unfold. Depending on the requirements of the picture groups, the usable area and its double-column layout are adjusted according to certain rules. Only the Futura series has the liberty to accompany the pictures, seemingly free of rules, in the places where the viewer looks for explanation. Two sizes of type were used to indicate the hierarchy between the introductory texts and the descriptions for the pictures. Large masses of information are stabilized into blocks by means of very small paragraph indents. Smaller masses are also permitted to flutter like little flags, unjustified, flush left on a common axis.

Capitals in Steinschrift, by Schelter & Giesecke, in bold condensed were used as a display type. This sans serif makes reference to the exactitude of stock-market prices and machine advertisements from the turn of the century without losing its connection with modernism, which gives it its narrow proportions and static rhythm. In the third edition of the Bauhaus exhibition catalogue in 1955, the first German-language edition, the contrast between text and display is weaker because Futura Bold Condensed had been used to replace Steinschrift, indicating a change in the function of the book: the updated ideas of the Bauhaus had resulted in the unification of the book's design.

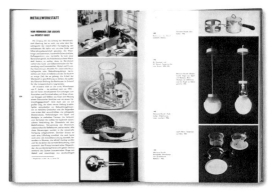

6

A comparison of the exhibition catalogue designed by Herbert Bayer, *Bauhaus 1919–1928*, double spreads from the English and German editions (1938 and 1955 respectively).

U.S. 48 States light the road
to world peace and commerce.

Container Corporation of America

 Save waste paper

FUTURA AND AMERICAN ADVERTISING

'The Type of Today and Tomorrow' was the alliterative slogan coined by the Bauer Type Foundry office in New York to announce the release of Futura in the United States. There were other popular home-grown and imported sans serifs available in the US, including Jakob Erbar's Erbar (1926/7), Rudolf Koch's Kabel (1928), W. A. Dwiggins' Metro (1927), Lucian Bernhard's Bernhard Gothic (1929), but neither these nor other typefaces at the time were as geometric. Futura was the epitome of modernism.

Introduced in the US in 1928 as a metal type family in various size and weight variations, it was promoted with great fanfare, including lavish specimen sheets showing the type in use – a very common marketing practice during that period. These specimens emphasized Futura's crisp, modern look and showed how well it functioned in large and small sizes for many purposes. It had immediate appeal throughout the advertising world, in large part because it did not revive an existing typeface, and yet was not so radically loud as to overpower a message. It managed to symbolize both 'today and tomorrow'.

Most American advertisements used sans serif typefaces that were either bold condensed or bold expanded. With Futura, ad typography was effectively altered from conventional to novel; even the name itself had great allure. Futura quickly became one of the most popular typefaces in use, and remained so for many years, until Helvetica was created.

7

Paul Rand: Container Corporation of America, advertisement in *Fortune*, April 1946.

8

For the American public – The Bauer Type Foundry Inc.: 'Futura. The Type of Today and Tomorrow'.

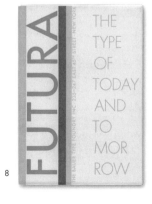

8

PAUL RAND AND FUTURA

Paul Rand's typeface preferences included a limited number of sans serifs, including Trade Gothic and Helvetica. He once even tried out A. M. Cassandre's Peignot, the first time it appeared in the United States. He also frequently used Futura Bold for advertisements and books that he designed during the 1940s, including a typographical ad for Benzedrine that featured a Futura Bold lowercase **b**, enlarged to fill the page. Owing to its near-perfect geometry, this sculptural letterform was very effective as an identifying mark, particularly at such huge proportions.

For a series of Stafford Fabrics ads, Rand spaced out lower-case Futura Bold letters for the company's name, and used the same type – regularly spaced, in smaller sizes – for both headline and body text on all the company's advertisements. When these Futura Bold letters were printed in alternating colours and paired with Rand's signature abstract-photo illustrations, the ads projected a powerful sense of modernity.

Similarly, the Futura Bold lower-case title *jazzways* – the nameplate for a hybrid book–magazine devoted to music – perfectly complemented Rand's witty Paul Klee-inspired symbolic cover illustration of four abstracted musical instruments to suggest modern jazz. For a collection of Hans Arp's poems and essays, Rand spaced Futura Bold out wide on the title page, making the letters **a-r-p** virtually dance on the page.

Yet, although he used it numerous times, Futura was not Rand's favourite typeface. He liked that it was 'functional, devoid of doodads and ringlets and hair curlers', but after a decade or more he grew tired of it, much preferring the thick and thin of the classic Bodoni, without the hair curlers.

9
Paul Rand: advertisement for Coronet Brandy, 1945–48.

10

top — Paul Rand: cover design for Hans Arp's *On My Way: Poetry and Essays 1912–1947* (Documents of Modern Art/ MoMA). New York: Wittenborn, Schultz, Inc., 1948.

bottom left — Paul Rand: cover design for László Moholy-Nagy's *The New Vision and Abstract of an Artist* (Documents of Modern Art/MoMA). New York: Wittenborn, Schultz, Inc., 1949.

bottom right — Paul Rand: cover design for Guillaume Apollinaire's *The Cubist Painters: Aesthetic Mediations* (Documents of Modern Art/MoMA). New York: Wittenborn, Schultz, Inc., 1944.

11

Paul Rand: cover design for Rudi Blesh's *Modern Art USA*. New York: Alfred A. Knopf, 1956.

12

Paul Rand: 'jazzways', cover for the magazine *The Architectural Forum*, March 1945.

13–14

Paul Rand: advertisements for Stafford Fabrics, 1942–44.

10

11

12

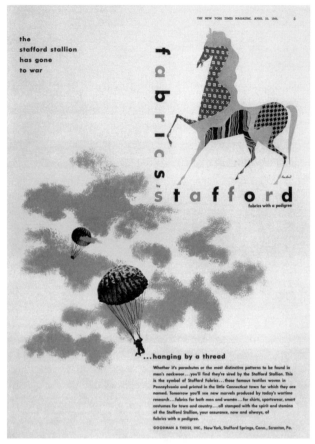

13

14

The building market in **1** package

architects & engineers

realty owners & managers

builders & contractors

lending institutions

public officials

distributors & dealers

The Architectural

FORUM

15

15

Paul Rand: advertisement for the magazine *The Architectural Forum*, 1943.

16

Paul Rand: *Thoughts on Design*. New York: Wittenborn & Company, 1947.

17

Paul Rand: cover design for Ann and Paul Rand's *Sparkle and Spin: A Book About Words*. New York: Harcourt, Brace and Co., 1957.

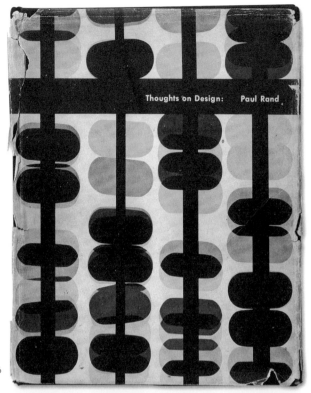

16

17

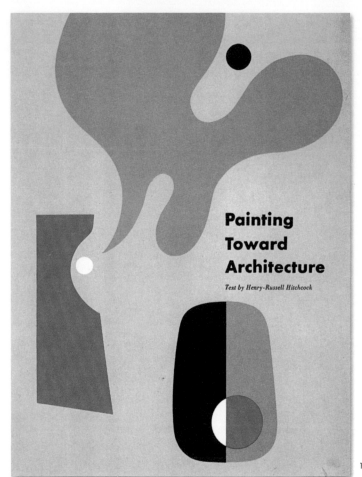

18

Bradbury Thompson: cover design for *Painting Toward Architecture*, ed. Henry-Russell Hitchcock. Meriden, Connecticut: Miller, 1948.

19

Bradbury Thompson: 'horsepower'.

20

Bradbury Thompson: *Alphabet as Image*, 1948.

21

Bradbury Thompson: *Seven Inspirations*. Symbols translated into graphic design by the author, from paintings by Miró, Braque, Helion, Le Corbusier, Tunnard, Léger and Gris, 1948.

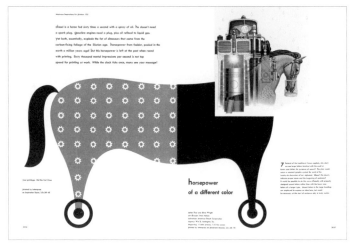

19

the newly designed ADDO-X quality Viking model 154

big performance

at economy price

ask now for "on-your-job" proof
that "addo-x" economy priced
model 44E will save you money

STEVEN HELLER

LADISLAV SUTNAR AND FUTURA

Futura had been introduced in the United States before the Czech modernist designer Ladislav Sutnar's arrival in New York City in 1939. Yet the typeface took on emblematic status once Sutnar had employed it for a series of industrial trade catalogues for the Sweet's Catalog Service, designed between 1941 and 1960.

Sutnar preferred lower-case Futura Bold and Medium, owing to their functionality, legibility and personality. In his book *Catalog Design Progress*, an erudite guide to modern catalogue creation, Futura dominates as the typographic complement to Sutnar's obsessive application of geometric icons as chapter markers and subject tabs. The typeface was part of an equation that also included shape, colour and line, leading to what Sutnar called 'traffic signs that quickly transmit the identifying information' to the users of Sweet's respective catalogues.

Sutnar was not a late adopter, but rather a Futura devotee; he had begun using the typeface while still in Czechoslovakia, designing book and magazine covers from as early as 1929 for Družstevní práce, Prague's largest publishing house (see pages 271–4). Sutnar wrote prolifically about the design process and, while he never explicitly wrote about the virtues of Futura, the face conformed to his basic credo of good visual design: 'Its aim is not to attain popular success by going back to the nostalgia of the past, or by sinking to the infantile level of a mythical public taste.' Most importantly, Futura was a typeface that never became passé.

22
Ladislav Sutnar: Flyer for Add-o, c. 1956–59, from *Visual Design in Action*, 1961.

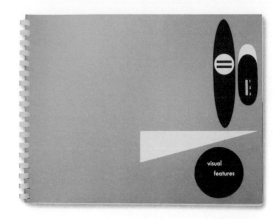

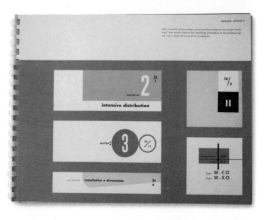

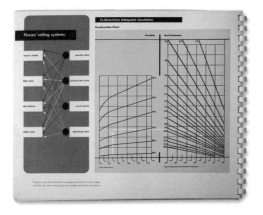

23

23

Ladislav Sutnar and Knud Lönberg-Holm:
Catalog Design Progress. New York:
Sweet's Catalog Service, 1950.

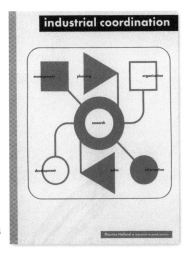

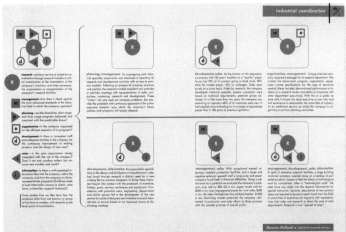

24

26

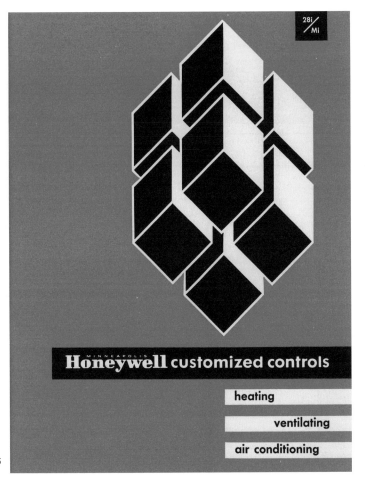

24

Ladislav Sutnar (design): title and double spread for *industrial coordination*, a catalogue for Maurice Holland. New York: Sweet's Catalog Service, c. 1947.

25

Ladislav Sutnar and Knud Lönberg-Holm: *Honeywell Customized Controls* catalogue. New York/Minneapolis: Sweet's Catalog Service for Honeywell, c. 1952.

26

Ladislav Sutnar: advertisement for Fiat Volunteer, in *Catalog Design Progress*, 1950.

'At first, everything new seems novel and exciting, but once we become adults, the novel becomes invisible to the trained eye.'

Publisher VANITY FAIR.

STEVEN HELLER

VANITY FAIR: THE AMERICAN MAGAZINE THAT PROMOTED FUTURA

There was no more influential advocate for Futura in the United States than *Vanity Fair* magazine, Condé Nast's highly respected culture, art and literature monthly. In 1929 its esteemed art director, the Ukraine-born Dr Mehemed Fehmy Agha, not only introduced Futura in the magazine, but also went a step further by removing all capital letters in *Vanity Fair*'s headlines. The lower-case result was at once jarring and elegantly modern.

The 'experiment', which lasted for only five issues, defined *Vanity Fair*'s progressive design style. However, just as suddenly as the capitals had disappeared, they reappeared in the March 1930 issue, in which the editors published an explanatory editorial entitled 'A Note on Typography'. Although the case was more important than the face in this context, the editors implied that this trial was best done with a face representing the New Typography of the European avant-garde. 'Typography without capital letters was introduced in Europe soon after the Great War and has been working westward ever since,' they wrote. 'It has not been used so much in text, but in all situations where the value of display is paramount it has been extremely popular. Thus, the intense competition of advertising, where the least optical advantage makes itself felt at once, has already made some modern typography familiar to Americans.'

This passage was followed by a particularly astute observation that could pass as the *raison d'être* for the very design of Futura in the first place: 'Any art, particularly any art with a function as utilitarian as that of typography, consciously or unconsciously conforms itself to the peculiar temper of the living and contemporary civilization.'

As for how experimental typography acts as an adaptive force, the editors explained: 'An innovation stands out at first like a sore thumb but before it has passed its infancy it has become invisible to the conscious eye. ... In using, and continuing to use, the new typography, *Vanity Fair* believes that it knows very well what it is doing. In modifying one of the conventions of the new typography by returning to the use of capital letters in titles, it is obeying considerations that outlast any mere "revolution in style." The issue is thus one between attractiveness and legibility, or between form and content, and *Vanity Fair*, not wishing to undertake a campaign of education, casts its vote by returning to the use of capital letters in titles, to legibility, and to the cause of content above form.'

The general readership at whom this statement was aimed did not buy typefaces, but they were certainly made aware of their importance. For the designers and production managers who did buy and use type, Futura was promoted in the US in trade magazines, and through articles and examples in *PM/ AD*, *American Printer* and *Print* magazine, but almost nothing was as impressive as seeing Futura being used (with or without capitals) in *Vanity Fair*.

27

Jean Carlu (design): cover of
Vanity Fair, September 1930.

1
Bauer, Konrad Friedrich: *Werden und Wachsen einer deutschen Schriftgiesserei*. On one hundred years of existence of the Bauer Type Foundry Frankfurt am Main 1837–1937, Frankfurt am Main: Bauersche Giesserei, 1937, p. 66.

2
Renner, Paul: 'Modern, traditionell, modisch'. In: *Imprimatur* (Munich), vol. 3, 1932, p. 67.

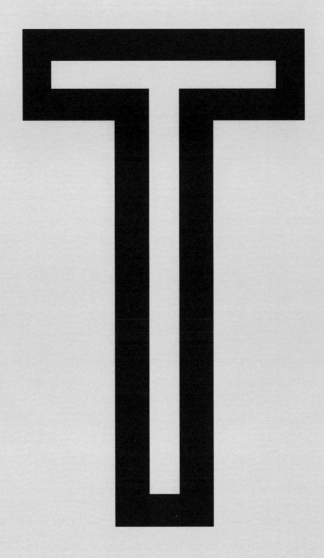

T, Futura Light.

O, Futura Light.

MOON

The internet is awash with references to the conspiracy theory that NASA engaged Stanley Kubrick to direct fake footage of the Apollo 11 moon landing, which was then broadcast to the world while the astronauts circled the Earth in low orbit, waiting to return. An adherent of such a theory would not hesitate, perhaps, to add that the stainless-steel plaque attached to the ladder of the lunar module – announcing, 'Here Men from the Planet Earth first set foot upon the moon, July 1969 AD. We came in peace for all mankind' – was composed in Futura because this was Kubrick's favourite typeface.

There seems to be no documented reason for choosing Futura to be the first typeface on the moon, but the thought that some inspiration came from its prominent use on the poster for 2001:

A *Space Odyssey*, Kubrick's masterpiece about space exploration released one year before the moon landings, cannot be ruled out. The name Futura may also have seemed appropriate to NASA for commemorating this most futuristic of endeavours. (The typeface Univers could have been even more appropriate, but was perhaps not sufficiently well known in the US by the late 1960s.)

CB

HOW DID FUTURA
GET TO THE MOON?

The plaque was designed and made in the Technical Services Division of the Manned Spacecraft Center, Houston, under the direction of Jack Kinzler and David McCraw. This division employed numerous technicians skilled in machining and metalwork. Two copies of the plate were curved around each side of the ladder on the descent stage of the lunar module – its lower part – which served as a launch pad for the upper part to blast off from, and was therefore left behind on the moon's surface.

Soon after the moon landing, the Bauer Type Foundry learned of the extraterrestrial adventure taken by its best-known typeface. Wolfgang Hartmann, grandson of Georg Hartmann and director of Bauer's Spanish subsidiary, Neufville, arranged for replicas of the NASA plaque to be made. He presented one to the minister of tourism at a trade fair, and this led to a request that he present one each to Spain's 'Chief of State', Francisco Franco, and Prince Juan Carlos. Wolfgang Hartmann was able to explain to them that the lead type used by NASA on the plaque had been cast in Spain, as had all Bauer foundry type supplied to the US market since World War II.

1
Landing of the *Eagle*.
Captured by Michael Collins,
Apollo 11 mission, NASA, 1969.

'I said, "Well, the first thing I'm caught up in is the idea we should have a plaque. We ought to have something with words on it indicating the crew's names and when they landed and where they came from." So my first suggestion was we ought to build something that we could put that information on. So I got an action item out of the committee saying, It's up to you. You go do it.'

JACK A. KINZLER
Interview with Paul Rollins
'Oral History 2 Transcript'
Seabrook, Texas, 16 January 1998.

357 HOW DID FUTURA GET TO THE MOON?

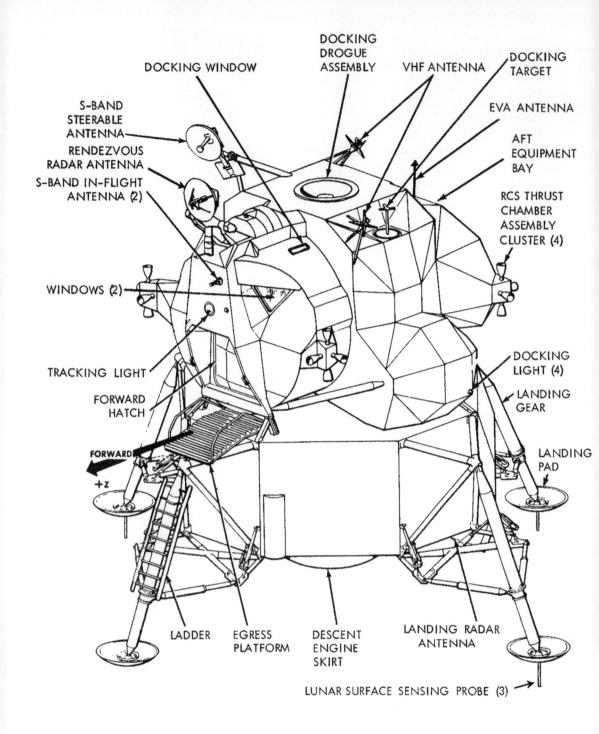

DOCKING
DROGUE
ASSEMBLY

DOCKING WINDOW

VHF ANTENNA

DOCKING
TARGET

S-BAND
STEERABLE
ANTENNA

EVA ANTENNA

RENDEZVOUS
RADAR ANTENNA

AFT
EQUIPMENT
BAY

S-BAND IN-FLIGHT
ANTENNA (2)

RCS THRUST
CHAMBER
ASSEMBLY
CLUSTER (4)

WINDOWS (2)

DOCKING
LIGHT (4)

TRACKING LIGHT

LANDING
GEAR

FORWARD
HATCH

LANDING
PAD

FORWARD

+Z

LADDER   EGRESS
PLATFORM

DESCENT
ENGINE
SKIRT

LANDING RADAR
ANTENNA

LUNAR SURFACE SENSING PROBE (3)

APOLLO LUNAR MODULE

2

P. 357 – The astronaut Edwin E. Aldrin leaves the space capsule and climbs down the ladder on to the moon's surface. Photo by Neil Armstrong, NASA, 1969.

3

Apollo lunar module, infographic, p. 97, from press kit, Apollo 11 mission of 6 July 1969.

4

An engineer holds the Apollo 11 plaque with its folding protective cover prior to its final installation on the ladder of the *Eagle*, July 1969.

5

(IN) A press release of 6 July 1969 (ten days before lift-off) painstakingly described what Armstrong's first action should be if the moon landing was suc-cessful – i.e. to unveil the plaque, the mes-sage of which also symbolized the entire mission of the trip.

This plaque was located on the foot of the lunar landing vehicle, which was left behind on the moon, and bears the inscrip-tion: 'Here men from the planet Earth first set foot upon the moon, July 1969, A.D.,' and below, 'We came in peace for all mankind.' Above are images of the two hemispheres of the Earth. Everything is engraved and set in upper-case Futura. Below are the signatures of President Nixon and the three astronauts, Armstrong, Collins and Aldrin. The unveil-ing by Armstrong was followed worldwide by means of a brief film clip.

After Armstrong's death in August 2012, his widow, Carol, discovered a white cloth bag in one of her husband's cupboards containing the video camera that he had used to document the landing on the moon. This late find is now on permanent loan at the National Air and Space Museum in Washington, DC.

4

HERE MEN FROM THE PLANET EARTH
FIRST SET FOOT UPON THE MOON
JULY 1969, A. D.
WE CAME IN PEACE FOR ALL MANKIND

NEIL A. ARMSTRONG
ASTRONAUT

MICHAEL COLLINS
ASTRONAUT

EDWIN E. ALDRIN, JR.
ASTRONAUT

RICHARD NIXON
PRESIDENT, UNITED STATES OF AMERICA

5

It's ugly, but it gets you there.

6

'It's ugly, but it gets you there'. Advertisement for the Volkswagen Beetle in the US by DDB, 1969.

7

(IN) The NASA Graphics Standards Manual from 1976 by New York design studio Danne & Blackburn, with the 'worm' logo, is an icon of corporate design and was only recently reissued in a reprint.

8

(IN) NASA Graphics Standards Manual, January 1976. It is interesting to note that although Helvetica, with its new look, was proclaimed the most important corporate type, on the next page Futura in light and semibold is recommended because of its 'technical character' for the special projects and print materials of NASA.

P
R
E
S
S

K
I
T

**APOLLO 11
LUNAR LANDING MISSION**

NASA

NATIONAL AERONAUTICS AND SPACE ADMINISTRATION

10

11

9

The official Apollo 11 crew photo: Neil A. Armstrong, Michael Collins, Edwin 'Buzz' Aldrin Jr (from left to right).

10

(IN) The powerful 254-page original press kit of NASA for the Apollo 11 mission of 6 July 1969. The letterhead of the National Aeronautics and Space Administration (NASA) and the lettering of many infographics and technical drawings is set in Futura. Also printed is the famous NASA logo, referred to as 'the meatball', of employee James Modarelli from 1959. The actual press release is set in a typewriter font with various sans serif types. It can by no means be described as consistent in visual style.

11

The official emblem of the NASA Apollo 11 mission: 'the eagle', which is landing on the moon with an olive branch in its talons. Above, in negative capitals set in Futura Bold, is written 'Apollo 11'. In the background is the blue planet Earth. NASA, 1969.

12

Apollo moon landing sites, infographic, p. 83, from press kit, Apollo 11 mission of 6 July 1969.

13

The foot of astronaut Neil Armstrong presses into the surface of the moon and leaves prints.

APOLLO LUNAR LANDING SITES

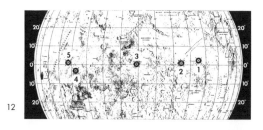

12

13

'It's Futura Extra Bold. It was Stanley's favourite typeface.'

TONY FREWIN
Stanley Kubrick's personal
assistant in an interview with Jon Ronson,
The Guardian, 27 March 2004.

14

Robert McCall: film poster for *2001: A Space Odyssey*, Stanley Kubrick, 1968. Title and subtitle in Futura. In the film, a modified Gill Sans was used for the title.

e, Futura Extra Bold.

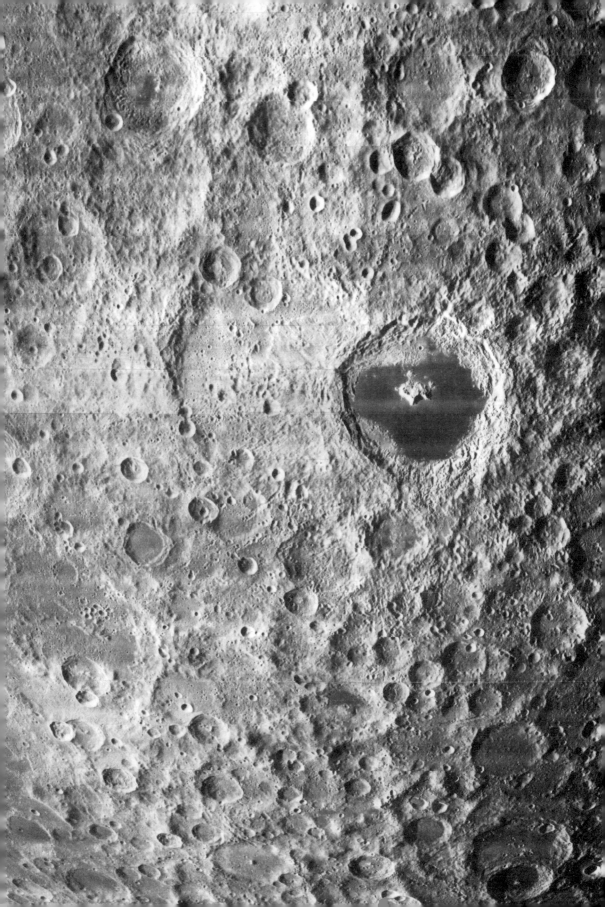

FUTURA. THE TYPEFACE IN DETAIL

1927	**Futura Light**
	Futura Medium
	Futura Schmuck
	Bauer Type Foundry

**TYPEFACES BY
PAUL RENNER**

1928 **Futura Bold**
Bauer Type Foundry

1928 **Plak; bold, bold condensed,
bold compressed**
D. Stempel AG

1929 **Futura Black**
Bauer Type Foundry

1930 **Futura Semibold
Futura Thin Italic
Futura Medium Italic
Futura Bold Condensed**
Bauer Type Foundry

1930 **Europe**
Deberny & Peignot

1931 **Futura Light
Futura Italic Semibold**
Bauer Type Foundry

1933 **Futura Book
Futura Schlagzeile**
Bauer Type Foundry

1937 **Futura Medium Condensed**
Bauer Type Foundry

1937 **Ballade Thin
Ballade Medium**
H. Berthold AG

1938 **Futura Bold Italic**
Bauer Type Foundry

1939 **Futura Book Italic**
Bauer Type Foundry

1939 **Renner Antiqua
Renner Kursiv**
D. Stempel AG

1950 **Futura Thin Condensed**
Bauer Type Foundry

1953 **Steile Futura Medium
Steile Futura Cursive Medium
Steile Futura Bold**
Bauer Type Foundry

1954 **Steile Futura Cursive Bold
Futura Heavy**
Bauer Type Foundry

1958 **Steile Futura Thin**
Bauer Type Foundry

1–48
Selected proofs of typefaces by
Paul Renner, 1927 to 1941.

WEILMÜNSTER

NIEDERLANDE

ABCDEFGHIKL

MNOPQRSTU

VWXYZÄÖÜ

ŒÆ.-:!'(§?*«»

gpqyJjiÇç,,;†

1234567890

Corps 72 Magere Futura ⁄ 23. August 1927

1

abcdefghijklm
nopqrstuvwxy
zæœçʃßchck&
àáâäèéêëïîìí
òóôöùúûü
ąăãåćčďđěęłľ
ñňŇøǿõőŕřşśštţǫůű

Corps 84 Magere Futura ⁄ 12. Oktober 1927

2

FUTURA PAUL RENNER
Kreuznach Ebernburg
84391 Flughafen 21083
Bauerſche Gießerei

ABCDEFGHIJKLMNO

PQRSTUVWXYZ

ÄÖÜÆŒÇØ$

abcdefghijklmmпnпop

qrsſtuvwxyzäöüchck

ﬀﬁﬂﬅﬃſiﬆß áàâåãèéêë

.,-:;!?(’»«*†§&ᴇ

1234567890

1234567890

Corps 36 Magere Futura ⁄ Korrektur 10. Januar 1928

3

3. VOLKS-KONZERT
ŒDENBURG
28. JANUAR 1832

Die Braut von Messina

Goldene Medaille

362 Kunſtgewerbe 168

Rüdesheim am Rhein

Frankfurter Hof

Corps 48 Magere Futura / Korrektur 11. Januar 1928

4

DIE ZAUBERFLÖTE
MERGENTHEIM
ABCDEFGHIJKLM
NOPQRSTUVWX
YZÖÄÜŒÆÇ

1234567890

1234567890

., -:;!?(§†*'«»&

ɑgɱɳɾ℮

Gutenberg-Muſeum
Richard Wagner
Hotel Schweizerhof
Winterfahrplan
abcdefghijklmnop
qrsſtuvwxyzæœç
chckﬀﬃﬁﬂﬄſiſtß
äüöáàâéèêëìíîï
òóôùúûãõñå

Corps 60 Magere Futura ⁄ 18. Juni 1928

Offenbach a. M.
Wiſſenſchaft
Der Konfektionär
abcdefhiklmnor
stuvwxzæœ
àáâäéèêëìîí
òóôöùúûü
ck ch ff ffi fi ft fl fr ſi ſſ ſt ß &

Corps 72 Magere Futura ⁄ 23. August 1928

7

ABCDEFGHIJ
KLMNOPQR
STUVWXYZ
ÆŒÇÄÖÜ
1234567890
.,-:;!?'*(†§«»
ĄĐĘŁĽŞŢ

Corps 84 Magere Futura / 12. Oktober 1928

MORGENLIED
QUO VADIS
DREHBÜNHE
Wilhelm Busch
Rigoletto
Zeitungshalter
Präsidium

Corps 84 Magere Futura ⁄ 12. Oktober 1928

ABCDEFGHIJKLMN
OPQRSTUVWXYZ
ÄÖÜÆŒÇØ$
aabcdefgghijklmm
nnopqrsſtuvwxyz
æœchckçﬀﬁﬂﬀﬁſﬅß
äáàáâäòóóôöøùùúûü
.,-:,;!?('†§*«»&&
1234567890
1234567890
abdegpqréèêëàáâä
åãĩ1238

BILDER-GALERIE
FRÜHJAHRS-MODE
RASENSPORT
Homburger Kurhaus
Zeichen-Atelier
Maſchinen-Bauſchule
Photographie
Handel und Induſtrie
17 Meiſterwerke 36
5291 Ödenburg 680

Corps 48 halbfette Renner Futura ∗ Korrektur 19. Dezember 1927

AN DER SPITZE DER EUROPÄISCHEN
SCHRIFTEN STEHEN DIE RÖMISCHEN
Versalien, aufgebaut aus Kreis, Dreieck
und Geviert, den denkbar einfachsten
und denkbar gegensätzlichsten Formen.
Seltsam strahlt die vornehme und edle
Schlichtheit dieser Schrift in unsere Zeit,
wie ein letzter Schimmer von der hellen
Geistigkeit des alten Roms. Das Einfache

A B C D E F G H I K L M N O P Q R S T U
163429 J V W X Y Z Æ Œ Ç 372108
a b c d e f g h i j k l m m n n o p q r s ſ t
u v w x y z ch ck ff fi fl ﬀ ﬄ ﬁ ﬅ ß æ œ ç å
à á ä â ã ò ó ô ö õ . , - : ; ! ' ? (§ † & & * « »
1 2 3 4 5 6 7 8 9 o 1 2 3 4 5 6 7 8 0

abdegpqràáâäåãèéêë1238

Corps 20 Halbfette Renner-Futura / Korrektur 30. Dezember 1927

RENNER FUTURA

WÜRZBURG

POST   MESSE

ABCDEFGHIJKLM
NOPQRSTUVW
XYZÄÖÜÆŒÇ
.,:;-!?(«»†§*&
1234567890
1234567890

Corps 60 halbfette Futura ⁄ Korrektur 2. März 1928

RENNER FUTURA

WÜRZBURG

POST MESSE

ABCDEFGHIJKLM

NOPQRSTUVW

XYZÄÖÜ

1234567890

Zeitungs-Verleger
Fichtel & Sachs
Frankfurt a. d. O.
Berliner Stadion

abcdefghijklmno

pqrsſtuvwxyz

æœçchckﬀﬁﬂﬀﬃſi

ſtßíĩìïíóòôöùúûü

e

Corps 60 halbfette Futura / Korrektur 2. März 1928

14

KURGARTEN
EISENACH
Mode-Bazar
Rheinſtein
Taſchenbuch
Hamburg
Sängerfest

Corps 84 Halbfette Futura / 16. März 1928

ABCDEFGHI
JKLMNOPQ
RSTUVWXY
ZÆŒÄÖÜ

.,-.:;!?«»'*†§&&

1234567890
1234567890

Corps 84 Halbfette Futura / 16. März 1928

abcdefghijkl
mmnnnopqrr
sftuvwxyz
æœçchck
äöüèéêë
ﬀﬁﬂﬀﬀﬁﬂﬃß
ø $

abcdefghijkl
mmnnopqrr
sſtuvwxyz
ﬀﬁﬂﬀﬁﬃﬄﬁﬀﬁﬁß
ch ck æ œ ç & &
Øø$

Corps 72 Halbfette Futura / 22. März 1928

HANNOVER
MELDUNG
Koln am Rhein
Talsperre
Schriftgießer
Odenwald
Mannheim

Corps 72 Halbfette Futura / 22. März 1928

ABCDEFGHIJKLMN
OPQRSTUVWXYZ
ÆŒÇÄÖÜØ$
aabcdefgghijklmm
nпopqrsſtuvwxyz
ch ck ff fi fl fl ffl ffi ffl ß
æœàáâäåàáâäãéè
êëìíîïñòóôöõøùúûü
& .,-:;!?'(§†«»*&
1234567890
EFfl

BAUERSCHE GIESSEREI
FRANKFURT A. M.

Die Zauberflöte
Johannes Gutenberg
Wilhelm Tell
Über den Wellen
Feſtvorſtellung
Mülheim an der Ruhr
Opernhaus
Äther Öffnung

Corps 36 fette Renner Futura ∕ Korrektur 23. November 1927

KÖLN AM RHEIN
GEOGRAPHIE
Romeo und Julia

Rigoletto

Doppelquartett

Winterfeſt

Alt-Heidelberg

Odenwald

.,-:;!?(§†*'»«&ε

1234567890

JKOSZkcksſſſ/Mﬄ ß

ROTHENFELS

HAMBURG

Zeitschriften

Gutenberg

Schornſtein

Expreß-Zug

Barcelona

Flugwoche

Corps 72 Fette Futura / 2. Mai 1928

23

Zentral-Hotel
Reichswehr
Wochenend
abcdefghijkl
mnopqrsſtuv
wxyzæœç
ﬀﬁﬂﬃﬄﬆß
chckäöüàáâ
èéêìíîïöóôùúû

Corps 60 Fette Futura - 26. Mai 1928

24

abcdefghij
klmnopqrſ
stuvwxyz
æœ&chck
 fffiflﬀﬁﬂﬃﬄß
áàâãăéèêìíî
òóôöùúûü

Corps 84/72 Fette Futura / 3. Juli 1928

HERMELIN
MEXIKO
QUINTA
Offenbach
Sonate
Winterfeſt
Panzer

Corps 84/72 Fette Futura / 3. Juli 1928

BETON- U. EISENKONSTRUKTION
NEUZEITLICHE BAUKUNST

Der Ring des Nibelungen
Siegfried Götterdämmerung
Sonate in S-dur
Deutſches Tennis-Turnier
Hamburg Amerika
Olympiſche Spiele 1928
Winter-Feſt

A B C D E F G H I J K L M N O P Q R
S T U V W X Y Z Æ Œ Ç
Ä Ö Ü Á Ã Å È É Ê Ë Í Ñ Ó Ø Õ $ Ú
a a b c d e f g g h i j k l m m n n o
p q r s ſ t u v w x y z æ œ ç ä ä ö ü
ch ck ff fi fl ﬀ ſi ſſ ſt ß & ε
à à á á â â å å ã ã è é ê ë ì í î ï
ñ ñ ò ó ô õ ø ù ú û
. , - : ; ! ? ' († § * « » & ε
1 2 3 4 5 6 7 8 9 0

J K S Z e k ck s ſ ſſ ſi ſt ß

Corps 20 Fette Renner Futura - Korrektur 6. Dezember 1928

INDUSTRIE
MANIFEST
HOMBURG
Kanalisation
Hildesheim
Autowerke
Gartenlaube

Corps 72/60 Futura - Black — Korrektur 4. September 1929

OBERURSEL A. T.
GRIECHENLAND
ÖDIPUS ÄTHER
Rheinland-Feier
24. Juli 1930
MainzWiesbaden
Genoſſenſchaft
ch ck ff fi fl ﬅ ﬆ ﬀ ﬁ ﬂ ß
1234567890

Corps 60 Dreiviertelfette Futura - 21. Juli 1930

ABCDEFGHIJ
KLMNOPQRS
TUVWXYZÆ
ŒÇÄÖÜ œ æ ç

abcdefghijkl
mnopqrsſtuv
wxyzchckﬀﬁﬂ
ﬃﬄﬅﬆßÄàáâãë
èéêëïìíîïöòóôöüù

Byrd's Flug über den Südpol

Frankfurter Stadtparlament

Naſſauiſche Landesbank

Goethe-Denkmal zu Weimar

Hamburger Pferde-Lotterie

Deutscher Buchdrucker-Verein

Kurhaus Münſter am Stein

Erzeugnisse der Industrie

28. Juni 1769 14. Februar 1903

United States of America

Australia and New-Sealand

ſ æ ch ck ſ ſi ſt ß fi ſt † § ? ( ) 3 5 8

Corps 36 magere Futura Kursiv - Korr. 10. Januar 1930

NORDERNEY QUAST

BAD MERGENTHEIM

XYLOPHON ZITHER

1872 CARLTON 1905

Berliner Stadt-Theater

Rundfunk-Ausstellung

Hagen in Westfalen

Printed in Germany

Colt Manufacturing

Corps 48 Halbfette Futura Kursiv - 23. Oktober 1929

ABCDEFGHIJJKLM
NOPQRSTUVWXY
ZÄÖÜÆŒÇæœç
abcdefghijklmnop
qrrsftuvwxyzäöü
chckﬀﬁﬂﬀﬂßﬅﬆ
£ØC$ø
.,-:;!?)'*§†»«&&
1234567890

Corps 48 Halbfette Futura Kursiv — 24. Oktober 1929

33

(Gesangs-Quartett)

Minifterialerlaß § 17

Bücher, Deckel Eifel

Freytag; Imker Jod

Suppé 93658 Wàffe

Keffel Often! Reflex

O Q

Bauersche Gießerei, Frankfurt a. M.   23. September 1936   Schmale halbfette Futura 84 Punkt

SUNDAY TIMES
Milchkuranſtalt
Rettungs-Wache
Beton u. Tiefbau
Philipp Hofmann
Central-Bahnhof
Wiſſenſchaftler

Corps 84 Schmalfette Futura - 14. Juli 1930

BAUER TYPE FOUNDRY INC.

CAROLUS-DRUCKEREI

Bayrische Hypothekenbank

Arabische Vollblut-Pferde.

Fortſchritte, Erkennungsdienſt

Genoſſenſchaft; (Iphigenie)

John Miller & Son, NewYork

Küſtengebiet »Louiſiana«

Technik! Unterkunft? Wecker

Xenia Zähler Ärzte-Verband

17240 Öhre § 832 Überfluß

I b

Bauersche Gießerei, Frankfurt a. M.   29. Dezember 1936   Futura-Buchschrift 36 Punkt

VOLKSTAGE
WESTFALEN
REISENDER
1930 MUND
KING 2564

Corps 84 Lichte Futura - 2. März 1931

SONNE. WESPE
Arzt Bach Licht
Dame! Emden
Farbe Hufland
Rom Jota Kino
Mord 89 Irene
$ 21.35 List Ruf
(Teppich) Ulk

72 Punkt Schlagzeilen-Futura - 30. August 1932

ADLERWERKE FRANKFURT A. M.
THE SATURDAY EVENING POST

**Bohrung Choral, Deutz; Frucht
Excellenz Gruß Hoffnung Irrtum
Jahrmarkt Kampf London $ 45
Madison Square 126. New York
Oxford Philadelphia Railroad
(United States of America)
3896 William Vrous 1078**

**ABCDEFGHIJKLMNO
PQRSTUVWXYZ$
abcdefghijklmnopq
rstuvwxyz ff fi fl ft
äéòû&
.,-:;!?('1234567890**

Bauersche Gießerei, Frankfurt a. M.   31. März 1937   Fette Futura Kursiv 28 Punkt

WARENHAUS
KOLB & DEPHIR
Rheinstahl 916
Villa Urban
Zelt 2579.10
Sunday Times

Bauersche Gießerei, Frankfurt a. M.   1. April 1937   Fette Futura Kursiv 60 Punkt

Naſſauiſche Landesbank;
Erfinder – Flughafen
Drexel-Lichtſpiele. Jülich
Chrysanthemen, Haftung.
Auguſt Marſchall & Reuß
(Bockenheimer Warte)
£ 5276.40 $ 891 ¢ 60
., - : ; ! ? ([„ " » « – ' * § †
1234567890

Bauersche Gießerei, Frankfurt a. M.   15. Februar 1939   Futura-Buchschrift-Kursiv 48 Punkt

Advertising is a branch of human activtiy which emphasizes its selfish motive and admits it openly. The more a people is inclined by its education and mode of thinking to lay the chief weight on ideal viewpoints and to keep material matters in the background, by so much the less is

THE GENTLE HINT OF STYLE
SHOPS AND BAZARS OF BOSTON
GRAPHIC ARTS EXPOSITION
LIGHT ON A GROUNDED SUBJECT

International Studio of Philadelphia
Etching of contemporary films
A favorite pattern of the modern bride
The Spanish Interior Decoration
South Eastern Railway

BAUERSCHE GIESSEREI FRANKFURT A.M.

ABCDEFGHIJKLMNOPQRSTUVWXYZ
abcdefghijklmnopqrstuvwxyz
ÄÇÖÜÆŒáàâäçéèêëíìîïóòôöúùûü
æœchckfffifl ftß ´ ` ^ ¨
.,-:;!?)'·&1234567890

AUS DEN KIRCHEN HOLT MAN ALLE HEILIGEN
IKONEN UND RELIQUIEN UND ÜBERALL DORT,

wo eine Bresche in die Mauer geschlagen ist,
hängt man dann eines der Heiligenbilder hin,
damit es besser als irdische Waffen den Sturm
der Ungläubigen abwehren solle. Gleichzeitig
versammelt Kaiser Konstantin die Senatoren,
die Kommandanten und Heerführer um sich.

Bauersche Gießerei   23. Juli 1951   Futura schmal mager 28 Punkt

Hamburg arme gar geboren Organe ab Hammer graue Orb nur Obernburg bar

HOabegmnoru

Bauersche Gießerei, Frankfurt a. M.   30. September 1938   Normale Renner-Grotesk 48 Punkt

BERLINER ZEITSCHRIFTENVERLAG

FONDERIE BAUER / NEW YORK

Amtsgericht Frankfurt am Main

Bau- und Siedlungs-Gesellschaft.

Kriegs-Winterhilfswerk 1940

(Erstlings-Ausstattungen)

Teerprodukte, Chemische Industrie

Deutsche Lufthansa; Königsberg

J. Eckhard & Hänflin, Worms

Operntexte: „Undine" Richard IV.

Mühle! Quäker Paßzwang?

§652 £ 810.62 $ 3790 ₡ 25

Bauersche Gießerei, Frankfurt a. M.   7. Dezember 1939   Normale Renner-Grotesk 36 Punkt

Hamburg Obmann
genau ebnen gerne
Horn am Orangen
ungarn Herborn er
Orbra um Hanauer

HOabegmnoru

Bauersche Gießerei, Frankfurt am Main   8. März 1939   Normale Renner-Kursiv 48 Punkt

ABCDEEFGHIJKLMNOP
QRSTUVWWXYZ
abcdefghijklmnopqrstuv
wxyzy&.,:-;!?(´*†§
1234567890

ABCEGJKPRSTVWWXYZ
acdeikpqstvwx
&?§234569

Bauersche Gießerei, Frankfurt a. M. 2. Mai 1939 Normale Renner-Kursiv 28 Punkt

ABCDEEFGHIJKLMN
OPQRSTUVWWXYZ
ÄÖÜÆŒÇ$£¢
abcdefghijkklmnop
qrsſtuvwxyyz
œœchckckçﬀﬁﬂﬅﬆſiſtßß
.,-:;!?(§+*'„"&
1234567890
AGMNШVWvwy

Bauersche Gießerei, Frankfurt a. M.   30. Januar 1941   Magere Normal-Kursiv 28 Punkt

49
Booklet of type specimens, Bauer Type
Foundry, 1950s.

Aa Bb Cc Dd

Ee Ff Gg Hh

Ii Jj Kk Ll Mm

Nn Oo Pp Qq

Rr Ss Tt Uu Vv

Ww Xx Yy Zz

ä ö ü fi fl 1 2 3

4 5 6 7 8 9 0

ISABEL NAEGELE

THE ANATOMY OF FUTURA

The following letters are unmistakeable symbols for identifying Futura, suitable when performing a quick typeface check: **a**, **j**, **t**, **u**, **M**, **C**, and the figure **1**.

The single-storey lower-case **a** was one of the characteristic symbols of the German grotesque types. As such, it was not in any way an innovation and had been known primarily as a playful form in 'cursive' Antiqua. However, the radical concept underlying the formal motifs of Futura, with its single-storey, round lower-case **a** and its two-storey **g**, was unprecedented for its time and was adopted as a successful model by several renowned type foundries in their own typefaces, such as Ludwig & Mayer in Erbar.[1]

The lower-case **j** is one of the few symbols that was retained from Ur-Futura, apart from its original square 'point', which was replaced by a round point. It is a special symbol in that it has no curve. This is also the case for the lower-case **t**, with its characteristically low ascender. The lower-case **t** and **f** are also distinctive because of their asymmetrical crossbar. The lower-case **u** is symmetrical and has no downstroke. The capital **M** in the light, book and medium sets has a sharp vertex and apexes, as do the **A** and **N**.

The capital **C** is notable for its geometrically round form. The angle at the ends of the **C** and **c** is vertical, ending

at a 90-degree angle to the baseline. In this way, the special characteristics of German spelling and the frequent letter combinations **Ch**, **Ck**, **ch**, **ck** are taken into account. In the figures, the **1** is notable for its horizontal nose and diagonal terminal.

CLASSIFICATION

All things require their own order; this is also the case for typefaces, of which there are a vast number. In Germany, the Deutsche Institut für Normung (German Standardization Institute) is officially responsible for the classification of typefaces. The classification of DIN 16518 puts Futura in group 1.6 as a sans serif linear Antiqua and as a geometric linear Antiqua. However, upon closer inspection, the widths and proportions of the humanistic grotesque can be observed in Ur-Futura. The clear differences in the width of the letters are characteristic. Thus, the proportions of the narrow capitals **E**, **F**, **L**, **S** compared with the wide capitals **A**, **M**, **N**, **O**, **Q** correspond to the size ratios of the humanistic alphabet.

According to the Willberg Matrix, the principle of form must be differentiated from style.[2] In formal terms, Futura is a typical representative of the grotesque, with geometric principles of form, i.e. with equal stroke weights, constructed forms and an **R** with a diagonal downstroke.[3]

The French classification, according to Maximilien Vox, is historically based and considers Futura to be a 'monoline' type.

ANATOMICAL DETAILS

'So long as we use upper-case and lower-case letters next to each other, the artist has the task of executing the same formal motif in both of these very different alphabets. Since the form of the Roman capitals must be left untouched, it would be more appropriate to transfer the motif of their contrasting forms to the lower-case letters.'[4] This was Paul Renner's explanation in 1930 of his concept for the design of Futura. He drew inspiration for the construction of the upper-case letters from the forms of Capitalis Monumentalis, namely, the circle, square and triangle, while his particular innovation was the transfer of this formal language to the lower-case letters and, as a result, the harmonious combination of the upper- and lower-case alphabets. Thus, for example, **a**, **b**, **p** and **q** 'only' consist of a circle and a stroke.

Geometric clarity and the rejection of all superfluity are the hallmarks of Futura. Renner made the point succinctly in a letter to the Bauer Type Foundry in 1940: what made Futura special was that 'all its letters are rooted in a geometric substrate, which gives the typeface a very strict cohesion when used as rows of symbols.'[5]

Indeed, even though the 'geometric substrate' underwent significant revision before arriving at the final form, the consistency of the typeface's symbols in the capitals **E**, **F**, **G**, **S**, the figures **2**, **3**, **4**, **5** and the lower-case **a**, **e**, **g**, **s** distinguishes it significantly in terms of its look from the competing grotesque types of the time, such as Johnston and Erbar.

As a linear grotesque, Futura contains no serifs and employs no upstrokes or downstrokes in lower-case letters such as the **l** and **t**. Of course it is free of any remnants of handwriting, and is considered to be a 'true expression of the technical process'. One special characteristic of Futura, although not an innovation, is the upright, single-storey **a**.[6]

Although Futura was the first typeface that Renner designed, he had already addressed the issue of optical phenomena with the eye of a trained typographer in his early book-typography work. With Heinrich Jost and his team at the Bauer Type Foundry, the details of the typeface's design were refined over a period of more than two years before it was released in 1927. While some of the more radical alternates were abandoned during this process, the long-lasting success of the typeface justifies the pragmatic approach taken at the time: 'The artistic value of a typeface is determined purely in the eyes of the beholder, and therefore in the sphere of perception rather than the sphere of mathematical concepts.'[7]

Following the optical correction of the circle – stretching it vertically – the counters of the **a**, **b**, **d**, **g**, **o**, **p** and **q** are no longer round, but are optically balanced ovals. And in some intersections with the stem, the stroke weights at the points of intersection are, strictly speaking, no longer monoline and have been narrowed instead.

Renner defined the basis for this optical correction in his article 'Das Formproblem der Druckschrift' (The Problem of Form in Printed Type; 1930):

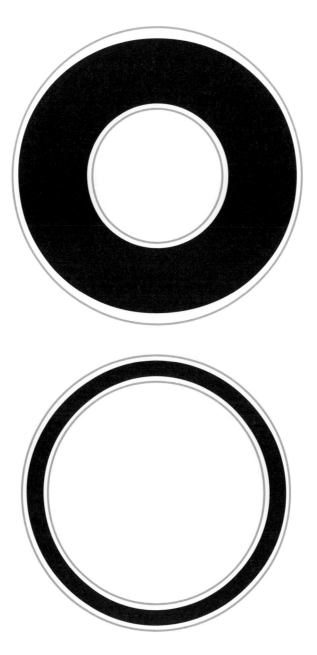

Top: Optical correction of the capital bold
O. To achieve an optical monoline effect,
the letter is narrower along the horizontal
than along the vertical. The rounding is
even somewhat wider at the widest horizontal point.
Bottom: Futura Light is actually almost
monoline.

Original construction of the a, with circle and stroke prior to optical correction.

After optical correction: the counter cuts into the stem. Enclosed lower-case a.

a a

Comparison of a circular and oval counter.

The counter is taller than it is wide. The oval counters cut into the stem.

Identical principle of construction for b, p, d and q. But the descenders are significantly shorter than the ascenders.

The arcs narrow towards the stem, and the strokes at the upper and lower points of connection are equal.

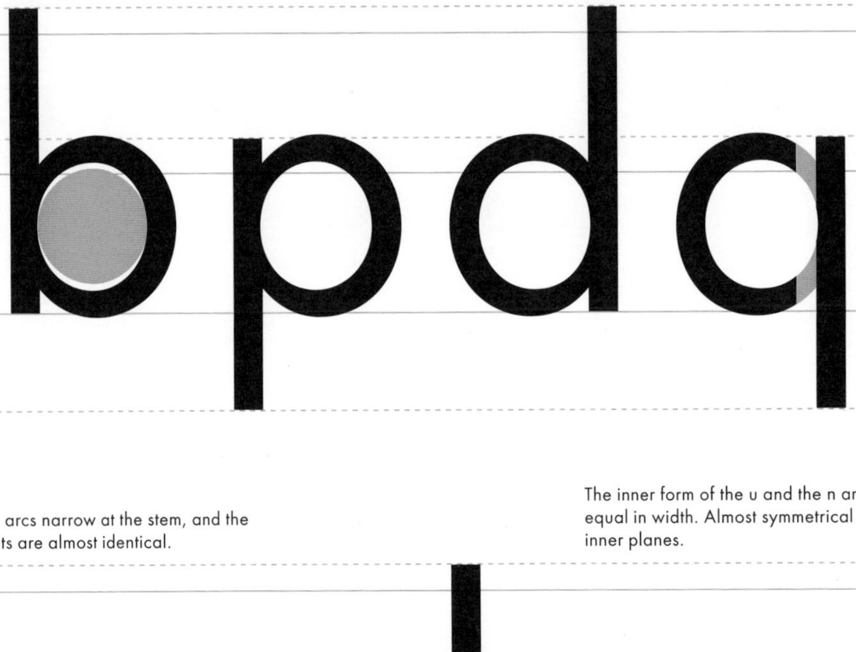

bpdq

The arcs narrow at the stem, and the joints are almost identical.

The inner form of the u and the n are equal in width. Almost symmetrical inner planes.

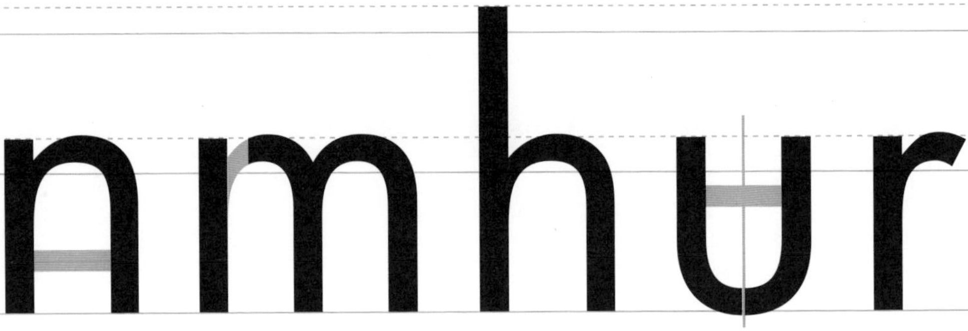

nmhur

scender
p height

eight
ean line

seline

scender

No arcs or downstrokes in the lower-case t, f and j.
Asymmetrical crossbar in the t and f.

The lower-case L overshoots the
capital i and is slightly lighter.

The ligature of the 'eszett' connects
the long s with a short s. Same stroke
as for f.

Ascenders overshoot the cap height.

Vertical terminal in
upper- and lower-case C.

Very wide, closed
lower-case e, horizontal
crossbars, oblique
terminal.

Oblique terminals in S.
The angles are discreetly varied.

Geometrically round form in C, G and Q.

O G Q

Vertical terminal in the C, which enables the letter to terminate close to the letters h and k.

The G has a very closed form and a vertical terminal. G, C and S end with different angles.

Horizontal terminal in the diagonal tail of the Q.

The sharp vertexes and apexes in the V, A and W overshoot the cap height and/or baseline.

W consists of two narrow V-shapes.

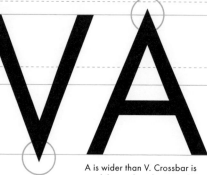

V A W

A is wider than V. Crossbar is much lower than the mean line.

The diagonal strokes narrow very slightly towards the point of intersection.

Sharp turning point at the top and bottom. The angles of the diagonal strokes vary between Z and z.

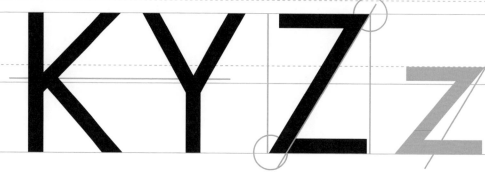

K Y Z z

ender

height

eight

an line

eline

cender

Upper and lower arms are equal in length.

HTEE

Contrast in stroke between the stem and the crossbar. The crossbar is somewhat lower than the middle arm of the E.

L and F are narrower than E; the middle arm lies at the same height, significantly above the mean line.

The arcs of the R and P go lower than in the B. Diagonal, straight leg in the R.

U is symmetrical; J has a smaller inner radius.

BRPU

The upper half of the B is larger than in the E. The lower bowl of the B is wider.

Horizontal nose in the 1 with an oblique starting stroke.

Sharp turning points in the 2 and 4. A closed 4 with a low crossbar creates a triangle shape.

!1246

Round points for the full stop, exclamation mark and question mark.

Circle and diagonal stroke in the 6.

Ligatures in Futura Medium and Light.
Top: f-i, f-l and f-t ligatures. The f-t ligature
is a remnant or alternate from Ur-Futura.
Bottom: f-f and f-f-i ligatures.

'Wherever two strong bars intersect at right angles or at a sharp angle, a zone forms which becomes more or less brighter as a result of irradiation. This results in dark spots.'[8]

With the first revision, the upper-case **A**, **N**, **M**, **V** and **W**, and the **v** and **w**, each received a sharp apex/vertex in light, book and medium in 1925. The horizontal arms of the **E** and **F** are all the same length.

The 'round' capital **G** has a horizontal end stroke, and the round **Q** has a distinctive diagonal tail.

The x-height is rather high in comparison with the types of the 1920s/30s and is also the reason for the type's relatively good legibility. Renner decided early on to 'strengthen' the lower-case letters optically by emphasizing the ascenders of many of them, such as the **b**, **d**, **f**, **h**, **k**, **l** and **ß**, and allowing overshoots over the cap height. He drew inspiration from examples taken from the humanist lower-case alphabet for this purpose.[9] As a result, the ascenders significantly overshoot the cap height. Looking back, Renner remarked: 'So, for example, I kept the capitals of Futura somewhat shorter than the ascenders of the lower-case letters. How many letters I received after the typeface's release, complaining that I needed to improve this sole error.'[10]

The secret of Futura's success can be found partly in its anatomy. While the typeface is impressive in its conceptual rigour and geometric principles of construction, it is also 'elegantly ungeometric' in its details — the result of intense and fine adjustment.[11]

FUTURA IS FUTURA?

At the beginning of the 1970s Futura was made available for photosetting in Germany by the companies Berthold and Linotype. Owing to the tastes of the time and the influence of typography from Switzerland and Ulm, a more compressed character spacing than was technically possible with the use of lead typesetting, with its rather light spacing, was demanded. This was compounded by the need in advertising typography for greater design independence. However, with all the freedom given to the typographers of the time with regard to the white spaces and innovative possibilities offered by design, it had to be accepted that in phototypesetting, regardless of type size, only one basic character form was used and photomechanically scaled. Only the kerning, the white space between the characters, could be adjusted automatically.[12]

The digital era began towards the end of the 1970s. By the mid 1980s, most fonts had been digitized. The enormous number of digitized versions of Futura in circulation – including by Linotype, Bitstream, Berthold, URW++ and Elsner+Flake, with their substantial differences in the details of the characters and spacing – is confusing for the layman, but can be attributed to the template used for each digitized version. As a result, the differences between suppliers of a typeface of the same name and size can be significant. On a micro-typographic level, these differences are small in terms of the radius and proportion of the characters, but they are substantial when it comes to cap height, stroke weight and spacing, resulting in a different look on a macro-typographic level, or a different grey tone in a body of text. Or, to put it simply: the body of text 'runs differently'. Hans Andree described this in his comparative analysis of the five most popular digital versions of Futura Book with a lead typeset version: 'Which digital and analogue templates were the basis of Futura and which technical methods were used to convert the characters for further processing has certainly been handled in different ways and is difficult to determine with historical accuracy.'[13]

During this process, certain sets were also abandoned or renamed. This concerns *Futura kräftig* and *Futura dreiviertelfett*, which are very similar in density. The name of the face in English is also a source of confusion: *Futura halbfett*(demibold) is known today as Futura ND Medium, and *Futura dreiviertelfett* corresponds most closely to Futura ND Demibold.

Today, through the OpenType format, the approximately 65,000 symbols, and thereby multiple glyphs for each symbol (so-called alternates), can be documented. After Architype Renner by The Foundry (1997), Futura ND Alternate (2015) by Neufville Digital (a joint venture between Bauer Types SL, Fundición Tipográfica Neufville and Visualogik) reverts to earlier lead versions, thereby bringing Futura back to its beginnings with many alter-nates, yet connecting it with the technical requirements of a typeface of our time.

A A **A** **A** **A** **A** **A** A A A A A A A A **A** **A** **A** A A

B B **B** **B** **B** **B** **B** B B B B B B B B **B** **B** **B** B B

C C **C** **C** **C** **C** **C** C C C C C C C **C** **C** **C** C C

M M **M** **M** **M** **M** **M** M M M M M M M **M** **M** **M** M M

Q Q **Q** **Q** **Q** **Q** **Q** Q Q Q Q Q Q Q **Q** **Q** **Q** Q Q

R R **R** **R** **R** **R** **R** R R R R R R R **R** **R** **R** R R

Z Z **Z** **Z** **Z** **Z** **Z** Z Z Z Z Z Z Z **Z** **Z** **Z** Z Z

a a **a** **a** **a** **a** **a** a a a a a a a **a** **a** **a** a a

b b **b** **b** **b** **b** **b** b b b b b b b **b** **b** **b** b b

c c **c** **c** **c** **c** **c** c c c c c c c **c** **c** **c** c c

n n **n** **n** **n** **n** **n** n n n n n n n **n** **n** **n** n n

o o **o** **o** **o** **o** **o** o o o o o o o **o** **o** **o** o o

t t **t** **t** **t** **t** **t** t t t t t t t **t** **t** **t** t t

l l **l** **l** **l** **l** **l** l l l l l l l **l** **l** **l** l l

Futura ND light/mager

Futura ND book/buch

Futura ND medium/halbfett

Futura ND demibold/dreiviertelfett

Futura ND bold/fett

Futura ND extrabold

Futura ND extrabold oblique

Futura ND bold oblique/fett schräg fett

Futura ND demibold oblique/dreiviertelfett schräg

Futura ND medium oblique/halbfett schräg

Futura ND book oblique/schräg buch

Futura ND light oblique/schräg mager

Futura ND Cn light oblique/schräg schmalmager

Futura ND Cn medium oblique/schräg schmalhalbfett

Futura ND Cn bold oblique/schräg schmalfett

Futura ND Cn extrabold oblique

Futura ND Cn extrabold

Futura ND Cn bold/schmalfett

Futura ND Cn medium/schmalhalbfett

Futura ND Cn light/schmalmager

FÜR DIE ELEMENTARE TYPOGRAPHIE

BAUERSCHE GIESSEREI FRANKFURT A. MAIN W 13

ist nach Aussagen ihrer vielen Anhänger unsere

VENUS

die geeignetste Schrift

Der bekannte und berühmte Bauhausmeister **L. MOHOLY-NAGY** urteilt in „Offset-, Buch- und Werbekunst" Nr. 7: ■ Als Auszeichnungs- und Titelschrift besitzen wir dagegen annähernd brauchbare, gute Schriften, deren geometrische und fonetische Urform, wie Quadrat oder Kreis, ohne Verzerrungen zur Geltung kommt. Das ist die Venus-Grotesk ■

ERIK SPIEKERMANN
FERDINAND ULRICH

FUTURA AND ITS ENVIRONMENT

Typefaces for use in book printing were made of a lead alloy — a soft and very heavy metal. They were sold according to weight and quickly wore out. Every new typeface was a major investment and a risk for both the buyer at the printing house and the manufacturer, the type foundry, because typefaces, even at that time, were subject to the prevailing taste. Just like hemlines in fashion, trends changed in typography, too. While today it takes just weeks, or even days, for a new type to be delivered as a digital font, back then it took years for an idea to develop into a design and reach the manufacturing stage. New lead typefaces were announced early, before a sketch had even been completed. This enabled the name to be registered and expressed an intention to produce the typeface, nothing more. Today it is difficult to determine who had which idea first, and exactly when a typeface came on to the market in its first version.

The idea of a sans serif without flourishes and free of any historical burden was hanging in the air. When *Typografische Mitteilungen* (Typography News) published Jan [Ivan] Tschichold's article 'Elementare Typographie' (Elementary Typography) in 1925, there was still no explicit mention of geometric sans serifs. Paragraph 4 in Tschichold's manifesto advocated: 'Elementary type form is the sans serif type in all its variations.' So-called static grotesque types began to enjoy increasing popularity at the beginning of the twentieth century, especially Venus (1907) by Bauer and Breite Grotesk (1890) by the Leipzig type foundry Schelter & Giesecke – both of which were frequently used by Herbert Bayer, Joost Schmidt and László Moholy-Nagy (and because this typeface was one of the sets in the possession of the Bauhaus printing house) – as well as

51

52

Akzidenz Grotesk, by H. Berthold AG in Berlin. In addition to their ideological superstructure, the facilities of the printing

50

P. 478 – Venus, type specimen 'Schmuck' from the Bauer Type Foundry, c. 1927.

51

P. 479 – Herbert Bayer: commemorative exhibition to celebrate the 60th birthday of Wassily Kandinsky, poster, 1926, set in Breite Grotesk.

52

P. 479 – H. Berthold AG: 'Die "klassische" Grotesk', specimen no. 462, Berlin/ Stuttgart, year not specified.

53

Comparison of Universalschrift by Herbert Bayer, Schablonenschrift by Josef Albers and Systemschrift by Kurt Schwitters with Paul Renner's Futura in Heinrich Jost's critical article 'Zweifel' (Doubt), in *Klimschs Jahrbuch* (Frankfurt am Main), vol. 21, 1928.

54

Josef Albers: Schablonenschrift, 1923–26. In: *Offset, Buch- und Werbekunst*, 1926 (special Bauhaus issue).

55

Herbert Bayer: design of Grotesk lower-case letters (probably 1926).

56

P. 482 – Ludwig & Mayer: 'Die schöne Erbar Grotesk', Frankfurt am Main (probably 1929).

bahnhofsplatz

Abb. 3. Versuch einer neuen Schrift von Herbert Bayer

einfacher Elemente

Abb. 4. „Schablonenschrift" von Josef Albers

neue plastische systemschrift

Abb. 5. „Systemschrift" von Kurt Schwitters

Internationale Buchkunst-Ausstellung

Das Gutenberg-Denkmal in Mainz

Abb. 6. „Futura"- Schrift von Paul Renner

53

54

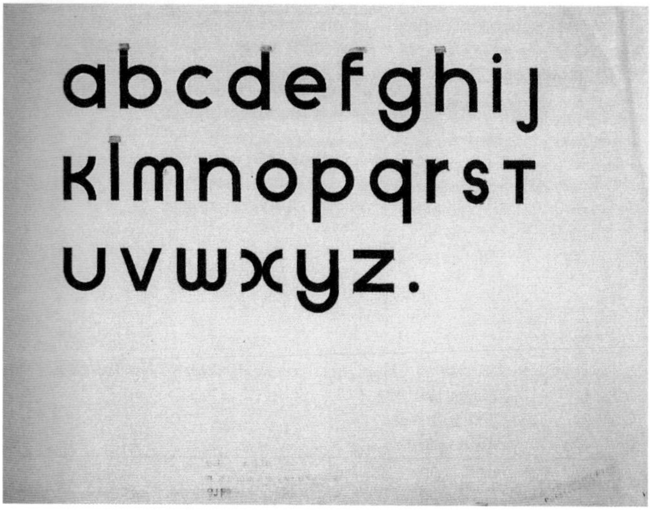

55

houses were also subject to the 'normative constraints of the factual': heavy lead types were difficult to transport, so local type foundries were at an advantage. Dessau was closer to the type foundries in Berlin, Dresden and Leipzig than to Frankfurt or Offenbach. If a new typeface became a success abroad, it was not exported in a cast form. Instead, new matrices were cast in a branch office. By the end of the 1920s, German type foundries were represented all over the world, from South and North America to Vienna and St Petersburg.

Back to the superstructure: the alphabets of Bayer and Schmidt at the Bauhaus in Dessau were basically drawn with a ruler and a pair of compasses. Like their colleague Moholy-Nagy, the ideas of the two designers corresponded to the views of the New Typography. Between 1925 and 1930, Bayer drew many variants of his 'Alfabet', which was presented to a wider audience for the first time in 1926 in a Bauhaus special issue of the specialist magazine *Offset*, no. 7. Certain parallels with Futura can be observed in the lower-case letters printed in this issue. The alphabet was eventually referred to in later publications as Universalschrift, but Bayer's as well as Schmidt's designs were never cast in lead. They were not optically corrected, and were simply not suitable for bodies of text for reasons of legibility.

Today Futura is the iconic representative of the class of sans serif grotesques. However, this does not mean that it was the first typeface of its kind. Every type foundry in the mid 1920s had its own version of this style, and the debate about 'Which typeface came first?' cannot be definitively settled by researching the archives.

The index cards of the Association of Type Foundries, which Hans Reichardt collected, contain a record by the Bauer Type Foundry regarding a geometric sans serif dated 26 February 1926. The first faces of Futura in light and medium gave rise in November the following year to the first print of the cast letters. The index card states: 'According to a letter of 14/11/1927'. On this basis, *Klimschs Jahrbuch* (Klimsch's Almanac) dates Futura back to 1928.

Judging from the date of registration of Jakob Erbar's Erbar Grotesk by the type foundry Ludwig & Mayer, also based in Frankfurt, the puzzle seems to be solved: the light face was registered on 10 August 1927 and is therefore one year younger than Futura. The first print was supposed to be produced in September the same year, but in *Klimsch's Almanac* for the printing industry, Erbar appears, like its competitors, for the first time only in 1928. This is not surprising, since the new releases of the previous year would have been shown in the Almanac after several months' delay, owing to the very lengthy manufacturing process of that time. The date of this letter, however, is another cause for much confusion: on this basis, Erbar had already been announced in October 1925. But what does this mean? Was such a design already in the air or did the designer sneak a peek over someone else's shoulder?

typeface became available in 1930. In 1931 Albers revised his design: simplified and based on ten basic forms, he developed the so-called combination type and had it made out of metallic glass for advertising purposes by Metallglas AG in Offenburg, Baden.

The impact of the prevailing zeitgeist can be demonstrated by the fact that Rudolf Koch's Kabel was registered in June 1927 by Gebrüder Klingspor in Offenbach, two months before Erbar Grotesk (initially only the light face), even though the first print was made only in October of the same year. Most sources date Kabel back to 1928. This date applies to the medium weight of the family Grobe Kabel. The name refers to the transatlantic telephone cable that was laid in 1927.

Next to typefaces such as Koch Antiqua (1922) and Locarno (1922), Kabel seemed strange among Koch's other work. However, the typeface designer remained true to his style in his

In his biography of Paul Renner, Christopher Burke describes a lecture given by the type designer at the Cologne Werbeschule, where Erbar was a teacher, during which Renner presented early designs for Futura.[14] Renner began the first sketches in 1924 but Erbar, according to his own statements, started work on his sans serif earlier.[15]

Renner may have registered the alphabets of the Bauhaus teacher. In any case, he definitely saw the designs of a Schablonenschrift by Josef Albers. His decorative type for Futura, called Black, was too closely reminiscent of it and also based on the idea of interrupted constructions of planes. However, Renner's design is simpler and more refined. Albers' Schablonenschrift was also shown in the aforementioned *Offset* edition in 1926. The first print of Futura Black was made in 1929, and the

letterforms, such as in the lower-case **a** and **g** — idiosyncrasies that Koch reintroduced in Marathon (1929). Koch created a modern typeface that combined the concept of the geometric sans serif with elements of art deco. This idea resulted in some slightly manipulated letterforms, which do not make the typeface very suitable for setting large quantities of text. Futura also initially had some purely geometrically constructed letterforms (a, g, m, n, r) that were soon replaced by more conventional forms.

In comparison with Futura, Kabel has a very low mean line – the lower-case letters sit almost below the optical middle. Also characteristic are the oblique ends of the downstrokes, which are especially apparent in the upper-case **K** and **R**, which give the typeface a lively style.

A series of ornamental faces followed: while the inline weight Zeppelin (released in 1930; in 1928 the largest airship that had ever been built at that time was named Graf Zeppelin after its inventor) reiterated the forms of Kabel in a bold and a thin stroke, the design of Prisma (1931, using five lines running in parallel) deviated from the actual alphabet. The Kabel family was enriched enormously by the Rundbuchstaben (1930), which were available for all upright faces in capitals, figures and some special characters from 6 to 96 point, as well as up to 60 cic as a display type. The circular letters once again emphasize the art deco background of the typeface and, in the words of the manufacturer, give 'the sentence a peculiar new character and a beautiful, calm rhythm'.[16] Later, even Zeppelin was supplemented with round letters.

In 1928 the Frankfurt type foundry D. Stempel AG also released to the market

its first geometric grotesque: Elegant Grotesk by Hans Möhring. The typeface is distinctive for the many sharply tapered forms in the upper-case letters, especially in the **A**, **M** and **N**, which, unlike those of

58

Futura, retain this characteristic in the bold weights, thereby living up to its name. The transitions of the stroke in the **K** and **R** are also sharp and make only minimal contact with the stem. Art deco elements can also be found here, such as the low waist of the **G**, **K** and **R**, which is positioned significantly below the mean line.

There are two versions of Elegant, which are fundamentally different in their lower-case letters. In the first version, the play of sharp apexes is continued: where there are open circular forms in joining strokes or downstrokes, such as in the **a**, **b** and **d**, as well as the **m**, **n** and **r**, Möhring drew sharp triangle-like transitions. The second version, however, has ordinary, blunt transitions. Additional differences can be observed in the single-eyed and two-storey **a**, and in the slightly more open **e**.

At Stempel, Elegant was available in light, normal, medium and bold sets as well as in the respective italics. It is worth mentioning the inline face, an upper-case alphabet drawn using a double line, with irregular interruptions and transitions. Outside Germany, the typeface was distributed by Caslon Machinery Ltd as Elegant Sans, and as Guildford Sans by the Stephenson Blake type foundry.

FÜR ELEGANTE, MODERNE MENSCHEN DER WENDIG-GESCHMEIDIGE UND ÜBERRASCHEND SCHNELLE WAGEN

EXCELSIOR

ER IST VON KLASSISCHER FORMUNG UND SIEGHAFTER KRAFT · ER IST DER MODERNSTE SPORTWAGEN DER WELT

Although Berthold was already well positioned with 'AG', as Akzidenz Grotesk was affectionately known, Berthold-Grotesk was released in 1929 as a proprietary design and response to the demands (and therefore the market) of the New Typography. Like Kabel, Berthold-Grotesk has a low mean line. While this makes the ascenders appear very long, the descenders look very short in comparison. The capital **M** is particularly conspicuous, with its unusually oblique legs, and a vertex that ends precisely in between the mean line and the baseline. The **G**, with the low positioning of its shaft, also provides a good way of differentiating it from Futura and Erbar in the capitals.

In the set of figures, especially in the **2** with its swan neck, and the **7** with its small serif, one can see the similarity with the type's older cousin Akzidenz Grotesk, from whose shadow Berthold-Grotesk, still largely unknown today, was never really able to emerge.

Arno Drescher's Super-Grotesk received much more attention, and its medium face was used by Schriftguss AG in Dresden (formerly Brüder Butter) in 1930 to make the first prints. In small sizes, Super-Grotesk is difficult to differentiate from Futura, so similar are many of the letterforms. Important differences can be found in the set of figures and the proportions of capital letters, and in some details, such as the vertical shaft of the **G**. Drescher also drew a set in a demibold weight (between medium and bold) for Super-Grotesk that was primarily familiar from Futura.

Drescher worked on Super-Grotesk until 1939 to create a well-developed family that included condensed sets as well as the ornamental typefaces Super-Reflex and Super-Elektrik — variants of Super-Grotesk Bold with integrated lines, simulating reflective lights. In addition, Super-Blickfang and Capitol were somewhat more distant from these letterforms, but were also advertised as related weights in the type specimens of Schriftguss.

With the expropriation of Schriftguss AG in East Germany, its collection of typefaces, and therefore also Super-Grotesk, became the property of VEB Typoart. Henceforth, it grew to become one of the most frequently used typefaces in East Germany; it adorned the letterheads of publishing houses (Volk und Wissen) and educational institutions (Hochschule für industrielle Formgestaltung Halle), and was a popular typeface for text. Its similarity to Renner's typeface and its great

60

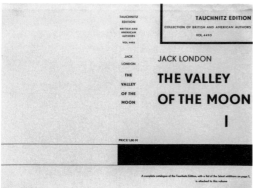

61

Orient-Teppiche

Meine diesjährige zweite sehenswerte
Ausstellung zeigt besonders schöne und
interessante Stücke aller Provenienzen

KIRMAN · AFGHAN · TÆBRIZ

BOCCARA · MAHAL · SENNEH

SAROUK · HAMADAN · HERIZ

Größtes Verkaufslager in Brücken und
Vorlagen aller Preislagen und Dessins

TEPPICH-KUNZE, BARMEN

62

57

P.482 – Kabel type specimen (1928), in
Klimschs Jahrbuch (Frankfurt am Main),
vol. 21, 1928.

58

P.483 –
left: Gebrüder Klingspor: the round letters
for Kabel Light, Offenbach am Main, 1930
right: Gebrüder Klingspor: the round
letters for Kabel Bold, Offenbach
am Main, 1930.

59

Type specimen of Elegant-Grotesk
in medium and an inline weight, in
Klimschs Jahrbuch (Frankfurt am Main),
vol. 23, 1930.

60–61

H. Berthold AG: Berthold-Grotesk,
Berthold-Series, no. 3, specimen no. 262,
Berlin, year not specified.

62

Type specimen of Super-Grotesk regular
and medium, *Klimschs Jahrbuch* (Frankfurt
am Main), vol. 28, 1935.

63

P.486 – Vogue Extra Bold.

64

P.486 – Vogue with the sets Special
Nos. 2–4 and 6–8.

65

P.487 – Rund-Grotesk type specimen, in
Klimschs Jahrbuch (Frankfurt am Main),
vol. 26, 1933.

popularity gave rise to the nickname 'Ost-Futura' (East-Futura) among West German typographers.

The 'multi-faceted' Vogue, available from 1929 onwards from the Intertype Corporation in Brooklyn, New York, consisted initially of a fixed standard set with a generic appearance that expressed its own style in only a few letters (in the medium face – although not in the light – the Q pushes down on its tail so that it lies vertically under the bowl). The typeface has a set of figures with several fractions, since this was needed by the US market with its duodecimal system, as well as many special characters and small caps, which was rare at the time among sans serif types.

However, a particular feature of the typeface is that it can be constantly transformed by changing the individual letters; in doing so, it clearly copies its successful German predecessors. On a whim, it can slip into the role of Futura (Special No. 2) or Kabel (Special No. 3). With the set Special No. 8, even Futura's constructed alternate letters **k**, **m**, **n**, **r** and **u** can be added. These would be referred to as stylistic sets.

Vogue   10 point

ABCDEFGHIJKLMNOPQRSTUVWXYZ
abcdefghijklmnopqrstuvwxyz   1234567890
[]%†§‡¶*()$,.-:';':!?&¹/₈¹/₄³/₈¹/₂⁵/₈³/₄⁷/₈

Special No. 2   Special No. 6   Special No. 8
GQ gq afgtu''1   Gag;   kmnru

Special No. 3
CGJMQUWY cgjmqwy abcefgijrt,.;''12

Special No. 4 Small Caps
ABCDEFGHIJKLMNOPQRSTUVWXYZ

64

Exchanging typefaces and licences was a common business model among type foundries that dealt in lead typesetting (and also later phototypesetting). A good example of this is a geometric sans serif that first appeared in 1931 as Polar Grotesk by J. John Söhne in Hamburg. It is not dissimilar to Futura in the capital letters. There are also blunt alternates for the letters **A**, **M**, **N**, **V** and **W**. The typeface develops a strong personality of its own through its lower-case letters. The most striking of these are the single-eyed **a**, the downstroke of which breaks the round inner shape; the **g**, with its abruptly truncated loop; and the angled downstrokes in the descenders of the **p** and **q**. Of the many ligatures of Polar Grotesk, the most conspicuous is the **ß**. As with Erbar, it has an ascender and descender that partially contribute

42 Point Vogue Extra Bold
These matrices are made without combination teeth. They are designed to be used with the Intertype Composing Stick Attachment.

ABCDEFGHIJKLM
NOPQRSTUV
WXYZ&
abcdefghijklmnop
qrstuvwxyz
.,-;:'!?()
$1234567890

Font No. 2492. Length of lower case alphabet 547 points. Figure size .394. Code word WJAEE. Use 6 point liners with molds U-35782 for 30 ems, U-35794 for 42 ems. The alphabet shown on this piece includes special No. 5 characters. They are regular in this size. Part No. T-3725.

63

to its somewhat foreign appearance compared with the other symbols of the typeface.

One year later, this very design was made available as Rund-Grotesk by C. E. Weber in Stuttgart. One of the few differences is the **f** with a descender and an **M** with a vertex that reaches only as far as the mean line. In 1937 the type-face began to appear again in a 'Polar design' under the name Kristall-Grotesk, from Wagner & Schmidt in Leipzig. It was also distributed outside Germany: in Denmark as Krystal Grotesk, by José Iranzo in Spain as Predilecta, and by the Swedish type foundry Berling under the name Saxo.[17]

One of the most successful typefaces of its time was Neuzeit-Grotesk, drawn by Wilhelm Pischner and released by D. Stempel AG in 1930, although at first it had only two weights. This date is referred to in Reichardt's index cards, but later type specimens indicate: 'Neuzeit-Grotesk light … was completed in 1928.'[18] For five long years, the typeface was

66

far is only available in Linotype matrices, is now also available as a manually set type and in the large sizes.'[19] At intervals of five years, the typeface was extended with medium and light sets (1935) and bold condensed and medium condensed sets (1940). The corresponding cursive sets appeared only in the 1950s.

Neuzeit-Grotesk differentiated itself from the other typefaces of its time primarily because of its raised mean line. Owing to its shorter ascenders and descenders, it was a more recognizable typeface. In type specimens, the type foundry indicates that 'the sans serif roman, which is generally known in Germany as the grotesque type … is today an elementary component of any printing house,' but the French term 'sans

65

available only in light and bold, without italics. In this regard, *Klimschs Jahrbuch* of 1932 mentions: 'This typeface, which so

NEUZEIT-GROTESK

D. STEMPEL AG

ELF GARNITUREN

Leichte Neuzeit-Grotesk
Leichte Neuzeit-Grotesk-Kursiv
Magere Neuzeit-Grotesk
Magere Neuzeit-Grotesk-Kursiv

Halbfette Neuzeit-Grotesk
Fette Neuzeit-Grotesk
Fette Neuzeit-Grotesk-Kursiv
Schmalhalbfette Neuzeit-Grotesk

Schmalfette Neuzeit-Grotesk
Neuzeit-Buchschrift
Kräftige Neuzeit-Buchschrift

D. Stempel AG
6 Frankfurt am Main S 10
Fernsprecher 60091
Postfach 10335

Figurenverzeichnis der Mageren Neuzeit-Grotesk

ABCDEFGHIJKLMNOPQRSTUVWXYZ
abcdefghijklmnopqrstuvwxyz ÄÖÜ äöü
1234567890 chckß & .,-:;!?'()„"»« §†* au

AEQS ajkory

D. STEMPEL AG · FRANKFURT AM MAIN   MAGERE NEUZEIT-GROTESK

Coup de foudre

MÄNSKLIGHET

Handsetzerei

67

sérif ... would be much more appropriate
for this sort of typeface'.[20] Consequently,
Stempel Gothic, as Neuzeit was initially
referred to in English-speaking countries,
was renamed Stempel Sans.

Notable letters are **J**, **R**, **S**, the
lower-case **a** and **u** with their alternates
(including a two-storey **a** and a **u** with

a stem), and the figure **3**. All in all, Neuzeit anticipated a design that was cited years later in ITC Avant Garde: large white spaces inside the letters and little space between them. After almost fading into oblivion, it was revived in 1970 as DIN 30640 by the Deutsche Institut für Normung (German Standardization Institute).

At the beginning of the 1930s, more and more type foundries wanted to have a slice of the geometric sans serif pie. In 1932 Schelter & Giesecke released Rhythmus, which took inspiration for many of its letters from Erbar and Kabel, and is strongly reminiscent in its figures of the foundry's own Breite Grotesk typeface. One year later Wilhelm Woellmer's Schriftgiesserei in Berlin registered its typeface Atlantis Grotesk, which was available only in light, medium and bold, without cursive. Like Neuzeit, Atlantis is characterized by a high x-height and featured much tighter tracking in its regular weight than most sans serif types of its time. In the Netherlands, Sjoerd de Roos and Dick Dooijes developed Nobel, which was released in about 1929 by Lettergieterij Amsterdam. The response in the United States to Futura, Erbar and Kabel was Metroblack No. 2 by William A. Dwiggins, which was released in 1931 by Mergenthaler Linotype Co. in New York.

In 1933 the German printing industry and, with it, the typographic landscape, began to change in anticipation of what was to come. These changes were reflected in *Klimschs Jahrbuch* of 1935, in which the articles are devoted almost exclusively to the so-called Deutsche Schrift (German type), and the type specimens are teeming with black letter types (such as Fraktur and Schwabacher) but primarily Gothic (*Gotische*) types dominate the volume. In 1934, looking back over the year, the typeface designer and publicist Friedrich Bauer wrote in praise of Gothic types: 'No other [typeface] offers so many possibilities to the artist's creative spirit,' adding: 'It will only be applicable in special cases as a book type, but then it will not fail to make an impact.'[21] His typeface, Friedrich-Bauer-Grotesk, is one of only two geometric sans serifs presented in the almanac of 1935.

At J. D. Isolert & Sohn, the typeface initially appeared only in the light, medium and bold weights, as well as a special display weight reminiscent of brick inscriptions on the facades of buildings. Almost six years after the publication of Futura, Friedrich-Bauer-Grotesk aimed for the same style, but overcame all the teething problems of its many predecessors and joined their circle as a mature, convincing geometric sans serifs. In addition, it brought with it many of its own, previously

Bericht der Handelskammer in Berlin
Spezialgeschäft für Feinkostwaren
Deutsche Gewerbeausstellung
MODENSCHAU IN DRESDEN 68

unseen, letterforms. Among these are the very special **C** and **S**, with the different positionings of their starting strokes and downstrokes.

One typeface that did not necessarily belong to the commercial environment of Futura at that time but that must be mentioned here as an influence is DIN-Schrift. DIN Engschrift and its younger sister DIN Mittelschrift – both better known as DIN 1451 – are constructed types in the best sense of the term, and belong chronologically to the beginning of this article. In 1936 DIN-Schrift was presented in an in-house publication, but its history goes much further back. In 1905 it was used as a guide for the labelling of vehicles in the early days of the Royal Prussian Railway Administration.[22] Judging from the strict grid on which DIN-Schrift was originally constructed, it is probable that Bayer and Schmidt were also aware of this grid idea.[23] Since this typeface is used on motorway signs, it is without doubt the most frequently seen geometric sans serif.

The mixing of black letter fonts with geometric sans serifs was still being suggested in the type specimens of German foundries in the early 1930s, but the release of Friedrich-Bauer-Grotesk marked the temporary end of this popular class of type in Germany.

66
P.487 – Stempel AG: Neuzeit-Grotesk type specimen, Frankfurt am Main, year not specified (probably 1950s).

67
P.488 – D. Stempel AG: Neuzeit-Grotesk. Eleven sets, Frankfurt am Main, year not specified (probably 1960s).

68
P.489 – *Klimsch Jahrbuch* (Frankfurt am Main), vol. 28, 1935.

69
Genzsch & Heyse: Friedrich-Bauer-Grotesk, Hamburg, year not specified (probably 1950s).

FRIEDRICH BAUER GROTESK

GENZSCH & HEYSE SCHRIFTGIESSEREI AG HAMBURG

69

'Elementary type form is the grotesque type in all its variations.'

FUTURA GOES INTERNATIONAL

In 1927, three years after the first sketches were made, the first casts of Futura were delivered to customers in the weights light and medium. The distribution of typefaces was already firmly established; the Bauer Type Foundry had a wide network of representatives with a well-stocked warehouse in Germany and in other European countries so that orders could be delivered within a very short time.

Abroad, it was mostly specialist retailers who sold typefaces for book printing, as well as book-printing machines and other accessories for typesetting and printing. Futura very quickly became the most popular typeface. The statement of a representative in Stockholm from 1962 seems particularly significant in this regard: 'Futura sells like Niagara. At that time, it generated a waterfall of orders. You did not have to do much to generate these sales.'

However, the Bauer Type Foundry did not produce Futura all by itself. It had an office in Spain called Fundición Tipográfica Neufville, SA. This company had gained an excellent reputation, not only by casting the Bauer types, but also by representing other leading German companies, including Schnellpressenfabrik Heidelberg, Roland, Koenig & Bauer, Goebel, Hoh & Hane, and Krause.

Immediately after the release of the typeface, the matrices of Futura were delivered to Spain and cast there, so that the lead letters of Futura soon became part of the collections of almost all the printing houses in the country. In addition, an agreement was made with the parent company that the typefaces could also be exported to Portugal and South America. The branch office in Spain was also of great importance for the American market because after the United States forbade imports from Germany in 1941, the orders could be delivered from Spain.

In 1927, the year in which Futura appeared in its first three sets, a subsidiary of Bauer was founded in New York. There, Futura was a great success right from the start, particularly because of its use in artistic and commercial applications. In 1938 the Museum of Modern Art in New York held the exhibition 'Bauhaus 1928–1938', organized by László Moholy-Nagy and Herbert Bayer, and the exhibition catalogue was set in Futura. FIG.6 P.329 Soon afterwards Futura was prescribed by agencies for the setting of the advertisements and catalogues of large companies.

Another important stop in the typeface's journey was France. Charles Peignot, director of the type foundry Deberny & Peignot, who had recognized the new trends in typography, contacted the Bauer Type Foundry at the end of 1929 on the advice of his artistic consultant, Maximilien Vox, and signed a licensing agreement for the casting of Futura. Peignot received the right to cast Futura under the name Europe, and to sell it in

French-speaking countries. In this way, Europe-Futura became the highest selling manually set type in France. FIG.2 P.290

Shortly after World War II, Futura also arrived in South America. After high import duties began to be imposed on book-printing materials, Serra Hermanos, a major dealer in Buenos Aires, which had been representing, among others, the printing presses of Schnellpressenfabrik Heidelberg and the typefaces of the Bauer Type Foundry, acquired a foundry in Argentina in order to cast Futura as well as other typefaces in its own country.

In about 1960 the first phototype-setting machines came on to the market, the historical event that led to the end of the type foundry business. There were still no signs of this development in the 1960s at the Bauer Type Foundry: the demand for manual typesetting, especially after Futura, was still so high that the means of production of the various foundries were not sufficient to fulfil the orders on time. For this reason, the production of matrices for Futura was agreed with the English foundry Stephenson Blake, which used its own casting machines to cast the typeface.

With the Apollo 11 mission, the first moon landing took place in July 1969, and the NASA team left behind a plaque with an inscription set in Futura on the moon's surface. With that, the application of Futura had surely reached its climax. FIG.5 P.359

In 1972 the production of manually set types by the Bauer Type Foundry was suspended; it was continued in Barcelona by Fundición Tipográfica

Neufville, SA. At the same time, the Spanish company had acquired the rights to the typefaces of other foundries such as Fundición Tipográfica Nacional, Fonderie Typographique Française, Ludwig & Mayer, Lettergietterij Amsterdam and Fonderie Dib. With the purchase of Fonderie Typographique Française, it also took over the foundry's employees and founded a subsidiary in Chennevières-sur-Marne near Paris in 1974, called Neufville France. Futura was sold in France for another 20 years, but under its original name and not as Europe, because Deberny & Peignot had gone bankrupt.

The head of the subsidiary, Sarah Benhamou, was born in Algeria. She focused particularly on the sale of typefaces in large quantities, including Futura, in Algeria, Morocco and Tunisia. The exports of the Spanish parent company were so high in 1982 that 80 per cent of its production of manually set types, cast with 120 casting machines, was delivered abroad.

An attempt was made to sell the typefaces in the Middle East, especially in Egypt, Yemen, Syria and Lebanon, after the takeover of the Lebanese foundry Dib. There, the former owner of the company, Georges Dib, had very good personal contacts with local printers. Unfortunately, these contacts could not be maintained after Dib fell ill and could no longer travel.

Neufville France was forced to close down in 1995 after 20 years of successful business. Then, the entry into the digital market began in Barcelona. The production of fonts, dominated by the Netherlands, was still not common in Spain at that time. In this way, a collaboration developed with the company Visualogik, which is still successful to this day. Various types are currently sold under the name Neufville Digital, including 36 fonts of Futura. Futura is now very widespread through the issue of licences to the world's leading digital-content publishers, such as Monotype, Linotype, Bitstream, Adobe, ParaType, URW++, Elsner & Flake, Berthold and FontDeck. For some of these companies, Futura remains at the top of the sales rankings, year on year.

Typefaces continued to be cast in Barcelona until 2008. Then, the last type caster retired, leaving no successors. The fourth generation of the Hartmann family has kept the business going with the sale of digital types only, under the name Bauer Types, SL, and Renner's Futura remains its most important source of revenue. It is indeed the typeface of our time – yesterday in lead, today digital.

1

Cf. Hermann Zapf: expert opinions for the Frankfurt am Main local court, 1979.

2

Hans Peter Willberg first published this matrix in: Hans Peter Willberg: *Wegweiser Schrift. Erste Hilfe mit dem Umgang mit Schriften. Was passt – was wirkt – was stört*, Mainz 2001, with clear influences from the concepts of Indra Kupferschmid and Max Bollwage.

3

Indra Kupferschmid: *Buchstaben kommen selten allein. Ein typografisches Handbuch*, Sulgen/Zurich 2004.

4

Paul Renner: 'Das Formproblem der Druckschrift'. In: *Imprimatur* (Munich), vol. I, January 1930, pp. 27–33.

5

Paul Renner, letter to the Bauer Type Foundry, Hödingen, 14 March 1940.

6

Albert-Jan Pool addressed the topic in detail in his lecture on 'The grotesque single-storey **a**', ATypl 2014, Barcelona.

7

Renner: 'Das Formproblem der Druckschrift'.

8

Ibid.

9

Paul Renner: 'Drei Jahre Futura'. In: *Type specimen Futura: die Ergänzungsgarnituren*. Frankfurt am Main: Bauersche Giesserei, 1930/31.

10

Paul Renner: 'Aus der Geschichte der neuen deutschen Typografie'. Lecture given at the annual assembly of Grafisches Gewerbe in Freiburg im Breisgau, 1947. Copy of a typewritten manuscript, p. 13.

11

Christopher Burke: 'Futura, Biographie einer Schrift'. In: Harzmuseum der Stadt Wernigerode (ed.), *Paul Renner, dem Schöpfer der Futura zum 125. Geburtstag*. Catalogue of Harzmuseum Wernigerode, 2003.

12

Hans Andree and Rolf Zander (eds): *Kritik der reinen Futura/Katharina Strauer*. Hochschule für Bildende Künste Hamburg, typography seminar, 2003.

13

Ibid.

14

Christopher Burke: *Paul Renner: The Art of Typography*, London 1998, p. 88 et seq.

15

Ibid.

16

In: *Klimschs Jahrbuch* (Frankfurt am Main), 1930, p. 185.

17

Philipp Bertheau: *Buchdruckschriften im 20. Jahrhundert. Atlas zur Geschichte der Schrift*, Darmstadt 1995; W. Turner Berry/ W. Pincus Jaspert/A. F. Johnson: *The Encyclopedia of Type Faces*, London: Blandford Press, 1991, p. 300; see also the undated specimen (probably 1959/60) D. Stempel AG: *Neuzeit-Grotesk*. Eleven sets, Frankfurt am Main, year not specified.

18

See also Neuzeit-Grotesk specimen. Eleven sets.

19

In: *Klimschs Jahrbuch* (Frankfurt am Main), 25th ed., 1932, p. 201.

20

See also the undated specimen of Neuzeit Grotesk referred to previously.

21

Friedrich Bauer: 'Die gotische Schrift'. In: *Klimschs Jahrbuch* (Frankfurt am Main), 25th ed., 1934, p. 27 et seq.

22

Albert-Jan Pool: 'FF DIN. The History of a Contemporary Typeface'. In: Erik Spiekermann and Jan Middendorp (eds): *Made with FontFont: Type for Independent Minds*, Amsterdam 2006, p. 68.

23

Ibid, p. 70.

70

P. 496 et seq. – typeface specimen for Futura Bold Condensed, 8 cic, after 1950.

BAUERSCHE GIESSEREI · FRANKFURT AM MAIN

SCHMALFETTE FUTURA

Berchtesgaden

FORTBILDUNG

1234567890

Nr. 93008
8 Cicero

Ornamentik
BARCELONA
123456789

Nr. 93010
10 Cicero

FUTURA

r°
AaCc
Futura
Initial designs of
Paul Renner

aaaabbþbc
ddefgghij
klmnooopp
qqrrſstuv
wxxyz
ΛΠΠ ck ß

THE COMPANIONS OF FUTURA

K

Breite Grotesk
In-house design
Type foundry:
Schelter & Giesecke

1880
Scheler Grotesk
In-house design
Type foundry:
Schelter & Giesecke

1903
Royal-Grotesk
In-house design
Type foundry: H.Berthold AG

V

Venus Grotesk
In-house design
Type foundry: Bauer-
sche Griesserei
Schmale Steinschrift
Type foundry: Schelter &
Giesecke

1908
Reform-Grotesk
In-house design
Type foundry:
D. Stempel

1909

n

Feder Grotesk
Jakob Erbar
Type foundry:
Ludwig & Mayer

---

b

Koralle
1913–1931
In-house design
Type foundry: Schelter &
Giesecke
Industria
Hermann Zehnpfundt
Type foundry: Schrift-
giesserei Emil Gursch

1914
Akzidenz-Grotesk
Type foundry: H. Berthold
AG

1916

J

Johnston
Underground
Edward Johnston
Type foundry: London
Transport

1922
Universal
Type foundry:
Grafotechna

Edel Grotesk
In-house design
Type foundry: Ludwig
Wagner AG

O

---

a

Erbar
1925–1931
Jakob Erbar
Type foundry: Ludwig &
Mayer
(first drawings 1922)

1926

ſ

Schablonenschrift
Josef Albers
(draft)

x

Universalschrift
Herbert Bayer
(draft)

TIMELINE

9 Aug. 1878 Paul Renner is
born in Werningerode.
He studies architecture and
painting. He then becomes
a painter in Munich.

From Nov. 1899 The first
vignettes by Renner in the
Munich magazine *Simplicissimus*.

1904 Renner visits Rome.

1905 Renner establishes
an office in Schleissheim,
near Munich.

1906 Renner visits the
Debschitz School in Munich.

1907 Renner's works
are exhibited at the
Glass Palace in Munich.

1907 Founding of the
Deutsche Werkbund.

1907–17 Renner works as
producer and supplier at
Georg Müller Verlag in
Munich.

1910 Renner joins the
Deutsche Werkbund.

1911 Together with Emil
Preetorius, Renner founds
the Munich School of Illustration and Publishing.

1914–19 Renner is assistant
director of the Münchner
Lehrwerkstätten.

1914 Start of World War I.

1915–17 Renner serves in the
military in Landsberg/Lech.

1918 End of World War I.

1919 Founding of the State
Bauhaus in Weimar.

1922 Renner publishes
Typographie als Kunst.

1922/23 Renner works as a
book designer for Deutsche
Verlags-Anstalt in Stuttgart.

1924 The magazine *Gebrauchsgraphik* is published
for the first time.

1924 Encounter with
Siegfried Buchenau
and Jakob Hegner, who
engage Renner to design
'the typeface of our time'.
Renner draws the first drafts
of Futura.

1924/25 Heinrich Jost
presents Renner's designs of
Futura to Georg Hartmann
of the Bauer Type Foundry.
Experimental designs and
an initial test print.

1925 Renner joins the
Kunstschule in Frankfurt.

1925 The Bauhaus moves
to Dessau.

1925 Frankfurt Kunstschule
exhibition with initial specimens of Renner's Futura.

1925/26 Renner col-
laborates with the urban
planning authority.

1926 Opening of the
Bauhaus Dessau.

1926 Renner becomes head
of Munich's Berufsschule für
das Graphische Gewerbe.

1927

AaCc
Futura Light

AaCc
Futura Medium

Futura Schmuck

Kabel
Rudolf Koch
Type foundry:
Gebr. Klingspor

Gill Sans Serif
Eric Gill
Type foundry: Monotype

1927 Founding and opening of the Meisterschule für Deutschlands Buchdrucker in Munich, of which Renner is also director.

1927 Futura appears.

1927 Founding of the 'ring neue werbegestalter'.

1927 Weissenhof housing estate in Stuttgart.

1928

AaCc
Futura Bold

Plak
Paul Renner
Type foundry:
D. Stempel AG

Lux
Jakob Erbar
Type foundry: Ludwig & Mayer

Elegant-Grotesk
1928–1940
Hans Möhring
Type foundry:
D. Stempel AG

1928 Jan Tschichold's publication *Die Neue Typographie: Ein Handbuch für zeitgemäss Schaffende* appears.

1929

AaCc
Futura Black

Nobel
1929–1931
Sjoerd de Roos /
Dick Dooijes
Type foundry: Lettergieterreij Amsterdam

Berthold-Grotesk
1929–1935
In-house design
Type foundry:
H. Berthold AG

Vogue
In-house design
Type foundry: Intertype Corporation

Stephenson Blake
In-house design
Type foundry: Intertype Corporation

Bernard Gothic
Lucian Bernhard
Type foundry: American

1929 'Black Friday' at the New York Stock Exchange; the Depression years follow.

1930

r

AaCc
Futura Light Oblique

AaCc
Futura Medium Oblique

AaCc
Futura Heavy

AaCc
Futura Bold Condensed

AaCc

Europe
Paul Renner
Type foundry: Deberny & Peignot

phonetic alphabet
Jan Tschichold
(draft)

Super-Grotesk
Arno Drescher
Type foundry:
Schriftguss AG
(formerly Brüder Butter)

Zeppelin
Rudolf Koch
Type foundry:
Gebr. Klingspor

**Neuzeit-Grotesk/
DIN 30640**
1930–1954
Wilhelm Pischner
Type foundry: D. Stempel AG

1931

n

AaCc
Futura Heavy Oblique

AC
Futura Inline

Prisma
Rudolf Koch
Type foundry:
Gebr. Klingspor

Polar-Grotesk
In-house design
Type foundry: J. John Söhne

Metro
William A. Dwiggins
Type foundry: Mergenthaler Linotype.

Semplicita
Type foundry: Nebiolo

1931 Renner publishes *Mechanisierte Grafik: Schrift, Typo, Foto, Film, Farbe.*

1932	**1933**	**1937**	**1938**	**1950**

V

AaCc
Futura Book

e

AaCc
Futura Medium Condensed

/

AaCc
Futura Bold Oblique

X

AaCc
Futura Light Condensed

t

AaCc
Futura Display

1939

†

AaCc
Futura Book
Oblique

b

Rhythmus
In-house design
Type foundry: Schelter
& Giesecke

ff

Rund-Grotesk
In-house design
Type foundry: C. E. Weber

Friedrich-Bauer-Grotesk
Friedrich Bauer
Type foundry: Trennert
& Sohn

1936
Spartan Classified
Linotype Staff
Type foundry: Mer-
genthaler Linotype Co.
& ATF

Acier Noir
A. M. Cassandre
Type foundry: Deberny
& Peignot

d

Twentieth Century
1937–1947
Sol Hess
Type foundry:
Monotype
Kristall-Grotesk
In-house design
Type foundry: Wagner
& Schmidt

Fundamental
1938
Arno Drescher
Type foundry: Ludwig &
Wagner

1932 Renner publishes
Kulturbolschewismus?

1932 The Bauhaus moves
to Berlin.

1932 The NSDAP becomes
the strongest party in the
Reichstag elections.

30 Jan. 1933 Hitler's
'seizure of power'.

1933 Renner receives a
commission to design the
German exhibit at the
5th Milan Triennale, for
which he is awarded the
Gran Diploma d'honore
and the Officer's Cross
of the Italian Crown. Renner's home and office are
searched; he is suspended
as school director, ar-
rested and released, and
eventually the charges are
withdrawn.

1937 Appointment to the
jury of the Paris World Exhibition for the book industry.

1939 Renner publishes
Die Kunst der Typographie.

1939 Start of World War II.

1945 End of World War II.

1945 Renner's vindication
as director of the Meisterschule für Deutschlands
Buchdrucker.

1947 Renner publishes *Das
moderne Buch* and *Ordnung
und Harmonie der Farben.*

1950s Futura Light, Medium and Bold appear at
Intertype; later, Futura Book
appears at Linotype.

1953

O

AaCc
Steile Futura Medium

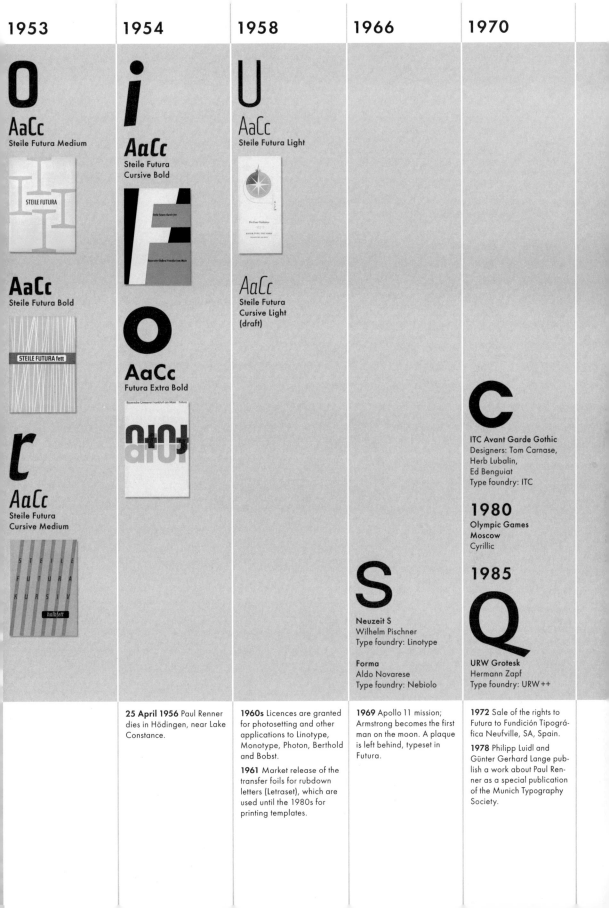

AaCc
Steile Futura Bold

r

AaCc
Steile Futura
Cursive Medium

1954

i

AaCc
Steile Futura
Cursive Bold

F

O

AaCc
Futura Extra Bold

1958

U

AaCc
Steile Futura Light

AaCc
Steile Futura
Cursive Light
(draft)

1966

S

Neuzeit S
Wilhelm Pischner
Type foundry: Linotype

Forma
Aldo Novarese
Type foundry: Nebiolo

1970

C

ITC Avant Garde Gothic
Designers: Tom Carnase,
Herb Lubalin,
Ed Benguiat
Type foundry: ITC

1980
Olympic Games
Moscow
Cyrillic

1985

Q

URW Grotesk
Hermann Zapf
Type foundry: URW ++

---

25 April 1956 Paul Renner
dies in Hödingen, near Lake
Constance.

1960s Licences are granted
for photosetting and other
applications to Linotype,
Monotype, Photon, Berthold
and Bobst.

1961 Market release of the
transfer foils for rubdown
letters (Letraset), which are
used until the 1980s for
printing templates.

1969 Apollo 11 mission;
Armstrong becomes the first
man on the moon. A plaque
is left behind, typeset in
Futura.

1972 Sale of the rights to
Futura to Fundición Tipográfica Neufville, SA, Spain.

1978 Philipp Luidl and
Günter Gerhard Lange pub-
lish a work about Paul Renner as a special publication
of the Munich Typography
Society.

1987

k

AaCc

Futura
Type foundry: Linotype

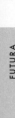

FUTURA
F FUTURA
FUTURA
LINOTYPE-POST

1988

O

Odessa
Peter O'Donnell
Type foundry: ITC/
Fontek

r

Avenir
Adrian Frutiger
Type foundry: Linotype

1990

Q

DTL Nobel
1990–1993
Fred Smeijers,
Andrea Fuchs
Type foundry: Dutch
Type Library

1991

f

AaCc

Futura Futuris
+Vladimir Yefimov,
Isabella Chaeva
Type foundry: ParaType

h

Century Gothic
Sol Hess
Type foundry: Monotype

1992

a

Proxima Sans
1992–1994
Mark Simonson
Type foundry: Um-
brella Type

1995

п

AaГг

Futura Futuris Cyrillic
+Vladimir Yefimov,
Isabella Chaeva
Type foundry: ParaType

1997

g

AaCc

Archetype Renner
+David Quay, Freda Sack
Type foundry: The Foundry

1995 Renaming of Neufville as Bauer Types.

1997 Collaboration between Bauer Types and Visualogik.

1998 Charles Leonard publishes *Paul Renner and Futura: The Effects of Culture, Technology, and Social Continuity of the Design of Type for Printing.*

1998 Christopher Burke publishes *Paul Renner: The Art of Typography.*

1999

f

AaCc

Futura ND
+Marie-Thérèse Koreman
Type foundry:
Neufville Digital

F

FF Super-Grotesk
Svend Smital
(after Arno Drescher)
Type foundry: FontFont

2000

e

AaCc

Futura BQ
+Dieter Hofrichter
Type foundry: Berthold

AaCc

2003
Futura EF
Type foundry:
Elsner+Flake

Gotham
Tobias Frere-Jones
Type foundry: Hoefler
& Co.

2001

T

Drescher Grotesk
Nicolai Gogol
(after Arno Drescher)
Type foundry: Bitstream

2002

R

Neutraface
Christian Schwartz
(after upper-case origi-
nals by Richard Neutra)
Type foundry: House
Industries

2003 Exhibition to mark
the 125th birthday of
Paul Renner at the Harz-
museum, Wernigerode,
Germany.

2006

s

AaCc

Futura No. 2
Type foundry: URW++

a

LL Brown
2007–2011
Aurèle Sack
(after Johnston,
Super-Grotesk)
Type foundry: Lineto

2009

e

Planeta
Dani Klauser
Type foundry: Gestalten

2010

g

Brandon Grotesque
2010–2012
Hannes von Döhren
Type foundry: HVD
Fonts

2011

Semplicita
Patrick Griffin
Type foundry: Canada
Type

2013

k

FF Mark
Hannes von Döhren,
Christoph Koeberlin
Type foundry: FontFont

2014

Neology deco
Nick Shinn
Type foundry:
Font-Shop

2011 Futura exhibition
at the Galerie Anatome
(Paris) and French
publication of *Futura: Une
gloire typographique* by
Alexandre Dumas de Rauly,
Éditions Norma and Michel
Wlassikoff.

2015

t

AaCc

Futura ND Alternate
+Marie-Thérèse Koreman
Type foundry: Neufville Digital

THE ALL NEW
The Futura
ORIGINAL
is now
VERSION

Futura ND
Alternate

Note: The dating of the individual type designs and type families is based on the publication date. Personal letters from archives and advertisements in *Gebrauchsgraphik* were taken into account as well as the official registration date, the date of dispatch of the first print, the publication date determined by the type foundry and dated proofs.

APPENDIX

BIOGRAPHIES

Ute BRÜNING (UB)

*Born in 1949, art teacher, studied art history, economic history and Dutch studies. Publications on graphic design history include *The Alpha and Omega of the Bauhaus*, Bauhaus Archive, Berlin 1995. Brüning works in Berlin as a web designer and art historian.

Christopher BURKE (CB)

*Born in 1967, England. Typographer, type designer and design historian. Principal Research Fellow at the Department of Typography and Graphic Communication at the University of Reading, UK. Designer of four typefaces: Celeste, Celeste Sans, Pragma and Parable. Author of two books: *Paul Renner: The Art of Typography* (1998) and *Jan Tschichold and New Typography* (2007). Co-editor of *Isotype: Design and Contexts, 1925–1971* (2013) and *History of the Monotype Corporation* (2014).

Carina DANZER

*Born in 1982, Frankfurt am Main. Danzer works as a research volunteer at the Bauhaus Archive/Museum of Design, Berlin. She previously studied art history at the University of Heidelberg and museum studies at the École du Louvre in Paris. She defended her dissertation, which examines the work of the art historian Fritz Wichert, in 2015 at Goethe University Frankfurt. During her PhD studies, she received a scholarship from the foundation Polytechnische Gesellschaft Frankfurt am Main foundation and was awarded the Johann Philipp von Bethmann Prize.

Petra EISELE (PE)

*Born in 1966, Rottweil am Neckar. Studied art history and German studies; four-year research project 'Bauhaus in the media', on how the Bauhaus was received in the media, University of Trier; PhD from Berlin University of the Arts on the postmodern development of design since the 1960s (scholarship from the IKEA Foundation); 2000–2003: researcher of design history and theory at Bauhaus University Weimar; lecturer at Zurich University of the Arts (ZHdK), faculty of design; since 2006, Professor of Design History and Design Theory at the University of Applied Sciences Mainz; 2008: founding member and board member of the Society of Design History (GfDg); since 2011, member of Institut Designlabor Gutenberg, University of Applied Sciences Mainz; since 2012, curator; many guest lectures, exhibi-

tion designs and publications, including *Classics of Product Design* (2014). www.designlabor-gutenberg.de

Wolfgang HARTMANN

*Born in 1936, Frankfurt am Main. Studied law in Genf and business management in Munich and Frankfurt. Advanced Management Programme at the IESE Business School in Barcelona. Trained at the Bauer Type Foundry from 1958 to 1963. Member of the advisory board of the Bauer Type Foundry and EMDA until 1972. Member of the management board of the Association of German Type Foundries. From 1963, managing director of Fundición Tipográfica Neufville, SA, and Chairman of Neufville France until 1995. Managing Director of Bauer Types, SL, and Abezeta, SA, until 2005, when he became Chairman. Chairman of the committee of the type foundries of ATypI; later Chairman of the state delegates and Vice-Chairman of ATypI. President of the ASAG (Agrupación de Suministradores para las Artes Gráficas). Board member of the German Chamber of Commerce in Spain. Senator of the International Gutenberg Society Mainz. www.bauertypes.com

Steven HELLER

*Born in 1950, studied at New York University and the School of Visual Arts, N.Y. Heller is Co-Chairman and joint founder of the MFA in Design/The Designer as Author and Entrepreneur, as well as a co-founder of the MFA in Design Criticism (Dcrit) for the MFA Interaction Design Program at the School of Visual Arts. He was Senior Director and Art Director for the *New York Times* as well as editor of *AIGA VOICE*; he is co-editor of *Print*, *Eye* and *Baseline* magazines. He has published numerous articles and over 170 books as author, co-author and editor, particularly on the history and practice of graphic design, illustration and satire. He has also curated exhibitions, including 'The Art of Simplicissimus', 'Art Against War', 'Malik Verlag' and 'Typographic Treasures: W. A. Dwiggins'. Awards: 2016 Eric Carle Award; 2014 Ladislav Sutnar Award and Honorary Doctorate in Fine Arts from the University of Westböhmen, Czech Republic; 2013 Honorary Doctorate in Fine Arts from the College for Creative Studies, Detroit; 2011 Smithsonian National Design Award for Design Mind; 1999 AIGA Medal for his life's work; 1998 laureate, Art Director Hall of Fame, Herschel Levitt Award from the Society of Illustrators. www.Hellerbooks.com, www.printmag.com/daily-heller

Stephanie KAPLAN

*Born in 1975, Pretoria, South Africa. Long-time member of the Freie Kunstschule Schwäbisch Hall, then a foundation course in design at Freie Kunstschule Stuttgart. Later studied communication design at Fachhochschule Mainz with, among others, Prof. I. Naegele and H.P. Willberg. Internship at Projekttriangle Design Studio/Stuttgart, 2001. Worked as a freelance graphic designer from 2003 to 2007 in Frankfurt am Main and Amsterdam. Now based in Basel. Through her close collaboration with 'Designlabor Gutenberg Institut', she has remained in contact with 'Mainz'. Design works include *Texte zur Typografie. Positionen zur Schrift* (with Isabel Naegele; 2012).

Klaus KLEMP

*Born in 1954; Professor of Design Theory and Design History, HfG Offenbach. After studying design, art history and history in Dortmund, Münster and Marburg, Klemp was head of the cultural department of the City of Frankfurt am Main, as well as head of the city's galleries in the Karmeliterkloster and Leinwandhaus from 1989 to 2006. From 1995 to 2005 he was also a member of the committee of the German Design Council. Since 1998 he has lectured in design history and theory as well as public design at various universities. In 2008 he became an honorary professor at the RheinMain University of Applied Sciences in Wiesbaden. In 2006 he became exhibition manager and curator for design, a position he still holds, at the Museum of Applied Arts in Frankfurt am Main. Since the winter term 2014/15 he has been Professor of Design Theory and Design History at HfG Offenbach. He has published many works on architecture, design and the fine arts.

Iva KNOBLOCH (IK)

*Born in 1964; studied art history at Charles University Prague and the University of Geneva. Worked as a curator of the print graphics collection at the Museum of Decorative Arts in Prague. Taught graphic design history at the Academy of Art, Design and Architecture in Prague. Publications and writings: *Ladislav Sutnar: Prag – New York*, *Design aktuell* (Prague 2003); *Ladislav Sutnar: Mental Vitamins* (Prague 2010); *Ladislav Sutnar: American Venus* (Prague 2011); *Václav Cigler: Design* (jointly with Hubatová-Vacková; Prague 2016); *Václav Cigler: Design in the Czech Lands 1900–2000* (Prague 2016).

Andreas KOOP

*Born on Pentecost, 1970, in Sonthofen in the Allgäu region. Following an education and further training in business, he received a degree from SFG Ravensburg and later an MAS from the 'Design2context' institute at ZHdK Zurich. Works as a communication designer, author (*NSCI*, *Die Macht der Schrift*, etc.), columnist for *Novum*, lecturer and design researcher. Owner of the koop design group, whose work has received many national and international prizes and is intended to be both useful and meaningful. Member of the project advisory committee Bundesdesign Ecodesign and the development team for the redesign of design courses offered at the FHV in Dornbirn, which is also planning to found an institute for design research. Initiator of the interdisciplinary conference 'Stadt. Land.Schluss', which is driven by the same concerns as the work of the firm – namely, a belief in 'the designability of the world' and the associated imperative to make it not only more beautiful, but also better.

Annette LUDWIG (AL)

*Born in Karlsruhe, studied art history, modern German literature and history of architecture at the University of Karlsruhe (TH). Master's degree. Her PhD dissertation on the Rasch Brothers, which examines the crossroads between utopian architecture, typography and design, received many awards. Curator, most recently (2002–2010) for the Städtische Museen Heilbronn association. Since 2008, lecturer at the Centre for Applied Cultural Studies at the Karlsruhe Institute of Technology (KIT) and at the Academy for Continuing Education in the Sciences (AWWK). Since 2010, director of the Gutenberg Museum Mainz, responsible for overseeing the content and restructuring of the 'Weltmuseum der Druckkunst' (World Museum of the Printed Arts) concept. Established the new typography theme; design and curation of many special exhibitions, some of which have received awards; numerous lectures and publications on topics relating to the 19th to 21st centuries. Jury member. Among other things, first chairman of the Bibliophile Society (Munich), the advisory board of the Saarländ Cultural Heritage Foundation (Saarbrücken), the board of trustees for the award of the Gutenberg Prize Mainz and Leipzig, and committee member of Internationale Gutenberg-Gesellschaft.

Isabel NAEGELE (IN)

*Born in Plainfield/NJ, USA; studied visual communication at HfG Offenbach.

Studied medicine and received PhD from Goethe University Frankfurt. Worked as a doctor and designer with a focus on culture. Workstations at Intégral Ruedi Baur, Paris, and Studio Dumbar, The Hague, and the 'corporate design' course at HGB-Leipzig. Since 1998, intense collaboration with 'Dialog im Dunkeln' and Ruedi Baur for signage projects. Since 1999, Professor of Typography and the Fundamentals of Design at University of Applied Sciences Mainz. Numerous awards and publications, including *Texte zur Typografie* and *Neue Schriften. New Typefaces* (together with Petra Eisele and Annette Ludwig). Since 2011, concepts for exhibitions on typography and collaboration with the Gutenberg Museum. Head of Institut Designlabor Gutenberg. Devoted fan of Futura.

www.designlabor-gutenberg.de

Erik SPIEKERMANN

*Born in 1947 in Stadthagen; studied art history in Berlin; in 1979 founded MetaDesign Berlin (including work for Audi, Skoda, Volkswagen, Springer Verlag, Heidelberg, management systems for the BVG and Düsseldorf Airport), with additional offices in London and San Francisco; in 1989 founded FontShop (with Joan Spiekermann), the first German re-seller of computer fonts; in 2002 founded Edenspiekermann (with Susanna Dulkinys), which now has offices in Amsterdam, Berlin, Los Angeles, San Francisco and Singapore. Columnist (including for *Blueprint* and *Form*); typeface designer (including FF Meta, ITC Officina, FF Info, FF Unit, FF Real, LoType, Berliner Grotesk and many corporate typefaces for *The Economist*, Cisco, Bosch, Deutsche Bahn, Mozilla and Autodesk); author of many publications on type and typography; honorary professor at HfK Bremen; honorary doctorate from Pasadena Art Center. In 2006 he received the Gerrit Noordzij Prize from the Royal Academy of Art in The Hague; in 2011 he received the Design Prize of the Federal Republic of Germany for his life's work from the committee of the German Design Council; 25th laureate of the TDC Medal and many other awards. In 2013 founded p98a berlin.

www.spiekermann.com,
www.p98a.com

Ferdinand ULRICH

*Born in 1987 in Schönebeck/Elbe; grew up in the USA and Germany; studied visual communication at Berlin University of the Arts with Erik Spiekermann, David Skopec and Siegfried Zielinski, as well as typography at Carnegie Mellon University in Pittsburgh/PA, USA (with a scholarship

from the German–American Fulbright Commission); since 2012, assistant to Erik Spiekermann (from 2013, at Studio p98a) and independent design work (including for Bauhaus Archive Berlin); 2012-2015, assistant lecturer of Anna Berkenbusch at the Burg Giebichenstein University of Art and Design Halle; since 2013, editor for FontShop (essays and typeface reviews); since 2015 researcher (PhD in typographic research) at the University of Reading, UK; in 2016, lecturer at Potsdam University of Applied Sciences. Many lectures and publications in the USA, UK and Germany.

www.ferdinandulrich.com,
www.p98a.com

Michel WLASSIKOFF

*A graphic designer and typography historian. Degree from École des Hautes Études en Sciences Sociale (EHESS). He teaches at the École Estienne in Paris, at the ESAG Penninghen and at the HEAD in Genf. Publications: *Signes de la collaboration et de la résistance* (Édition Autrement, 2002), *Histoire du graphisme en France* (Les Arts décoratifs/Dominique Carré Éditeur, 2005, 2008), *Mai 68 l'affiche en héritage* (Éditions Alternatives, 2008), *Futura. Une gloire typographique* (in collaboration with Alexandre Dumas de Rauly, Éditions Norma, 2011). Publication of contributions to www.garamond.culture.fr and responsible for the platform www.signes.org, which is dedicated to the history of graphic design and typography. He has also curated exhibitions about contemporary and historical graphic design, including for the Centre Pompidou, the Shoah Memorial and the Design Festival in Chaumont, France.

BIBLIOGRAPHY

Paul Renner: Texts (chronological order)

RENNER, Paul: 'Typografische Regeln'. In: *Börsenblatt für den deutschen Buchhandel* (Leipzig), vol. 84, March 1917, no. 65, pp. 265–66.

RENNER, Paul: 'Der Künstler zur Rechtschreibreform'. In: *Archiv für Buchgewerbe und Gebrauchsgraphik* (Leipzig), vol. 57, 1920, no. 5/6, p. 102.

RENNER, Paul: 'Münchner Typographie'. In: *Archiv für Buchgewerbe und Gebrauchsgraphik* (Leipzig), vol. 57, no. 5/6, 1920, pp. 112–20.

RENNER, Paul: *20 Jahre Münchner Typographie*, Munich 1920.

RENNER, Paul: 'Künstler und Gewerbe'. In: *Das Werk. Mitteilungen des Deutschen Werkbundes* (Berlin), February/March 1921.

RENNER, Paul: *Typographie als Kunst*. Munich: Georg Müller, 1922.

RENNER, Paul: 'Das Ende des Historismus'. In: *Gebrauchsgraphik* (Berlin), vol. 1, September 1925, no. 9, pp. 45–48.

RENNER, Paul: 'Neue Ziele des Schriftschaffens'. In: *Die Bücherstube* (Munich), vol. 4, 1925, no. 1, pp. 18–28.

RENNER, Paul: 'Entbehrliche Künste, notwendige Kunst'. In: *Die Bücherstube* (Munich), vol. 4, 1925, no. 1, pp. 238–46.

RENNER, Paul: 'Revolution der Buchschrift'. In: Gutenberg commemorative publication to celebrate the 25th anniversary of the Gutenberg Museum in Mainz 1925, ed. A[loys] Ruppel. Mainz 1925, pp. 279–82.

RENNER, Paul: 'Die Zukunft unserer Druckschrift'. In: *Typographische Mitteilungen* (Leipzig), vol. 22, 1925, no. 5, pp. 86–87.

RENNER, Paul: 'Bildungskrise'. In: *Die Form* (Berlin), vol. 1, no. 10, 1925, pp. 205–6.

RENNER, Paul: in: *Kampf um München als Kulturzentrum. Sechs Vorträge von Thomas Mann, Heinrich Mann, Leo Weismantel, Willi Geiger, Walter Courvoisier und Paul Renner*. Munich: Pflaum, year not specified [1926], p. 49.

RENNER, Paul: 'Vom Stammbaum der Schrift'. In: *Das Neue Frankfurt* (Frankfurt am Main), no. 4, February 1927, pp. 85–87.

RENNER, Paul: 'Rede des Oberstudiendirektors Paul Renner bei der Eröffnung der Meisterschule für Deutschlands Buchdrucker'. In: *Börsenblatt für den deutschen Buchhandel* (Leipzig), vol. 95, February 1927, no. 36, pp. 179–80.

RENNER, Paul: *Futura. Die Schrift unserer Zeit*. Specimen of the Bauer Type Foundry Frankfurt am Main, year not specified [1927], p. 4.

RENNER, Paul: 'Die Schrift unserer Zeit'. In: *Die Form* (Berlin), vol. 2, 1927, no. 4, pp. 109–10.

RENNER, Paul: 'Die alte und neue Buchkunst'. For the Leipzig international book exhibition. In: *Die Literarische Welt* (Berlin), vol. 3, 17 September 1927, p. 3.

[RENNER, Paul:] 'Paul Renner on his typeface "Futura"'. In: *Börsenblatt für den deutschen Buchhandel* (Leipzig), vol. 94, 20 September 1927, no. 220, pp. 1134–35.

RENNER, Paul: 'Zu den Arbeiten von Ferdinand Kramer'. In: *Die Form* (Berlin), vol. 2, 1927, no. 10, pp. 320–22.

RENNER, Paul: 'Über die Schrift der Zukunft'. In: *Typographische Mitteilungen* (Berlin), vol. 25, August 1928, no. 8, pp. 189–92.

RENNER, Paul: 'Gegen den Dogmatismus in der Kunst'. In: *Die Form* (Berlin), vol. 3, 1928, no. 11, pp. 313–24.

RENNER, Paul: 'Kunst, Natur, Technik'. In: *Münchner Mitteilungen für künstlerische und geistige Interessen* (Munich), vol. 2, 8 December 1928, no. 49, pp. 745–47.

RENNER, Paul: *Kunst und Technik im Buchgewerbe*. Series of lectures presented to the German Book Industry Association in the winter of 1928. Second lecture 'Type and Typography'. In: *Archiv für Buchgewerbe und Gebrauchsgraphik* (Leipzig), vol. 65, 1928, no. 6, pp. 453–67.

RENNER, Paul: 'Asymmetrie im Buchdruck und in der modernen Gestaltung überhaupt'. In: *Die Form* (Berlin), vol. 5, 1930, no. 3, pp. 57–59.

RENNER, Paul: 'Das Formproblem der Druckschrift'. In: *Imprimatur* (Munich), vol. 1, January 1930, pp. 27–33.

RENNER, Paul: 'Das Lichtbild'. Speech at the opening of the international exhibition 'Das Lichtbild', Munich 1930, on 5 June. In: *Die Form* (Berlin), vol. 5, 1930, no. 14, pp. 377–78.

RENNER, Paul: 'Drei Jahre Futura'. In: *Type specimen Futura: die Ergänzungsgarnituren*. Frankfurt am Main: Bauersche Giesserei, 1930/31.

RENNER, Paul: 'Wie müssen die Arbeitskräfte des Buchdruckgewerbes ausgebildet werden?' In: *Deutscher Buchdrucker-Verein. Zeitschrift für Deutschlands Buchdrucker Hauptversammlung 1930* (Berlin), vol. 42, 1930, no. 75, pp. 753–55.

RENNER, Paul: *Mechanisierte Grafik: Schrift, Typo, Foto, Film, Farbe*. Berlin: Hermann Reckendorf, 1931.

RENNER, Paul: 'Modern, traditionell, modisch'. In: *Imprimatur* (Hamburg), vol. 3, 1932, pp. 65–85.

RENNER, Paul: *Kulturbolschewismus?* Zurich/Munich/Leipzig: Eugen Rentsch, 1932.

RENNER, Paul: 'Verkehrswerbung, deutsche Lebensform und Kulturpropaganda'. In: *Die Form* (Berlin), vol. 7, 1932, pp. 233–47.

RENNER, Paul: 'Gegen den Schematismus in der Typografie'. In: *Klimschs Jahrbuch des graphischen Gewerbes* (Frankfurt am Main), 1933, pp. 25–31.

RENNER, Paul: date not specified [examination of the current status of graphic design]. In *Gebrauchsgraphik* (Berlin), vol. 10, January 1933, no. 1, pp. 34–35.

RENNER, Paul: 'Das Geheimnis der Darstellung in der Bildenden Kunst'. In: *FUTURA Book*. Specimen 1937.

RENNER, Paul: *Die Kunst der Typographie*. Berlin: Frenzel & Engelbrecht, 1939.

RENNER, Paul: 'Erinnerungen aus meiner Georg-Müller-Zeit'. In: *Imprimatur* (Munich), vol. 7, 1940, page not specified.

[RENNER, Paul:] 'Vom Georg-Müller-Buch bis zur Futura und Meisterschule. Erinnerungen Paul Renners aus dem Jahrzehnt 1918 bis 1927'. In: *Imprimatur* (Munich), vol. 9, 1940, pp. 1–12 (supplement).

RENNER, Paul: 'Das Ende des Schriftstreites'. In: *Die Literatur* (Stuttgart), vol. 44, February 1942, no. 5, pp. 187–89.

RENNER, Paul: 'Vom Georg-Müller-Buch bis zur Futura und Meisterschule'. In: *Gebrauchsgraphik* (Berlin), vol. 20, May 1943, no. 5, page not specified.

RENNER, Paul: *Kunststil und Kunstismen.* Supplement in the magazine *Gebrauchsgraphik* to mark Renner's 65th birthday (Berlin), vol. 20, May 1943, no. 5, p. 4.

RENNER, Paul: *Aus meinem Leben.* Frankfurt am Main: Bauersche Giesserei, year not specified (c. 1945).

RENNER, Paul: 'Schrift und Rechtschreibung'. In: *Pandora* (Ulm), 1946, p. 31–37.

[RENNER, Paul:] Interview with Paul Renner. In: *Der Druckspiegel* (Frankfurt am Main), vol. 2, May 1947, pp. 6–7.

RENNER, Paul: *Das moderne Buch.* Lindau: Jan Thorbecke, 1947.

RENNER, Paul: *Typografische Regeln.* Lindau: Jan Thorbecke, 1947.

RENNER, Paul: 'Diktatur in der öffentlichen Kunstpflege'. In: *Die Pforte* (Urach), vol. 1, 1947, no. 2, pp. 160–81.

RENNER, Paul: 'Psychoanalyse und moderne Kunst'. In: *Zeitschrift für Kunst* (Leipzig), vol. 1, 1947, no. 4, pp. 68–71.

RENNER, Paul: *Ordnung und Harmonie der Farben. Eine Farbenlehre für Künstler und Handwerker.* Ravensburg: Maier, 1947.

RENNER, Paul: 'Mensch und Maschine'. In: *Grafische Berufsschule* (Leipzig), vol. 14, March 1948, no. 1, pp. 1–2.

RENNER, Paul: 'Die moderne Typographie wird funktionell sein'. In: *SGM* (Schweizer Graphische Mitteilungen; Zollikofer and St Gallen), vol. 67, July 1948, no. 7, pp. 310–12.

RENNER, Paul: 'Fraktur und Antiqua'. In: *SGM* (Schweizer Graphische Mitteilungen; Zollikofer and St Gallen), vol. 67, August 1948, no. 8., pp. 345–47.

RENNER, Paul: *Die Kunst der Typographie.* 2nd ed. Berlin: Druckhaus Tempelhof, 1948.

RENNER, Paul: 'Die Farbe als Kunstmittel der Formgebung'. In: *SGM* (Schweizer

Graphische Mitteilungen; Zollikofer and St Gallen), vol. 67, November 1948, no. 11, pp. 451–56.

RENNER, Paul: 'Kleine Farbenlehre'. In: *SGM* (Schweizer Graphische Mitteilungen; Zollikofer and St Gallen), vol. 67, December 1948, no. 12, pp. 487–88.

RENNER, Paul: 'Funktionelle Typografie'. In: A chapter from the book *Mechanisierte Grafik.* Frankfurt: Deutscher Typokreis, 1953.

RENNER, Paul: *Der Künstler in der mechanisierten Welt.* Ed. Max Gleissner, Munich: Akademie für das Grafische Gewerbe, 1977.

RENNER, Paul: *Der Künstler in der mechanisierten Welt.* Munich: Akademie für das grafische Gewerbe, 1977.

Paul Renner: Manuscripts

RENNER, Paul: *Was ist modern.* Typewritten manuscript, archive of Haushofer Schröder.

RENNER, Paul: *Die moderne Buchform.* Typewritten manuscript, archive of Haushofer Schröder.

RENNER, Paul: *Vom echten und falschen Zeitstil.* Typewritten manuscript, archive of Haushofer Schröder.

RENNER, Paul: *Der Kampf um die neue Kunst.* Typewritten manuscript, archive of Haushofer Schröder.

RENNER, Paul: *Tyrannei der Maschine.* Typewritten manuscript, archive of Haushofer Schröder.

RENNER, Paul: *Zum Raumproblem in der bildenden Kunst.* Typewritten manuscript, archive of Haushofer Schröder.

RENNER, Paul: *Kunstdenkmäler.* Typewritten manuscript, archive of Haushofer Schröder.

RENNER, Paul: *Die monumentale Inschrift.* Typewritten manuscript, archive of Haushofer Schröder.

RENNER, Paul: *Neue deutsche Typographie.* Typewritten manuscript, archive of Haushofer Schröder.

RENNER, Paul: 'Aus der Geschichte der neuen deutschen Typografie'. Lecture at the annual assembly of Grafisches

Gewerbe in Freiburg im Breisgau, 1947, 13 pages, Gutenberg Museum Mainz.

Texts about Paul Renner (in chronological order)

CONRAD, Rudolf: 'Frankfurt-Offenbach und die Deutsche Schriftentwicklung seit der Jahrhundertwende/Frankfurt-Offenbach and the Development of German Type Since the Beginning of the New Century.' In: *Gebrauchsgraphik* (Berlin), vol. 3, March 1926, no. 3, pp. 38–48.

HOFFMANN, Hermann: 'Reform und Bolschewismus'. In: *Zeitschrift für Deutschlands Buchdrucker und verwandte Gewerbe* (Leipzig), vol. 38, no. 23, 1926, p. 191.

RODENBERG, Julius: 'Neues aus den Werkstätten der Schriftgießereien'. In: *Gutenberg Jahrbuch.* Mainz: Gutenberg-Gesellschaft, 1927, pp. 215–51.

WIEYNCK, Heinrich: 'Probleme der Druckschriftgestaltung'. In: *Gutenberg-Jahrbuch.* Mainz: Gutenberg-Gesellschaft, 1927, pp. 7–11.

GUÉGAN, Bertrand: 'Le Futura'. In: *Arts et métiers graphique,* July 1928, no. 6, pp. 388–89.

[Bauer Type Foundry Inc.:] *Futura Black. Introducing the Latest Member of the Futura Family, a Unique and Powerful Letter for Display.* New York: Bauer Type Foundry Inc., c. 1929.

BAUER, Konrad: 'Heinrich Jost'. In: *Gebrauchsgraphik* (Berlin), vol. 7, April 1930, no. 7, pp. 41–56.

K. R.: 'Die "Zeitschrift" im neuen Gewand'. In: *Zeitschrift für Deutschlands Buchdrucker und verwandte Gewerbe* (Leipzig) 1930, no. 1, pp. 1–2.

EHMCKE, Fritz Helmuth: 'Wandlung des Schriftgefühls'. In: Hans H. Bockwitz (ed.): *Buch und Schrift – Schriftprobleme.* Jahrbuch des Deutschen Vereins für Buchwesen und Schrifttum zu Leipzig (Leipzig), vol. 4, 1930, pp. 101–6.

HAUSMANN, Raoul: 'Das Buch als Gegenstand der Gebrauchsgraphik'. In: *Gebrauchsgraphik* (Berlin), vol. 6, June 1930, no. 7, pp. 50–55.

JOST, Heinrich: 'Zweifel'. In: *Klimschs Jahrbuch des graphischen Gewerbes* (Frankfurt am Main), 1933, pp. 6–15.

CONRAD, Rudolf: 'Heinrich Jost als Typograph'. In: *Klimschs Jahrbuch des graphischen Gewerbes* (Frankfurt am Main), 1933, pp. 34-41.

'Probleme über Probleme'. In: *Typographische Mitteilungen* (Berlin), vol. 30, 1933, no. 2, pp. 35-44.

Sch., Ttt.: 'Das deutsche Buchgewerbe auf der V. Triennale in Mailand'. In: *Gebrauchsgraphik* (Berlin), vol. 5, 1933, no. 6, pp. 70-71.

MEINER, Annemarie: 'Die Münchner Renaissance'. In: *Gutenberg Jahrbuch 1935*. Mainz: Gutenberg-Gesellschaft, 1935, pp. 313-25.

BAUER, Konrad Friedrich: *Werden und Wachsen einer deutschen Schriftgiesserei.* On one hundred years of existence of the Bauer Type Foundry Frankfurt am Main 1837-1937, Frankfurt am Main: Bauersche Giesserei, 1937.

HÖLSCHER, Eberhard: 'Zu den neuen Futura-Proben'. In: *Gebrauchsgraphik* (Berlin), vol. 14, July 1937, no. 7, pp. 46-49.

BEALL, Lester/SANDUSKY, L.: 'The Bauhaus Tradition and the New Typography'. In: *PM* (New York), vol. 4, June/July 1938, no. 7, pp. 1-34.

MEGAW, Denis: 'Twentieth-Century Sans Serifs Types'. In: *Typography*, Winter 1938, no. 7, pp. 27-35.

GRUBER, L. Fritz: 'Some German Types and Their Evolution'. In: *Art & Industry* (London), August 1939, pp. 74-77.

HÖLSCHER, Eberhard: 'Paul Renner'. In: *Gebrauchsgraphik* (Berlin), vol. 20, May 1943, no. 5, pp. 6-11.

JOST, Heinrich: 'Paul Renner. Siebzig Jahre'. In: *Der Druckspiegel* (Frankfurt am Main), vol. 3, 1948, no. 9, p. 9.

HUNTER MIDDLETON, Robert: 'Historical Development of Sans Serif Type'. In: *Graphic Arts abc* (Chicago), vol. 2, 1949, p. 82-91.

OLSEN, Mogens Greve: *Omkring en visit hos Paul Renner.* Copenhagen: Rasmussen, 1953.

ETTENBERG, Eugene M.: 'A Typeface for Our Times'. In: *American Artist* (New York), June 1954, pp. 44-47, 98-99.

'Paul Renner'. In: *Gebrauchsgraphik* (Berlin), vol. 31, January 1954, no. 1, p. 16.

BAUER, Konrad: 'Der Schöpfer der Futura'. In: *Linotype Post* (Berlin), 1954, no. 21, pp. 3-7.

KÄUFER, Josef: *Paul Renner. Mahner und Erzieher.* Special publication in: *Der Druckspiegel* (Frankfurt am Main), no. 6.

SCHAUER, Georg Kurt: 'Das Bauhaus und Paul Renner'. In: *Deutsche Buchkunst 1890 bis 1960* (vol. 1), Hamburg: Maximilian-Gesellschaft, 1963.

BECK, Heinrich: 'Paul Renner'. In: *Berufen und bewährt. Vier verdienstvolle Typographen und Berufspädagogen,* Bielefeld: Graph. Bildungsarbeit Bezirk Bielefeld, 1967.

WILLBERG, Hans Peter: *Schrift im Bauhaus. Die Futura von Paul Renner* (Monographien und Materialien zur Buchkunst II). Neu-Isenburg: Tiessen, 1969.

LUIDL, Philipp/LANGE, Günter Gerhard (eds): *Paul Renner.* A special publication of the Munich Typography Society. Munich: Typographische Gesellschaft, 1978.

LUIDL, Philipp: 'München – Mekka der Schwarzen Kunst. Die typografische Avantgarde der Zwanziger Jahre: Renner, Tschichold, Trump'. In: *Die Zwanziger Jahre in München* (Schriften des Münchner Stadtmuseums 8), ed. Christoph Stölzl, catalogue for an exhibition at the Munich City Museum, May-September 1979. Munich: Munich City Museum, 1979, p. 195 et seq.

BULLOCK, Nicholas: 'Modern Design and Municipal Patronage. Frankfurt 1924-1930'. In: *Oxford Art Journal* (Oxford), vol. 2, April 1979, no. 2, pp. 21-24.

GERHARDT, Claus: 'Die Entstehung der funktionellen Typographie in den zwanziger Jahren in Deutschland'. In: *Gutenberg Jahrbuch 1982*, Mainz: Gutenberg-Gesellschaft, 1982, pp. 282-95.

BEAUCAMP, Eduard et al. (eds): *Städelschule Frankfurt am Main. Aus der Geschichte einer deutschen Kunsthochschule.* Frankfurt am Main: Kramer, 1982.

LUIDL, Philipp: 'Kursiv oder schräg'. In: *tgm Werkstattbrief*, no. 5. Munich: Typographische Gesellschaft, 1985.

PONOT, René: 'Les années trente et l'innovation typographique française'. In: *Communication et langages* (Paris), 1988, no. 78, pp. 15-28.

LANE, John A.: *Futura in 26 Letters.* Munich: Typostudio Schumacher-Gebler, 1989.

STRESOW, Gustav: 'Gedenkblatt für Heinrich Jost'. In: *Philobiblon* (Stuttgart), vol. 33, 1989, pp. 218-26.

LEMOINE, Serge: 'Merz, Futura, DIN et cicéro'. In: *Art & pub. Art & publicité 1890-1990*, catalogue of Centre Georges Pompidou, Paris, 1990.

'Paul Renner'. In: *Typographische Gesellschaft Munich: Hundert Jahre Typographie, hundert Jahre Typografische Gesellschaft.* Munich: TGM, 1990.

CAFLISCH, Max: *Die Schriften von Renner, Tschichold und Trump* (TGM Library). Munich: TGM, 1991.

HELLER, Steven: 'Ladislav Sutnar. The Czech Years'. In: *Print* (New Haven), January/February 1991, no. 435, pp. 50-55.

OWEN, William: 'Fortune Magazine Was a Visual Encyclopedia of American Business Life'. In: *Eye* (London), vol. 1, Winter 1991, no. 2.

NEUMANN, Eckhard: 'Frankfurter Typografie. Bemerkungen zur Futura und zur angeblichen Kramer-Grotesk'. In: *Der Charme des Systematischen,* ed. Claude Lichtenstein, catalogue of Museum für Gestaltung/Frankfurt/Dessau. Giessen: Anabas, 1991.

SPIEKERMANN, Erik: 'Futura – a typeface of its time'. In: *Type & Typographers.* London: Architecture and Technology Press, 1991, pp. 84-88.

AYNSLEY, Jeremy: 'Gebrauchsgraphic as an Early Graphic Design Journal, 1924-1938'. In: *Journal of Design History* (Oxford), Vol. 5, 1992, no. 1, pp. 53-72.

'Tradition und Avantgarde. Buchkunst der Zwanzigerjahre'. In: *Wittmann, Reinhard: Hundert Jahre Buchkultur in München.* Munich: Hugendubel, 1993, pp. 130-35.

RÜCK, Peter: 'Die Sprache der Schrift. Zur Geschichte des Frakturverbotes von 1941'. In: Jürgen Baurmann/Hartmut Günther and Ulrich Knoop (eds): *Homo Scribens. Perspektiven der Schriftlichkeitsforschung.* Tübingen: Niemeyer, 1993, pp. 231-71.

MEGGS, Philipp B./CARTER, Rob: *Typographic Specimens. The Great Typefaces.* New York: Van Nostrand Reinhold, 1993.

HELLER, Steven: 'Sutnar'. In: *Eye* (London), vol. 4, Summer 1994, no. 15, pp. 44–57.

HEINE, Peter: '"Futura" Without Future. Kurst Schwitters' Typography for Hanover Town Council, 1929–1934'. In: *Journal of Design History* (Oxford), vol. 7, 1994, no. 2, pp. 127–40.

STRESOW, Gustav: 'Paul Renner und die Konzeption der Futura'. In: *Buchhandelsgeschichte*, book 2, 1995, supplement in *Börsenblatt für den deutschen Buchhandel* (Frankfurt am Main), no. 51, 27 June 1995, pp. B41–B51.

BURKE, Christopher: 'The Authorship of Futura'. In: *Baseline International Typographics Journal* (East Malling), 1997, no. 23, pp. 33–40.

BARRON, Stephanie/ECKMANN, Sabine/AFFRON, Matthew: *Exiles + Emigrés: The Flight of European Artists from Hitler,* catalogue of the Los Angeles County Museum of Art; the Montreal Museum of Fine Arts; Neue Nationalgalerie, Berlin. New York: H. N. Abrams, 1997.

BURKE, Christopher: *Paul Renner: The Art of Typography.* London: Hyphen Press, 1998.

MOSLEY, James: *The Nymph and the Grot: The Revival of the Sans Serif Letter.* London: Friends of the St Bride Printing Library, 1999.

BURKE, Christopher/KINROSS, Robin (eds): 'The Dispute between Max Bill and Tschichold of 1946, with a Later Contribution by Paul Renner'. In: University of Reading, Department of Typography & Graphic Communication: *Typography Papers 4,* Reading: University of Reading/ Department of Typography & Graphic Communication, 2000.

NESBITT, Alexander: 'Futura'. In: *Texts on Type: Critical Writings on Typography,* ed. Steven Heller and Philip B. Meggs. New York: Allworth Press, 2001, pp. 82–87.

Harzmuseum der Stadt Wernigerode (ed.): *Paul Renner, dem Schöpfer der Futura zum 125. Geburtstag,* catalogue of Harzmuseum Wernigerode 2003.

STRAUER, Katharina: *Kritik der reinen Futura (Zum Buch 4),* ed. Hans Andree and Rolf Zander, Hamburg University of Fine Arts, seminar on typography. Hamburg: Material, 2003.

WALTHER, Rudolf: 'Die Richtung ändern. Paul Renner über den Vorwurf des "Kulturbolschewismus" (1932)'. In: *Süddeutsche Zeitung* (Munich), 28 June 2004.

LEONHARD, Charles: *Paul Renner and Futura. The Effects of Culture, Technology, and Social Continuity on the Design of Type for Printing.* MA dissertation, Georgia State University, Atlanta, 2005.

FRUTIGER, Adrian: 'The History of Linear Sans Serif Types'. In: *Linotype Matrix* (Bad Homburg), vol. 4, 2005, no. 1.

DODD, Robin: *From Gutenberg to OpenType: An Illustrated History of Type from the Earliest Letterforms to the Latest Digital Fonts.* Vancouver: Hartley & Marks, 2006.

BOUIGE, Caroline: 'Futura puissance 104'. In: *Étapes* (Paris), no. 153, February 2008.

LEONARD, Charles: *Paul Renner and Futura: The Effects of Culture, Technology, and Social Continuity on the Design of Type for Printing.* Saarbrücken: VDM, 2008.

HANSERT, Andreas: *Georg Hartmann (1870–1954). Biografie eines Frankfurter Schriftgießers, Bibliophilen und Kunstmäzens.* Vienna/Cologne/Weimar: Böhlau, 2009.

NERDINGER, Winfried/HOCKERS, Hans-Günter (eds): *München und der Nationalsozialismus.* Catalogue of the Munich Documentation Centre for the History of National Socialism. Munich: Beck, 2015.

Other references (in alphabetical order)

ALBERS, Josef: 'Zur Ökonomie der Schriftform'. In: *Offset, Buch- und Werbekunst* (Leipzig), 1926, no. 7 (the so-called Bauhaus issue), p. 395.

ALBINUS, Philipp: *Grundsätzliches zur Neuen Typographie.* Berlin: Educational Association of German Book Printers, 1929.

ANNA, Susanne (ed.): *Das Bauhaus im Osten: Slowakische und tschechische Avantgarde 1928–1939,* catalogue of the Bauhaus Dessau Foundation et al., Ostfildern-Ruit: Hatje, 1997.

BAUER, Konrad Friedrich: 'Elementare Typographie'. In: *Klimschs allgemeiner Anzeiger für Druckereien* (Frankfurt am Main), vol. 52, 1925, no. 8, p. 3.

BAUER, Konrad Friedrich: 'Zukunft der Schrift'. In: *Klimschs Druckereianzeiger* (Frankfurt am Main), vol. 54, 1927, no. 56, pp. 1329–30.

BAUER, Konrad Friedrich: 'Heinrich Jost'. In: *Gebrauchsgraphik* (Berlin), vol. 7, April 1930, no. 4, p. 47.

BAUER, Konrad Friedrich: *Werden und Wachsen einer deutschen Schriftgießerei.* On one hundred years of existence of the Bauer Type Foundry Frankfurt am Main 1837–1937, Frankfurt am Main: Bauersche Giesserei, 1937.

BAUER, Konrad Friedrich: *Aventur und Kunst. Eine Chronik des Buchdruckgewerbes von der Erfindung der beweglichen Letter bis zur Gegenwart.* Frankfurt am Main: Bauersche Giesserei, 1940.

BAUMEISTER, Willi: 'Neue Typographie'. In: *Die Form* (Berlin), vol. 1, July 1926, no. 10, pp. 215–17.

BAYER, Herbert: 'Versuch einer neuen Schrift'. In: *Offset, Buch- und Werbekunst* (Leipzig), 1926, no. 7 (the so-called Bauhaus issue), p. 398 et seq.

BAYER, Herbert: 'typografie und werbsachengestaltung'. In: *bauhaus* (Dessau), vol. 2, 1928, p. 10.

BEHNKEN, Klaus/WAGNER, Frank (eds): *Inszenierung der Macht. Ästhetische Faszination im Faschismus,* catalogue of the NGBK. Berlin: Nishen, 1987.

BERRY, W. Turner/ JASPERT, W. Pincus/ JOHNSON, A. F.: *The Encyclopedia of Type Faces*. London: Blandford, 1993.

BERTHEAU, Philipp: *Buchdruckschriften im 20. Jahrhundert. Atlas zur Geschichte der Schrift*. Darmstadt: Technische Hochschule, 1995.

BONFILS, Robert: *La Gravure et le Livre*. Paris: Edition Estienne, 1938.

BOTHE, Rolf (ed.): *Kunstschulreform 1900-1933. Bauhaus Weimar, Dessau, Berlin, Debschitz Art School, Munich, Frankfurt Art School, Breslau Academy, Reimann School Berlin* (exhibition catalogue, Bauhaus Archive Berlin 1977). Berlin: Mann, 1977.

BREUER, Gerda (ed.): *Kramer, Ferdinand. Design für variablen Gebrauch*. Tübingen/ Berlin: Wasmuth, 2014, pp. 194-95.

BRINGHURST, Robert: *The Solid Form of Language: An Essay on Writing and Meaning*. Nova Scotia: Gaspereau Press, 2004.

BROOS, Kees: 'Das kurze, aber heftige Leben des "rings neue werbegestalter"'. In: Exhibition catalogue. *Typographie kann unter Umständen Kunst sein*.

BRÜNING, Ute (ed., for the Bauhaus Archive Berlin): *Das A & O des Bauhauses*. Bauhaus advertising: typefaces, print materials, exhibition design, catalogue. Leipzig: Ed. Leipzig, 1995.

BURKE, Christopher/KINDEL, Eric/ WALKER, Sue: *Isotype: Design and Contexts, 1925-1971*. London: Hyphen, 2013.

CONRAD, Rudolf: 'Frankfurt-Offenbach und die Deutsche Schriftentwicklung seit der Jahrhundertwende/Frankfurt-Offenbach and the Development of German Type Since the Beginning of the New Century'. In: *Gebrauchsgraphik* (Berlin), vol. 3, March 1926, no. 3, p. 41.

CONRAD, Rudolf: 'Heinrich Jost als Typograph'. In: *Klimschs Jahrbuch des graphischen Gewerbes* (Frankfurt am Main), vol. 26, 1933, p. 39.

DEXEL, Walter: 'Reklame im Stadtbilde'. In: *Das Neue Frankfurt* (Frankfurt am Main), vol. 1, 1927, no. 3, p. 45 et seq.

DIEHL, Robert: *Heinrich Jost (Deutsche Buchkünstler und Gebrauchsgraphiker der Gegenwart)*. Leipzig: German Book Industry Association, 1926.

EHMCKE, F. H.: *Schrift. Ihre Gestaltung und Entwicklung in neuerer Zeit*. Munich: Wagner, 1925.

EHMCKE, Fritz Helmuth: 'Wandlung des Schriftgefühls'. In: Hans H. Bockwitz (ed.): *Buch und Schrift — Schriftprobleme. Jahrbuch des Deutschen Vereins für Buchwesen und Schrifttum zu Leipzig*, vol. IV, Leipzig 1930, p. 13.

FRANZEN, Brigitte: 'Die Großstadt — ein gewaltiges Merzkunstwerk? Versuch über Kurt Schwitters und die Architektur'. In: *New Architecture of the 1920s. Gropius, Haesler, Schwitters and the Dammerstock Housing Estate in Karlsruhe 1929*, (exhibition catalogue, Baden State Museum et al.), Karlsruhe 1997, pp. 123-38.

HALLER, Rudolf/KINROSS, Robin (eds): 'Otto Neurath: Bildstatistik nach Wiener Methode in der Schule (1933)'. In: *Otto Neurath. Gesammelte Bildpädagogische Schriften*. Vienna: Hölder-Pichler-Tempsky, 1991.

HANSERT, Andreas: *Georg Hartmann (1870-1954). Biografie eines Frankfurter Schriftgießers, Bibliophilen und Kunstmäzens*. Vienna/Cologne/Weimar: Böhlau, 2009.

HEINE, Werner: 'Der kurze Frühling der Moderne, oder — Futura ohne Zukunft. Kurt Schwitters' typografische Arbeiten für die Stadtverwaltung Hannover 1929-1934'. In: Exhibition catalogue. *Typographie kann unter Umständen Kunst sein*.

HOCHULI, Jost: *Das Detail in der Typografie. Buchstabe, Buchstabenabstand, Wort, Wortabstand, Zeile, Zeilenabstand, Kolumne*. Munich/Berlin: Deutscher Kunstverlag, 1990.

HOFFMANN, Hermann: 'Reform und Bolschewismus'. In: *Zeitschrift für Deutschlands Buchdrucker und verwandte Gewerbe* (Leipzig), vol. 38, 1926, no. 23, p. 191.

JOST, Heinrich: 'Zweifel'. In: *Klimschs Jahrbuch des graphischen Gewerbes* (Frankfurt am Main), 1933, p. 6.

Kampf um München als Kulturzentrum. Sechs Vorträge von Thomas Mann, Heinrich Mann, Leo Weismantel, Willi Geiger, Walter Courvoisier und Paul Renner. Munich: R. Pflaum, year not specified [1926].

KANDINSKY, Wassily: *Punkt und Linie zu Fläche. Beitrag zur Analyse der malerischen Elemente* (Bauhaus-Buch no. 9). Munich: A. Langen, 1926.

KANDINSKY, Wassily: *Über das Geistige in der Kunst*. With an introduction by Max Bill. 10th ed. Bern: Benteli, 1980.

KAPR, Albert: *Schriftkunst. Geschichte, Anatomie und Schönheit der lateinischen Buchstaben*. Dresden: Verlag der Kunst, 1996.

Abridged: 'Eine Bauausstellung auf der Frankfurter Frühjahrsmesse'. In: *Das Neue Frankfurt* (Frankfurt am Main), February/ March 1927, no. 4, pp. 90-91.

KLEMP, Klaus: *Design in Frankfurt 1920-1990*, ed. Matthias Wagner K. (exhibition catalogue, Museum of Applied Arts Frankfurt am Main), Stuttgart: AV Edition, 2014.

KLEMP, Klaus/WAGNER K., Matthias/ FRIEDL, Friedrich/ZIZKA, Peter (eds): *Alles neu! 100 Jahre neue Typografie und neue Grafik in Frankfurt am Main*, catalogue of Museum of Applied Arts Frankfurt am Main. Stuttgart: AV Edition, 2016.

KNOBLOCH, Iva (ed.): *Ladislav Sutnar v. textech. (Mental Vitamins)*. Prague: Kant, 2010.

KOOP, Andreas: *Die Macht der Schrift. Eine angewandte Designforschung*. Sulgen/Zurich: Niggli, 2012.

KUPFERSCHMID, Indra: *Buchstaben kommen selten allein. Ein typografisches Handbuch*. Sulgen/Zurich: Niggli, 2003.

LANGE, Günter Gerhard: 'Weg, Werk und Zeitgenossen Paul Renners'. In: *Paul Renner. A special publication of the Munich Typography Society*, ed. Philipp Luidl with the collaboration of Günter Gerhard Lange. Munich: TGM, 1978.

LEMOINE, Serge: 'Merz, Futura, DIN et cicéro'. In: *Kurt Schwitters*, exhibition catalogue, Centre Georges Pompidou, Paris 1994/95.

Lentos Kunstmuseum Linz (ed.): *Ahoi Herbert! Bayer und die Moderne*. Weitra: Verlag Bibliothek der Provinz, 2009.

LICHTENSTEIN, Claude (ed.): *Ferdinand Kramer. Der Charme des Systematischen. Architektur, Einrichtung, Design*. Giessen: Anabas, 1991.

LIHOTZKY, Grete: 'Rationalisierung im Haushalt'. In: *Das Neue Frankfurt* (Frankfurt am Main), April/June 1927, no. 5, pp. 120-23.

LISSITZKY, El: 'Topographie der Typographie'. In: *Merz*, no. 4, July 1923.

LUDWIG, Annette: *Die Architekten Brüder Heinz und Bodo Rasch. Ein Beitrag zur Architekturgeschichte der zwanziger Jahre*. Tübingen/Berlin 2009.

LUPTON, Ellen/MILLER, J. Abbott (eds): *The ABCs of the Bauhaus. Bauhaus and Design Theory*. London: Thames and Hudson, 1993.

M[AY], E[rnst]: 'Reklamereform'. In: *Das Neue Frankfurt* (Frankfurt am Main), 1927, no. 3, p.64.

[MEYER, Peter:] 'Mechanisierte Grafik'. In: *Das Werk* (Zurich), vol. 19, April 1932, pp.118–20.

MOHOLY-NAGY, Ladislaus: 'Zeitgemässe Typographie – Ziele, Praxis, Kritik'. In: Gutenberg commemorative publication to celebrate the 25th anniversary of the Gutenberg Museum in Mainz 1925, ed. A[loys] Ruppel. Mainz 1925, pp.307–17.

MOHOLY-NAGY, László: 'Zeitgemässe Typographie (Ziele, Praxis, Kritik)'. In: *Offset-, Buch und Werbekunst* (Leipzig; special 'Bauhaus' issue) 1926, no. 7, pp.375–85.

MOHOLY-NAGY, László: '(Reply to) Im Kampf um neue Gestaltungsfragen'. In: *Typografische Mitteilungen*. Magazine of the Educational Association of German Book Printers (Berlin), vol. 30, January 1933, p.3.

'Neue Reklame in Frankfurt am Main'. In: *Das Neue Frankfurt* (Frankfurt am Main), vol. 1, 1927, no. 3, p.61.

NOSBISCH, Werner: 'Die neue Wohnung und ihr Innenausbau. Der neuzeitliche Haushalt'. In: *Das Neue Frankfurt* (Frankfurt am Main), 1927, no. 6, pp.129–33.

OSTERER, Heidrun/STAMM, Philipp (eds): *Adrian Frutiger. Schriften. Gesamtausgabe*. Basel: Birkhäuser, 2008.

PICARD, Tobias: 'Durch den Kopf des Auftraggebers denken. Der Gestalter Hans Leistikow'. In: *Archiv für Frankfurts Geschichte und Kunst* (vol. 69), ed. Dieter Rebentisch and Evelyn Hills. Frankfurt am Main 2003, pp.99–126.

PORSTMANN, Walter: *Sprache und Schrift*. Berlin: Verein Deutscher Ingenieure, 1920.

RASCH, Heinz und Bodo (eds): *Gefesselter Blick*. 25 short monographs and contributions on modern advertising design, with the support of the 'Ring d. Werbegestalter d. Schweizer Werkbundes' et al. Stuttgart 1930, reprint Baden (Switzerland): Müller, 1996.

REICHEL, Peter: *Der schöne Schein des Dritten Reiches. Faszination und Gewalt des Faschismus*. Munich/Vienna: Hanser, 1991.

RÖSSLER, Patrick (ed., for the Bauhaus Archive Berlin): *Herbert Bayer: Die Berliner Jahre – Werbegrafik 1928–1938*, on the occasion of the exhibition 'Mein Reklame – Fegefeuer'. Berlin: Vergangenheitsverlag, 2013.

ROSSMANN, Zdeněk: *Typographic Designs*. Prague: State Institute for Professional Schools, 1936.

SALDEN, Hubert (ed.): *Die Städelschule Frankfurt am Main von 1817 bis 1995*. Mainz: Schmidt, 1995.

SARKOWICZ, Hans (ed.): *Hitlers Künstler. Die Kultur im Dienst des Nationalsozialismus*. Frankfurt am Main/Leipzig: Insel, 2004.

SCHAUER, Georg Kurt: 'Das Bauhaus und Paul Renner'. In: *Deutsche Buchkunst 1890 bis 1960* (vol.1), Hamburg: Maximilian-Gesellschaft, 1963.

SCHREIBER, Justina: 'Die Avantgarde der Buchstaben. Vor 80 Jahren erfand Paul Renner die Futura. Nach einer steilen Karriere treibt die Schrift ihren Fans noch heute Tränen in die Augen'. In: *Süddeutsche Zeitung* (Munich), 16 March 2006 (weekend supplement).

SCHWITTERS, Kurt: 'Der Rhythmus im Kunstwerk'. In: *Hannoversches Tageblatt*, 17 October 1926.

SCHWITTERS, Kurt: 'Anregungen zur Erlangung einer Systemschrift'. In: *i 10. Internationale Revue* (Amsterdam), vol. 1, August/September 1927, no. 8/9, pp.312–16.

SCHWITTERS, Kurt: *Das literarische Werk*, 5 vols, Munich 2005 (first published Cologne 1973).

SCHWITTERS, Kurt: *Wir spielen, bis uns der Tod abholt. Letters over five decades*. Collected, selected and commentary by Ernst Nündel. Frankfurt am Main/Berlin 1986.

SCHWITTERS, Kurt: *Typographie und Werbegestaltung*, produced by Volker Rattemeyer and Dietrich Helms with the collaboration of Konrad Matschke, Wiesbaden State Museum et al. Wiesbaden 1990.

SELLE, Gert: *Geschichte des Design in Deutschland*. Updated and expanded. New edition, Frankfurt am Main: Campus, 2007.

SEMBACH, Klaus-Jürgen: *Stil 1930/ Style 1930*. Tübingen: Wasmuth, 1971.

SPIEKERMANN, Erik/MIDDENDORP, Jan (eds): *Made with FontFont: Type for Independent Minds*. Amsterdam: BIS Publishers, 2006.

Städtische Kunstgewerbeschule Frankfurt am Main: first exhibition. *Grafische, malerische, plastische Kräfte* (no. 23) (exhibition catalogue, Kunstgewerbemuseum/49 Neue Mainzer Strasse, Frankfurt am Main). Frankfurt am Main 1925.

STRESOW, Gustav: 'Gedenkblatt für Heinrich Jost'. In: *Philobiblon* (Stuttgart), vol. 33, 1989, p. 219.

STRESOW, Gustav: 'Paul Renner und die Konzeption der Futura'. In: *Buchhandelsgeschichte* (Frankfurt am Main), 2/1995 (supplement in *Börsenblatt für den Deutschen Buchhandel*, no. 51, 27 June 1995, p. B44).

SYLVESTROVÁ, Marta/JINDŘICH, Toman (eds): *Zdeněk Rossmann. Horizonty modernismu (Horizons of modernism: Zdeněk Rossman, 1905-1984)*. Brno: Moravská Galerie, 2015.

TSCHICHOLD, Iwan: *Elementare Typographie*. Facsimile edition of the 1925 edition. Mainz: Hermann Schmidt, 1986.

TSCHICHOLD, Iwan: 'Elementare Typographie'. In: *Typographische Mitteilungen* (Leipzig), vol. 122, October 1925, no. 10, pp. 198-200.

TSCHICHOLD, Jan: *Die neue Typografie. Ein Handbuch für zeitgemäss Schaffende*. (Org. Berlin: Educational Association of German Book Printers, 1928); 2nd ed. Berlin/West: Brinkmann & Bose, 1987.

TSCHICHOLD, Jan: 'Noch eine neue Schrift. Beitrag zur Frage der Ökonomie der Schrift'. In: *Typographische Mitteilungen* (Berlin), vol. 27, March 1930, no. 3, supplement.

TSCHICHOLD, Jan: 'Schriftmischungen'. In: *Typographische Monatsblätter* (Bern), vol. 3, 1935, no. 2, pp. 32–37.

VOX, Maximilien: 'Charles Peignot et son temps'. In: *Communication et Langages* (Paris), no. 14, June 1972, pp. 58–59.

WANETZKY, Harald: *Typotektur. Architektur und Typografie im 20. Jahrhundert – der Modellfall einer Zusammenführung.* Dissertation, Freiburg im Breisgau 1995.

WICK, Rainer: *Bauhaus – Kunstschule der Moderne.* Ostfildern-Ruit: Hatje Canz, 2000.

WILLBERG, Hans Peter: *Ungedruckte Illustrationen von Willi Baumeister. Schrift im Bauhaus. Die Futura von Paul Renner* (Monographien und Materialien zur Buchkunst II). Neu-Isenburg: Tiessen, 1969.

WILLBERG, Hans Peter: *Wegweiser Schrift. Erste Hilfe mit dem Umgang mit Schriften. Was passt – was wirkt – was stört.* Mainz: Hermann Schmidt, 2001.

WINGLER, Hans Maria (ed.): *Kunstschulreform 1900–1933.* Berlin: Mann, 1977.

WINGLER, Hans M.: *Das Bauhaus 1919–1933. Weimar, Dessau, Berlin und die Nachfolge in Chicago seit 1937.* 6th ed. Cologne: DuMont, 2009.

WINGLER, Hans Maria/ DROSTE, Magdalena: *Herbert Bayer. Das künstlerische Werk 1918–1938* (exhibition catalogue, Bauhaus Archive Berlin). Berlin: Mann, 1982.

INDEX

Page numbers in **bold** refer to illustrations. The terms Futura, Bauer Type Foundry and Paul Renner are not included

PICTURE CREDITS

Many figures are based on the extensive collections of the Gutenberg Museum and the Gutenberg Library in Mainz. In addition, the legal inheritor of the Bauer Type Foundry, Mr Wolfgang Hartmann, Bauer Types, SL, generously granted the reproduction rights for the reprints.

Permission was kindly granted for the reproduction of all the other figures and copyrights from the following institutions and individuals:

Axel Mauruszat collection, Berlin 193
Andrea Haushofer Archive, Munich 27 (© Photo: E. Wasow), 43, 45, 48 et seq., 67, 203, 214, 218, 227, 233 et seq., 301
Badisches Landesmuseum 151
Bauhaus Archive, Museum of Design Berlin 187 et seq., 190, 479, 480
Baumeister Archive, at the Stuttgart Art Museum 128 (inv. no. ab-ty-0095; CC license CC BY-NC-SA)
Bertram Schmidt–Friderichs collection, Mainz 220 et seq.,
Christos Nikolas Vittoratos collection Frankfurt am Main 92 et seq., 177
City of Karlsruhe, Cultural Office, City Archive & History Museums, Dept. City Archive 150 Fig. 6 (Sign. Stadt AK7/NI Pflästerer 25)
DDB Worldwide Inc. 360
Erik Spiekermann Archive, Berlin 478, 479, 482, 484 et seq., 487–489
Etienne Robial Collection 307
Freese collection, Frankfurt am Main 120, 186, 190, 200, 206
Friedrich Vordemberge-Gildewart © Wiesbaden Museum and the Vordemberge-Gildewart Foundation, Rapperswil (Switzerland) 162
Gutenberg Museum Mainz Historical Picture Archive Wolff & Tritschler Offenburg 71, 73
History Museum Hanover 138 (©photo: Wilhelm Ackermann), 167 (©photo: Wilhelm Hauschild)
Institut für Stadtgeschichte (ISG), Frankfurt 60, 86 et seq., 139 (©photo: Hannah Reek)
Institut für Zeitgeschichte (IFZ) München 238 et seq. (©photo: Andreas Koop)
Klimschs Jahrbuch des graphischen Gewerbes Frankfurt am Main 480 (©photo: Erik Spiekermann)
Klingspor Museum Offenbach am Main 4–15, 38–41, 45, 78, 216, 218 et seq., 222 et seq., 326 et seq., 331, 483, 490

Kurt and Ernst Schwitters Foundation 148–150, 152, 156, 159
Kurt Schwitters archive 152 et seq.,155
Ladislav Sutnar family 270–273 (©photo: UPM Prague), 340, 342, 343
Library of the École Estienne/Archiv Signes Paris 289 et seq., 292–294, 296–298, 304 et seq., 310–314
Lilo Tschichold: 199 (©photo: Christopher Burke), 202–205 (©photo: Christopher Burke), 209 (©photo: Christopher Burke)
Magazine das Neue Frankfurt 65, 68B et seq., 70, 72, 74–77, 78, 79 (©photo: Hannah Reek), 91
Magazine Die Form 229–230
Magazine die neue linie Berlin 238
Magazine Gebrauchsgraphik Berlin 168, 172, 174, 238
Magazine Graphische Nachrichten Berlin 182, 183, 184, 203, 204
Magazine Typographische Mitteilungen Berlin 82, 123
Moravian Gallery Brno 277
Müchner Stadtmuseum 240
Munich Documentation Centre for the History of National Socialism 240 (©photo: Isabel Naegele)
Museum für Angewandte Kunst, Frankfurt 67, 94, 97, 112
Museum of Decorative Arts Prague (©photo: UPM Prague): 270–273, 275, 278
NASA 354, 357–361, 365
Otto and Marie Neurath Isotype Collection, University of Reading 254, 257–260
Pavel Rossmann 275 (©photo: UPM Prague), 276 (©photo: Moravian Gallery Brno)
Sprengel Museum Hannover
148 Fig. 1, 2 Sprengel Museum Hannover, on loan from the Kurt and Ernst Schwitters Foundation, Hanover (inv. no. obj06837851a-m)
149 Sprengel Museum Hannover, on loan from the Kurt and Ernst Schwitters Foundation, Hanover (inv. no. obj06837851a-m)
150 Fig. 4 (Sprengel Museum Hannover, Kurt Schwitters Archive (inv. no. KSA 2011,1)
150 Fig. 5 Sprengel Museum Hannover, on loan from the Kurt and Ernst Schwitters Foundation, Hanover (inv. no.obj06837408)
151 Fig. 8 Sprengel Museum Hannover, Kurt Schwitters Archive (inv. no. SH 77, 1996)
152 Fig. 9 Sprengel Museum Hannover, on loan from the Kurt and Ernst Schwitters Foundation, Hanover (inv. no.obj838492)
152 Fig. 10 Sprengel Museum Hannover,

Kurt Schwitters Archive (inv. no. SH 2015,0179)
153 Sprengel Museum Hannover, Kurt Schwitters Archive (inv. no. 215)
155 Sprengel Museum Hannover, on loan from the NORD/LB Cultural Foundation (inv. no. D9557)
156 Sprengel Museum Hannover, on loan from the Kurt and Ernst Schwitters Foundation, Hanover (inv. no.obj0683419)
159 Fig. 14 Sprengel Museum Hannover, on loan from the Kurt and Ernst Schwitters Foundation, Hanover (inv. no.obj06825135)
VG Bild-Kunst © VG Bild-Kunst, Bonn 2017 68 (© FLC/VG Bild-Kunst, Bonn 2017), 118, 119 (© The Josef and Anni Albers foundation/VG Bild-Kunst, Bonn 2017), 128, 148, 149, 150 Figs 5, 6, 151 Fig. 7, 160 Figs 16–17, 185, 190, 243 (© The Heartfield Community of Heirs/VG Bild-Kunst, Bonn 2017), 257, 258 Fig. 6, 259, 260, 307, 329, 346. 479 Fig. 51
Wien Museum 248, 253, 263

© Reproduced photographs and illustrations, unless otherwise stated, belong to Institut Designlabor Gutenberg (IDG), University of Applied Sciences Mainz.

Items from the comprehensive collections of the Gutenberg Museum and the Gutenberg Library are not indicated (with inventory numbers). All rights belong to the Gutenberg Museum.

The editors and publisher endeavoured to find the owners of rights to other images. Any individuals and organizations who could not be contacted and own the rights to any images used are requested to contact the publisher.

ACKNOWLEDGEMENTS

The editors would like to thank everyone who supported this project and made it possible. Our thanks to the authors and colleagues who made valuable contributions in the form of their expertise, writings and analyses.

—

We would also like to thank the following people and organizations (in no particular order) for their trust and support:

Andrea Haushofer (Andrea Haushofer Archive, Munich), Dr Annemarie Jaeggi (Bauhaus Archive/Museum of Design, Berlin), Prof. Dr Klaus Klemp (MAK, Frankfurt am Main), Wolfgang Hartmann (Bauer Types, SL, Barcelona), Katharina Pennoyer/Lore Kramer (Frankfurt am Main), Bernd Freese (Freese Collection, Frankfurt am Main), Dr Stefan Soltek and Martina Weiss (Klingspor Museum, Offenbach), Lilo Tschichold, Monika Stöckl-Reinhard and Karl Zimmermann (Hesse State Museum/House of Industrial Culture, Darmstadt), Erik Spiekermann, Dr Christopher Burke, Michel Wlassikoff and Alexandre Dumas de Rauly, Dr Christos Nikolas Vittoratos (Vittoratos Collection, Frankfurt am Main), Kerstin Preiss (BSZ Alois Senefelder, Munich), Renate Flagmeier (Werkbund Archive – Museum of Things, Berlin), Robin Kinross, Paul Barnes, Hans Dieter Reichert, Hans Reichardt.

—

We thank the following archives and institutions for their scientific expertise in support of the project:

Baumeister Archive at the Stuttgart Art Museum.
Andrea Haushofer Archive, Munich.
Bauer Types, SL, Barcelona.
Bauhaus Archive Museum of Design, Berlin.
Bernd Freese (Freese Collection, Frankfurt am Main).
Library of the École Estienne/Archive Signes, Paris.
Etienne Robial Collection.
Deutscher Werkbund Berlin.
Frankfurt Museum Library/State University of Fine Arts (Städelschule), Frankfurt.
German National Museum Nuremberg Gutenberg Library in the Gutenberg Museum, Mainz.
House of Industrial Culture/Hesse State Museum, Darmstadt.
Duchess Anna Amalia Library,

Klassik Foundation, Weimar.
History Museum, Vienna.
University and State Library RheinMain, Wiesbaden.
Institute of Urban History, Frankfurt am Main.
Institute of Contemporary History (IFZ) Munich-Berlin, Munich.
Klingspor Museum, Offenbach am Main.
Art Library of the Kulturforum/Berlin State Museums/Prussian Cultural Heritage Foundation.
Kurt and Ernst Schwitters Foundation, Sprengel Museum, Hanover.
Kurt Schwitters Archive, Sprengel Museum, Hanover.
Kramer archive, Frankfurt am Main.
Ladislv Sutnar Family.
Moravian Gallery (MG) Brno.
Munich City Museum.
Museum of Decorative Arts Prague (UPM).
Museum of Applied Arts (MAK) with the Albinus Collection, Frankfurt am Main.
Wiesbaden Museum, Vordemberge-Gildewart Estate, Bodo Rasch Estate.
Munich Documentation Centre for the History of National Socialism.
Otto and Marie Neurath Isotype Collection, University of Reading.
Saxony State Library/State and University Library, Dresden.
Freese Collection, Frankfurt am Main.
Schmidt-Friderichs Collection, Mainz.
Vittoratos Collection, Frankfurt am Main.
Sprengel Museum, Hanover.
City of Karlsruhe, Cultural Office, City Archive & History Museums.
Technical Information Library, Leibniz University, Hanover.
University Library, Johannes Gutenberg University, Mainz.
Victoria & Albert Museum, London.
Werkbund Archive – Museum of Things, Berlin/Deutscher Werkbund Collection, Berlin.
State Science Library, Mainz.

—

Our thanks go to all our co-workers at the Gutenberg Museum and the Gutenberg Library, particularly Natalja Lurje and Norbert Kaut (library), Rainer Huth (printing), Frank Obitz (building technician), Uta Böhnert (loans), Martina Illner and Petra Nikolic M.A. (press and publicity), Annette Lang-Edwards (restorer), Petra Bermeitinger and Tanja Dörflinger (head of the secretariat).

We are deeply grateful to the Gutenberg Museum of Internationale Gutenberg-Gesellschaft e.V., the Moses Foundation and Förderverein Gutenberg e.V. (Gutenberg

Foundation) for their financial support. From the university, the president, Prof. Dr Gerhard Muth; Dr Sabine Hartel-Schenk, Stefan Klein and Sabine Jackwerth from the library; Klaus Völker from the offset printing press; and Marion Gleissner from bookbinding, supported us with their advice and work – to them, also, our warmest thanks.

—

Not least, we thank the communication design tutors, Florian Schimanski, Bianca Rother, Tobias Wenz, Carina Willenbrink, Daniel Wolfrath, Erdem Yildirim and many others, for their scanning and reproduction work.

—

We would also like to thank the company BauerTypes for the usage rights to Futura ND and Futura ND Alternate, as well as all the typography designers for their permission to print their fonts.

—

For the organization of the exhibition, FUTURA. THE TYPEFACE we thank buero.us, Marc Ulm and LESS, Mainz.

—

We would like to give our very special thanks to Bertram Schmidt-Friderichs from Verlag Hermann Schmidt for his enthusiastic support for the project.

—

Our warm and very special thanks go to Stephanie Kaplan, for her sincere commitment to and passion for typography, which helped to make this publication possible.

Dates:
The dating of the individual type designs and type families is based, when possible, on the publication date. Since most type specimen booklets are not dated, their dates were determined on the basis of the following factors: official registration date, the date of dispatch of the first print, the publication date determined by the type foundry, the date of the proofs, advertisements in the magazine *Gebrauchsgraphik*, and correspondence.

LAURENCE KING

Published in 2017 by
Laurence King Publishing Ltd
361–373 City Road
London EC1V 1LR
Tel +44 20 7841 6900
Fax +44 20 7841 6910
E enquiries@laurenceking.com
www.laurenceking.com

German language edition:
Futura. Die Schrift.
© 2016 by Verlag Hermann Schmidt,
Germany and the Editors and Authors
www.verlag-hermann-schmidt.de

ISBN 978-1-78627-093-1

A catalogue record for this book
is available from the British Library.

The publication
Futura. The Typeface
was issued on the occasion of the
exhibition of the same name at
the Gutenberg Museum Mainz
3 November 2016 to 30 March 2017

A collaborative project of the
Gutenberg Museum Mainz
(Dr Annette Ludwig) and Designlabor
Gutenberg/University of Applied
Sciences Mainz (Prof. Dr Petra Eisele,
Prof. Dr Isabel Naegele)

www.gutenberg-museum.de
www.hs-mainz.de

CONCEPT & EDITING
Petra Eisele, Annette Ludwig,
Isabel Naegele

**GRAPHIC CONCEPT
& DESIGN**
Stephanie Kaplan, Isabel Naegele

ILLUSTRATIONS
Stephanie Kaplan

TRANSLATOR
Phyllis Elago

REPRODUCTIONS
Florian Schimanski, Bianca Rother,
Tobias Wenz, Carina Willenbrink,
Daniel Wolfrath, Erdem Yildirim

TYPEFACES
Futura ND
Futura ND Alternate
Architype Renner

Printed in China

With thanks to Mike Daines.

Landeshauptstadt
Mainz

Gutenberg
Museum
Mainz

DESIGNLABOR
GUTENBERG